FROM ONE EXTREME TO THE OTHER

First Edition published 2023 by

2QT Limited (Publishing) Settle, North Yorkshire BD24 9RH United Kingdom

Copyright © Mike Hartley 2023

The right of Mike Hartley to be identified as the author of this work has been asserted by him in accordance with the Copyright, Designs and Patents Act 1988

All rights reserved. This book is sold subject to the condition that no part of this book is to be reproduced, in any shape or form. Or by way of trade, stored in a retrieval system or transmitted in any form or by any means, electronic, mechanical, photocopying, recording, be lent, re-sold, hired out or otherwise circulated in any form of binding or cover other than that in which it is published and without a similar condition, including this condition being imposed on the subsequent purchaser, without prior permission of the copyright holder.

Cover Design by Charlotte Mouncey, photo by Martin Stone

Photographs by: Mike Hartley

Printed and bound in Great Britain by TJ Books Limited, Padstow, Cornwall

A CIP catalogue record for this book is available from the British Library

ISBN - 978-1-914083-76-1

Publisher Disclaimer:

The events in this memoir are described according to the Authors recollection; recognition and understanding of the events and individuals mentioned and are in no way intended to mislead or offend. As such the Publisher does not hold any responsibility for any inaccuracies or opinions expressed by the author. Every effort has been made to acknowledge and gain any permission from organisations and persons mentioned in this book. Any enquiries should be directed to the author.

FROM ONE EXTREME TO THE OTHER

MIKE HARTLEY

CONTENTS

Acknowledgements	7
Foreword	9
Chapter 1: Early Days – Naivety and Single-Mindedness	11
Chapter 2: A Dream Comes True	28
Chapter 3: Tested to Destruction	44
Chapter 4: Battered and Bruised, but Not Beaten	61
Chapter 5: The Pennine Way	73
Chapter 6: Round and Round and Round	99
Chapter 7: The Coast to Coast	112
Chapter 8: The Western States Endurance Run	129
Chapter 9: Ultra Track and Road	142
Chapter 10: Going with The Flow	159

Chapter 11:
Wind Vanes and Hallowed Land   169

Chapter 12:
A Solar-Heated Bivvy and a Floating Trailer 177

Chapter 13:
End to End Diary   183

Chapter 14:
From Dovedale to Dihedrals   193

Chapter 15:
The Little Voice   202

Chapter 16:
A Firmer Than Usual Handshake   217

Chapter 17:
The Strand   223

Afterword:
Three Score Years and Ten   226

Glossary   229

ACKNOWLEDGEMENTS

I cannot overstate how essential Gill's support and encouragement have been. Saying that she provided practical and emotional help on a multi-day run or passed me drinks in a road race does not, however, capture the essence of the support she has given me. Despite my obsessive desire to achieve my objectives, it would be a mistake to assume that without Gill's commitment I would have been capable of constantly striving. Without her endorsement and encouragement, I have no doubt that it would have been impossible to summon and sustain the total dedication required. I was entirely unfettered – unquestioned, even – as I pursued my dreams, indulged my obsession. She never once asked me to dilute my training or lower my ambitions. Gill knew it was all or nothing, from both of us. Jokingly, she once said, when questioned about her loyalty, 'behind every "great" man there is a gullible woman!'

For many years, Gill encouraged me to put pen to paper and record my exploits, primarily for the interest of friends and family. Eventually, I was persuaded, and embarked upon yet another and different challenge: the writing of this book. Displaying the same supportive patience, Gill spent hours explaining the simplest of keyboard skills to a very slow learner. Only in the later stages did I grasp how to highlight a paragraph. Cutting and pasting still remains a mysterious process. Gill would have gladly typed the entire manuscript herself; there were times when I wished she had. But, like running an ultra, with Gill's support, I got there in the end.

Gill's dad, Gerald, followed my progress from 1974, when Gill and I married. Although he had no previous knowledge of climbing, running or kayaking, he always showed a genuine interest in my exploits, but he had a wry sense of humour. 'Some people,' he once said, 'may consider your behaviour to be unreasonable. One of these days you might come home from a training run to find Gill has had the locks changed.' Gerald, and

Gill's mum, Betty, were probably the unwitting forerunners of the 'tracking' system now commonly used on ultras. Often manning the telephone all night, they provided a central point of reference on my progress, thereby allowing members of my support team to 'follow the dots'.

At the time, I may not have thanked all my pacers and supporters sufficiently. I have no valid excuse for that, except that I was often exhausted, preoccupied or simply too emotional. I am in no doubt that without the help of an expert team focussed entirely on my success, I simply would not have achieved anything at all, let alone set records. In the days before social media, when instant contact with a large number of people at the click of a button was not possible, the only way to arrange support was to pick up the telephone and ask. The result, inevitably, was one hundred per cent enthusiasm for my latest project – importantly, in my view, from people I already knew. I hope the accounts in this book go some way towards explaining just how vital that support was, and that my story conveys my abiding gratitude.

My friends Mike Cudahy and Inken Blunk, as well as being early and enduring sources of encouragement in my running, also provided much-needed assistance in the writing of this book. Their tireless proofreading and checking gave me the impetus to complete something which at times I thought I couldn't. Their forthright yet gracious and pertinent criticism is much appreciated, as are Inken's excellent illustrations. In one of my many moments of self-doubt, I confided in Mike that I was finding the whole process so difficult that I wasn't sure I could complete it. His simple, telling reply was, 'You can do difficult things.'

Many thanks to Tim Hancock for help with presentation and editing of photographs.

Thanks also to my nephew Paul Woolley for his pertinent opinion as a member of a younger generation.

FOREWORD

'Will you tell me, Master Shallow, how to choose a man?
Care I for the thews, stature, bulk and big assemblance of a man?
Give me the spirit, Master Shallow.'

William Shakespeare, *2 Hen. IV*

Shakespeare's Falstaff would surely have appreciated Mike Hartley. Mike once described his physical appearance as being 'like a piece of streaky bacon viewed from the side'. Matching Falstaff's ideal, Mike's stature lies not in the dimensions of his body but in his spirit.

It is, however, the physical parameters of Mike's achievements which may first capture your attention. His performances at the extreme ends of several sports are remarkable; none more so than his 'Three Rounds'. The physical challenge inherent in his attempt to complete the 293km and 25,150m of ascent (183 miles / 83,000 feet) of the three twenty-four-hour UK mountain circuits may at first overwhelm your imagination. But as you join Mike on the last round, with strength failing and all chance of success on this ultimate ultra fading, you will become acutely aware of a weary yet inextinguishable spirit. When Tennyson spoke of 'the sword outwearing the sheath', this is what he meant. This is the light which never need fade and in this is the only true merit of such endeavours.

The French mountaineer Lionel Terray gave his book the thought-provoking title *Conquistadores Of The Useless*. If he meant that, with respect to mountain climbing, conquest was of no importance, then what might be the merit in undertaking any such challenge? The mountain, like the blank rock face or the ultra trail, is indifferent. It can be climbed or completed, but it cannot be conquered. Terray's title, therefore, is both cynical and realistic, a barb to puncture the possible swell of hubris. By developing strength and skill, Terray did conquer – but only his own limitations and frailties. Here, again, is the measure and merit of such enterprises.

In Mike's book you will find achievements at the limit of human endeavour, but you will find no hubris. Instead you will find a single-minded, even quasi-romantic drive to sporting excellence, a gradual refinement of physical, mental and emotional attributes which merge to produce a complex harmony of spirit – a harmony which might be termed an 'emergent property'. This harmony, emerging from years of dedicated training, is what proved fundamental to Mike's outstanding achievements. Falstaff was an uncouth, blustering fellow, but he spoke with Shakespeare's insight when he said, 'Give me the spirit, Master Shallow.' Here, you have that spirit.

Mike Cudahy 2023

CHAPTER 1:

Early Days – Naivety and Single-Mindedness

Easter, 1965. The mist and driving snow merged; the sky and earth appeared as one, a wet white wall. Unable to distinguish hillocks from hollows, or even uphills from downhills, we stumbled blindly on. We were in a white-out. Alan Willis and myself were 13 years old and trying to get down off Sail Mhòr, a Corbett in the Scottish highlands.

We were on a school trip under the strict but rather inexperienced guidance of our metalwork teacher, Mr Griffiths. Our four classmates were impressed when Alan produced a map, and baffled when I produced a compass. Sceptical looks were cast my way when I explained the mysterious device was not for drawing circles but would be our salvation. After studying the map, I announced with as much authority as I could muster that Alan and I would make our way down by taking bearings off each other, the one in front being directed left or right from behind until on the correct bearing, and the whole group then moving forward, leapfrog fashion.

Acutely aware that my experience was limited to reading Alan Blackshaw's authoritative book *Mountaineering*, a birthday present from my uncle Ron, we set off down through the white wilderness, the one in front always stopping before being lost from view or, more permanently, over the edge of a cliff. My classmates were in awe, but Mr Griffiths remained uncharacteristically silent, even perplexed. He was not accustomed to receiving instructions from his pupils. Even as I dared to hope we might be on the verge of scoring a minor victory, I caught a glimpse of a vengeful eye through the ice-encrusted slit in his red balaclava. He knew his often-used aluminium cane might bring results in the classroom, but it would not help him here.

After a short while, buoyed by my rising sense of superiority, I called a halt at a snowdrift to demonstrate my snow-holing skills – something else I'd learnt only in theory from *Mountaineering*. A snow hole can be a lifesaver but requires the correct snow conditions and a certain level of practical experience; I had neither. Alan and I burrowed into the drift a few yards apart, the object being to meet in the middle. All went well until we both came up against rocks and grass; the drift wasn't deep enough. Alan burrowed left; I burrowed right. Just as we met, the whole side of the burrow collapsed. We were left facing each other on all fours on a sort of balcony. Our classmates thought it was hilarious, but the loud guffaws coming from the red balaclava had a more mocking tone.

Clutching the map and compass as if to prove our authority was still intact, we continued to leap and frog our way downhill. Eventually, visibility improved, snow gave way to rain, tussock grass and bog gave way to safe, solid tarmac. Through a combination of much luck and a little skill, we emerged from the sodden hillside, a mere 100 yards from the school minibus.

The remainder of our Easter trip went well. We even seemed on better terms with Mr Griffiths, but whenever he reprimanded us for some minor misdemeanour, we had to suppress a smirk as we thought about our victory on the hill. It seemed 'Sir' was also smirking but with little attempt at suppression. We guessed he was thinking about the aluminium cane!

Immediately after this episode, even before we returned home, my mind became occupied with thoughts of snowy and dangerous adventures in monochrome worlds. I dreamt of climbing through black, wet crags and crossing windswept icy plateaux, compass and ice axe in hand, crampons on boots. I didn't own an ice axe or crampons, but I knew what they were; I had seen them in the window of the Frank Davies Mountain shop in Birmingham.

I started spending a lot of time daydreaming about adventuring in the mountains, always on my own, always on my physical limit and only just surviving my latest imaginary epic. These daydreams were never about a particular climb or place; they were more a crystallisation of experiences I wanted above anything else. In effect, I was creating virtual scenarios with virtual difficulties and overcoming them with positive thinking. It was many years before I realised this was a sort of positive mental rehearsal, often practised by elite athletes. Never in my wildest dreams – and that is saying something for me – would I have envisaged that twenty-five years later I would be aspiring to be such an athlete. I would be trying to enhance my performance by practising this very technique.

*

I had been back at school for a few months, and it was winter. I had been dreaming endlessly about what I had discovered but I also felt very frustrated. I could not think of any way to get back to the mountains. Everything seemed against me. I was too young to hitch-hike; at least, that was what my mum said. I didn't have any money and I didn't know anybody apart from Alan who was interested in the same things. Then something happened that changed the rest of my life. A student teacher started working at our school and promptly set up an outdoor activities club. One day, after an easy walk on Cannock Chase which was far too tame for a dreamer like me, he said, 'Fancy going climbing, lads?' We could not believe our ears. 'Be at the school at 8 a.m. on Saturday. Bring sleeping bags, I'll bring everything else. We'll go to Stanage.' We were going climbing!

After what felt like a month of waiting, Saturday arrived and we met Mr Walters at the school. Fortunately, risk assessments, parental consents and CRB checks had not been invented, so we could quickly get on our way. No need to faff around with rear seat belts, either, as they also hadn't been invented; anyway, Mr Walters's van didn't have any rear seats.

I had no idea where Stanage was, or even what it was, but before long we were skidding and sliding our way along a very snowy minor road high above Hathersage. Trudging up the snow slope towards the crag, I was disappointed to see how small it was – only about fifteen feet high. 'It's OK,' said Mr Walters, 'It's actually a lot taller than this. Most of it is under the snow.' Over the course of the next few days, we did quite a few very short, albeit very cold, climbs.

Mr Walters had borrowed the climbing equipment from a friend, and this inspired him to persuade our PE department that, because the school now had a 'Climbing Club', we ought to have a rope and the necessary equipment. The 'Climbing Club' consisted of Mr Walters, Alan and myself. The shiny new nylon rope was a hawser-laid Viking No. 3 and the 'equipment' was an eight-foot sling and a massive steel screwgate carabiner.

After only a few months Mr Walters announced he was leaving the school. It hit me like a bombshell; he had introduced me to something I felt so in tune with, something that consumed my waking consciousness and fuelled my dreams. I had found climbing to be a true 'in the moment' experience, where nothing else mattered apart from my ability to maintain contact with a piece of rock, to tread the knife edge between success and failure, the outcome as dependent on confidence and self-control as on strength and balance. I was sure climbing would provide inspiration both physically and mentally for the rest of my life. Even through my running years, I never lost the longing to climb. I knew one day I would return to it.

At this time, climbing helmets were not in common use but, before he left, Mr Walters gave me an old motorbike helmet. If I close my eyes, I can still see it and smell it. He also passed on a couple of valuable tips. 'If you can find your way undetected into the girls' changing rooms' – I wondered what he was going to say next; I hoped he wasn't a mind reader – 'there is a rack full of black hockey boots with rubber soles. They've got studs, but you can cut them off with a hacksaw. They will make great rock boots.' And they did. They weren't quite PAs or EBs (early commercially available rock boots), but we thought they were excellent. Wearing them, we felt like 'proper' climbers. The second top tip was to find a brass machine nut, turn the thread out on a lathe, slide it onto a nylon sling and it would make an excellent runner. 'Go and see Mr Griffiths. You can borrow a hacksaw at the same time.'

After Mr Walters's departure we were left without transport and without an experienced mentor. We began searching for adventures near to home. Alan's attempt to abseil down the side of his house, with the rope attached to the top of a drainpipe, nearly ended in disaster. The drainpipe parted company from the brickwork, causing him to swing across the driveway, narrowly missing the ground. His aerial display ended abruptly as he crashed into his neighbour's back door. Miraculously, he was unharmed apart from the after-effects of a severe tongue-lashing inflicted by his mother.

One day, during a gym lesson, I noticed the roof of the sports hall was supported by steel beams, with six-inch-wide flanges separated by a web. My mind leapt with excitement as I visualised myself hanging ape-like from the beam, climbing to the middle of the hall then abseiling down to the floor. After a few more gym lessons, I had fully 'cased' the hall and soon formulated a plan. It was fraught with problems, not least the possibility of being expelled from school.

Undeterred, Alan and I pooled the proceeds of our paper rounds and bought four carabiners from the Frank Davis Mountain shop; 9*s.* 6*d.* each seemed an outrageous amount to pay, but we were one step closer to our objective. The next and potentially insurmountable challenge was one of access. A clandestine ascent during sports day, when everyone would be outside, was appealing, but we knew the hall was a favourite haunt of skivers. The end-of-term school assembly, when everybody was receiving a pep talk from the headmaster, seemed to offer the best chance of evasion. It also offered the highest chance of expulsion if we were caught. Fully expecting to be turned down flat, we simply decided to be bold and asked the head of PE for permission. Surprisingly, it was granted – with the proviso, 'Don't come crying to me if you kill yourselves.'

With Alan belaying, I scaled the wall bars to within a few feet of the roof. Then, making use of the modified but untried hockey boots, I made a couple of 'thin' moves to gain the steel beam. Its flanges provided ample purchase for my fingers, then, by employing some nifty 'heel hooking', I started out. Having clipped the rope into runners threaded through holes in the beam, I reached the middle without incident. I then clipped myself to a safety sling before rigging the abseil rope. Executing the next part of the plan was always going to be challenging. I hadn't been able to fathom exactly how I would achieve the crucial transfer of body weight from the safety sling to the abseil rope. I reckoned I would work something out when I got there. Attaching myself to the abseil rope was straightforward; supporting my body weight by one hand, while unclipping from the safety sling with the other, was not. After several failed attempts, I realised all I needed to do was cut through the safety sling.

'Alan,' I shouted down, 'chuck me some scissors up. I'll be down in no time.'

Thankfully, he hadn't got any. Making one more superhuman effort which involved poking my feet through the holes in the web and hanging upside down, I unclipped. At last, I completed the abseil and stood on the floor. I was just pleased Mr Griffiths wasn't there.

The local grammar school also had a climbing club, a bit bigger than ours (we were now down to two), and a master called Mr Jones, who strangely used to berate the kids for pronouncing 'Jones' incorrectly. To the 'grammar kids' and me he was a sort of climbing god; he'd been to the Alps and he'd climbed the Sloth, a fearsome overhang at the Roaches which we used to gawp at whenever we went there. As we made our way along the base of the crag at the end of the day's climbing, I would always glance back over my shoulder for one last look at its jutting profile. Despite the Sloth's apparent invincibility, I could feel a magnetism. I sensed my relationship with it would ultimately become much more than just a backward glance. Well, Mr Jones might have seemed like a climbing god, but the age and condition of his climbing gear left something to be desired. Often, I'd return home from a wet day on Stanage or the Roaches to find that when I rose from a chair I could still feel the weight of the sodden 100-foot hemp rope.

I climbed with the 'grammar kids' as much as possible, which wasn't nearly enough. On one memorable trip, Martin Nunn's mother gave us a lift to Stanage; our intention was to live in Robin Hood's Cave for a few days. We hadn't actually been inside the cave before, so we were pleased to find it quite clean – no sheep droppings, or worse. The cave is near the top of the crag. This ensured it was inaccessible to sheep but allowed us access via an easy scramble from above. The cave consisted of quite a large boulder-strewn balcony and a smaller inner sanctum. Martin and I climbed all day, leading as hard as we dared, top-roping more extreme climbs which dated back to the Brown/Whillans era of the 1950s. Bloody battles were fought with Right Unconquerable, Left Unconquerable and the Dangler, climbs as tough and uncompromising as their first ascensionists. Sometimes we succeeded, sometimes not. To succeed was a thrill; to fail was a disappointment; both were the stuff of adventure. Eventually, at dusk – ropes coiled over our shoulders, knuckles skinned, fingertips worn smooth by the rough gritstone – we scrambled down to the cave. Sleeping inside to avoid the rain wasn't as comfortable as we had hoped; the floor was sandy and sloping, not to mention hard. When it was dry, we slept out on the balcony, gazing at the stars, drinking tea and smoking. At least, I smoked. Martin thought it was a disgusting habit. I knew he was correct, but I persevered for another fifteen years, only quitting in pursuit of a faster marathon time. We were living our dream.

The year before I left school, I began climbing with a new partner, Steve Hudson. We started hitching to the Roaches at weekends. This became a sort of habit and it soon developed into a competition. Getting there in the fastest time was an obvious victory, but did it trump a lift in a Jag or a Merc? On one occasion, I arrived at the campsite first and while I was musing about the best way to pour scorn on Steve's pathetically slow time, a Lotus pulled up. Steve jumped out with the smuggest of smug grins on his face. Swaggering up to the tent, he said, 'Well, I think that trumps everything.'

We soon tired of lugging the tent all the way to the Roaches, and got to know an obliging farmer, who allowed us to leave it in his outbuilding. We eventually persuaded him to allow us to sleep in his hayloft if we promised not to use stoves or to smoke. We became friendly with his daughters, who used to come into the loft to chat and sometimes play jokes on us. Soon after this, he stopped us from using the loft, citing the risk to his property. We knew what he meant.

Steve and I spent the next few years hitching or scrounging lifts to various places – often the Roaches, albeit back in the tent, but also North Wales. We once spent ten consecutive nights sleeping in 'Willie's Barn' in the Ogwen Valley. One day, a climber gave us a lift to the Llanberis Pass. We were aware of its reputation; we knew you had to be an expert to climb in the 'Pass'. So, not wasting any time and in full 'positive thinking' mode, I promptly led 'Trilon', my first Very Severe graded lead.

By 1969, four years after my first climbing experience, with dreams of adventure fully embedded, I wanted to move on. I contacted my nearest 'proper' climbing club. The Stafford Mountain Club was well established and had many experienced members. I made some good friends and achieved some of my best climbs with them. Based at Bryn Hafod, the club's hut in Cwm Cywarch, Stuart Grant and I made the third ascent of 'The Grafter'. At grade E3, it was one of the most difficult climbs I had done. We also shared many climbs in the Llanberis Pass, including the classics of Sickle, Spectre and Erosion Groove.

My strongest memory of this period was our ascent of 'Diagonal'. While not high in the scale of difficulty, the scarcity of runners, combined with its Hard Very Severe grade, ensures it is not a pushover. According to the guidebook, the climb requires 'finesse for success'. It was a freezing cold day, and the rock was damp. I tiptoed up the rising traverse on tiny sloping footholds, my frozen fingers trying to gain purchase on the smooth rock, my last runner an awfully long way below. With every move upwards came an increasing sense of danger and commitment. Doubt and indecision began to cast a shadow over my confidence. One more tricky move and I knew I had crossed the line; I could not climb down. The only way was up, but a mistake would be disastrous. I remembered what Edward Whymper had said: 'a momentary negligence may destroy the happiness of a lifetime.' For the next few minutes, the only thing that was important or even existed was the few square feet of rock in front of me. The way I placed the toe of my boot on a foothold and the way I positioned my numb fingertips were both crucial to preventing a slip and the appalling consequences. At last, I found the security of the belay ledge and an overwhelming sense of relief. In the pursuit of adventure and a desire to be as close to the edge as possible, both physically and mentally, one occasionally gets a bit too close. I rigged a solid anchor and shouted down 'I'm safe. Phew.'

Life with the club was great fun, but as well as hard climbing, there was also a fair amount of hard drinking and fast driving to contend with – a bad combination which was never going to end well. One particularly 'fast and drunk' weekend came to an abrupt halt when I, as an innocent passenger, was obliged to spend the following week in hospital in St Asaph.

The years of corrective facial surgery and dentistry that followed became a constant reminder that a seat belt is most definitely a good idea!

*

July 1970. I was staring up at the 'Sloth'; it was staring down at me. I knew this day would come. It was inevitable, just a question of time.

The climb starts easily enough, up cracks and steep slabs, to arrive at a ledge called the Pedestal, a large flake of rock with a flat top about two feet wide. A good place for a rest and a girding of loins. I had studied the overhang many times from the safety of the ground, but it looked a lot bigger and more menacing now I was at close quarters. I was having second thoughts. I tried to summon as much positivity as possible – after all, Mr Jones had climbed it. I wondered if he had used that awful hemp rope. Also, I was sure I had succeeded on climbs which were technically more difficult. But I had never tried to climb anything as dramatic and, frankly, outrageous as the 'Sloth'. Above the Pedestal the climbing becomes steeper and more difficult, with small finger and toeholds leading up to the overhang. I draped a sling over a block and, with the rope clipped in, reached out along the roof to place a wire nut. So far, so good. Gripping the series of flakes that lead out above the drop, I got my feet up and jammed my toes behind the flakes. Feeling insecure, I clipped the rope to the wire and started out across the roof.

Halfway along, I stopped, hanging 'sloth-like'. I knew I had made a mistake. I could feel the exposure sapping my resolve, gravity making my arms ache. I did not have the strength to continue up or to climb back down. I was going to fall.

Looking at my foot, I was horrified to see the rope tangled round it. If I fell now, I would be flipped upside down. I wondered if anyone had ever fallen out of a harness. The only solution was to untangle my foot, hang vertically from my fingertips, then let go – but it was impossible to let go voluntarily. As my strength ebbed away, I watched my fingers uncurl – slowly, reluctantly – and slide from the black and brown gritstone flakes. It was all over in seconds. I was left dangling on the end of the rope like a puppet. The wire nut held, and I was unhurt.

One week later, I stood again beneath the mighty overhang. It was my eighteenth birthday, and I had dreamt of nothing else for the past week. I wasn't frightened; I now knew how to do it. Speed and conservation of strength were the keys to success. I cruised along the flakes, my pulse racing, senses on high alert, tingling from head to toe. I was in full control. This time I would not be denied. Pulling round the lip onto verticality and safety, I shouted down, 'I've done it! It's OK really!'

The Lichfield Mountaineering Club was formed in the autumn of 1970 by local teacher John Brooks, who soon developed a friendly and active club. Meets stretching from Cornwall to Glen Coe were arranged most weekends. The club's inaugural meet was held in January, based at 'Willie's Barn' in the Ogwen Valley of North Wales. With everyone sleeping in the same barn, it was a good opportunity for us all to become acquainted, and I soon became friendly with a young lady called Gill. Norman, a colleague of Gill's, had persuaded her to go on the meet with the promise of a lift. Never having been near a mountain before, she was hoping for an adventure, and possibly to make some new friends.

Low cloud, rain, and snow on high ground provided challenging and potentially dangerous conditions for the club's first meet. We split into two groups, according to experience and ambition. The most experienced group, in view of the poor conditions, lowered our expectations and enjoyed a good day of low-level walking. The totally inexperienced and ill-equipped group did the opposite. Norman, their self-appointed leader, announced, 'We will do Snowdon, up the Zig Zags.' Gill had no idea what the 'Zig Zags' were but must have thought they sounded just a bit adventurous, so joined the 'Snowdon' group. After a late start, they spent an hour or so hiring boots, followed by a leisurely visit to the café. Then, eventually, they set off from Pen-y-Pass towards Snowdon. Gill was soon to get her hoped-for adventure.

The 'Zig Zags' are a series of sharp bends on a steep path, prone to accumulations of snow and ice. In winter conditions, to the unprepared, they are extremely dangerous and have been the scene of many fatalities. Back at the barn, I was beginning to worry. It was getting dark. I didn't know anything about Norman, and Gill didn't know anything about adventures.

I was beginning to think I ought to call the mountain rescue when they returned.

'How did that go?' I asked Gill.

'It was awful. We got stuck. Some climbers with ropes helped us to get down. It was Norman's fault. I'm never going anywhere with him ever again.'

I could hardly believe my good fortune; with Norman sidelined, my path was clear. I was a keen adherent of the seventies' 'hippy-style' climbing culture, complete with long hair, headband and the obligatory roll-up. I could tell she was impressed. I swept her off her feet.

We became regular attendees on club meets, often in the Llanberis Pass. On one of those 'Pass' meets, John Brooks and I made an ascent of 'White Slab', an Extremely Severe graded climb on Clogwyn Du'r Arddu, one of the most impressive crags in Britain. Its high elevation and northerly aspect ensure it is often cold and shaded, both of which add to its aura of seriousness. An ascent of 'White Slab' requires at one point, while balanced on small finger and footholds, the ability to lasso a small spike of rock. The spike is about twenty feet away and once secured, the rope is used to make an exciting swing into a corner, allowing upward progress to continue. Before the climb was finished, it would provide me with another exciting swing, albeit a more unexpected one. It's a long climb of over 600 feet; very near the top, without warning, a handhold came loose. Almost falling, and left hanging by one hand, I shouted a warning to John and deflected the house-brick-sized block into the abyss.

*

Gill and I were married in 1974 and spent the following few years fell walking all over the UK. We discovered the unparalleled beauty of Scotland's west coast, an area we still visit and never tire of. We competed as partners in the Karrimor International Mountain Marathon (KIMM; now called the Original Mountain Marathon), a two-day event for teams of two. Teams are required to be self-sufficient for two days of mountain orienteering, including an overnight camp. Cycling trips and more latterly sea kayaking have fuelled our love of the outdoors and provided a constant source of enjoyment and fulfilment.

During 1977 Gill and I visited Horton in Ribblesdale, in the Yorkshire Dales. We learnt that the spectacular hill overlooking the village was Pen-y-ghent. We also discovered that it was, along with Ingleborough and Whernside, one of the famous Yorkshire 'Three Peaks', and we learnt that all three could be traversed in a single walk of twenty-four miles. The Pen-y-ghent café was the official starting point, operating a 'clocking in and out' system which allowed walkers to record their times. A distance of twenty-four miles was beyond our capabilities, so we were content to allocate a separate day for each peak, but the idea of completing the Three Peaks as a single walk implanted itself in my mind. I had never undertaken a walk of anywhere near twenty-four miles, but this one caught my imagination. I just had to do it. Three months later, I stamped my card in the clocking machine and set off on my first long walk. Exactly nine hours after that, I returned to the café and clocked back in. I knew this would be the first of many long walks.

A year later, in 1978, I read Thomas Firbank's book *I Bought a Mountain*. The book tells the story of his purchase of a hill farm on the southern flanks of Glyder Fach, in Snowdonia, in 1931. He was young and completely inexperienced in the ways of farming, but he was following a dream. After many miles of shepherding on the rough boulder slopes, his hill craft and fitness inevitably improved. He also developed great respect and love for his local mountains. In 1938 it came to his notice that all fourteen of the Welsh mountains whose summits exceed 3,000 feet had been visited in a total of 12h 30min during a continuous walk. His interest piqued, he began to undertake training walks to determine the best route. At 8 a.m. on a misty and wet August morning, Thomas and his friends, Capel and Rex, set off from Snowdon (Yr Wyddfa), the first and highest peak. They were intent on breaking the recently set new record time of 10h 29min. Despite thick mist and rain, they arrived at Foel Fras, the last summit, in 8h 25min.

Before I had even finished reading the book, the Welsh 3000ers had become my next 'must do' objective. At the end of June, only a month after turning the final page, I bivvied on top of Snowdon together with a small group of fellow LMC members. Our plan was to make an early start to take advantage of the long hours of daylight. We awoke to thick mist and pouring rain. In an odd way it seemed fitting that the weather should be as bad as on that August day forty years previously. We made our way northwards via Crib Goch, the Glyders and Tryfan, with no improvement in conditions. Eventually we plodded up onto the Carneddau. It was at this point, trudging along, that I noticed I was following a trail of soapy water. Spotting Phil Haswell in front, I noticed with some surprise that he was covered from the waist down in a thick layer of soap suds and was leaving a trail of foamy water like the overflow from a blocked drain. It transpired that Phil's mother had washed his tracksters but not rinsed them thoroughly. The combination of walking and flapping in the wind had caused the soap to expand like a bubble bath. When we were at our lowest ebb, Phil had unwittingly stepped into the breach and provided much-needed hilarity. It was the funniest thing we'd seen since starting out; in fact, it was the funniest thing we had ever seen on the mountains, or were ever likely to see. Our arrival at Foel Fras in 14h 15min was a bit of an anticlimax. We had done it and found it tough, but it hadn't been much fun. By way of compensation, the image of the bedraggled 'foaming Phil of the Carneddau' has stayed with me to this day.

Over the next two years, I followed a similar pattern, with more circuits of the Three Peaks and more crossings of the Welsh 3000ers. Dreams of walking further and faster were becoming insistent, but I would not have believed that one day I would run the Three Peaks a full 5h 30min faster than my first walk and go on to complete another thirteen circuits. I would complete three more crossings of the Welsh 3000ers. I felt I had turned a corner. I knew I was on the verge of something special; I wasn't sure what it was, but I knew I could not let it go. I felt as though I was part way through a dream and didn't want to wake up. As I stood unwittingly on the brink of a lifetime of physical endeavour and adventure, it became obvious that if I wanted to continue improving and find out how this 'special' stage in my life would develop, if I wanted to realise the conclusion of the dream, then attaining the highest possible level of fitness was essential.

The LMC held a climbing meet in Glen Coe at Whitsun 1979 and I relished climbing on the massive smooth slabs of Glen Etive. The serious and extreme climbs of 'Swastika', 'The Pause' and 'The Long Reach' were experiences I would never forget; they were surely some of the most exciting slab climbs anywhere. Having already walked many of the Glen Coe peaks with Gill, including the Aonach Eagach ridge, making a continuous traverse seemed an obvious if ambitious target. The day I completed a circuit of the Glen Coe skyline was sweltering and it proved to be a lot more arduous and testing than I expected. Walking the steep uphills and running the downhills was my first real attempt at fell running. The experience was only slightly marred by writhing in the agonies of cramp on my way to the pub later

I was now spending more time running than climbing, and over the next few years my focus shifted. My enthusiasm for the rock was being superseded by an overwhelming desire to run. But not just any run; it had to be long and testing, it had to be on my limit. I felt a reconnection with those early dreams from my schooldays.

In May 1980 I entered my first organised event, the Fellsman Hike, a tough and hilly course in the Yorkshire Dales. The event was established in 1962 and – apart from 2001, when it was cancelled due to foot-and-mouth disease – has been held every year since. The route starts at Ingleton, makes its way northwards over the tops of Ingleborough, Whernside and Gragareth to the village of Dent. It then swings east over Dodd Fell to Buckden Pike before turning south to Great Whernside. The last few miles of rough, featureless moorland provide a final navigational test before participants descend to the finish at Threshfield. Much rough, trackless terrain, together with 11,000 feet of ascent and difficult route-finding, ensures the Fellsman Hike is one of the toughest events on the ultra calendar. I was so exhausted at the end of this gruelling sixty-two-miler that I could barely walk. I was glad I had already booked a day off work from my job as a meter reader. The prospect of walking for six hours the following day had been more than I could face. (In years to come, my job became an integral part of my training and helped me to build mental and physical stamina.) I completed my first Fellsman Hike in 17h 49min, in forty-fourth equal place in the company of Michael Abbott and Christopher Johnson. On reflection, I was pleased I had completed a run that was 'long, testing and on my limit'. I just didn't expect it to be so testing or to happen so soon.

My dream had sustained a setback. I felt an inkling of doubt; surely such a monumental effort deserved not just a painful completion, but something more rewarding? A faster time and better finishing position would have been tangible and pleasing. But simply finding the undertaking easier would have been more gratifying.

So my initial satisfaction at finishing such a difficult challenge soon turned to disappointment. The more I thought about the struggle I'd had, the more disappointed I became. I had to do better than that. I vowed I would never feel that tired again – not because I didn't want to do anything else as hard, but because I didn't want to pay such a high price ever again. I resolved to improve my strength and fitness by embarking on longer and faster training walks, including short sections of jogging. I hoped this would ensure I could avoid sore feet and stiffness in the future.

Occasionally, during my long walks, I had noticed short spells of effortlessness. Even walking uphill, I would sometimes look back and think, 'I don't remember that steep section.' It didn't occur very often, and it only ever happened spontaneously. I reasoned that it might be possible, in the correct frame of mind, to engage in physical effort so easily that it would be unnoticeable. I started to believe that if I could achieve a supreme level of fitness and not be distracted by physical discomfort, then that effortless state was more likely to occur. Naively, I convinced myself that I possessed an inherent ability to achieve anything I wanted. I believed that ultimately, with enough training, I could reach a physical and mental state where no matter how far I ran or how hard I tried, it would feel undemanding. An effortless and serene application of energy.

In the years that followed, I did indeed become much fitter and stronger. The mountain challenges I undertook became more extreme, the road and track races faster, more intense and more punishing. It never got any easier, and I never had anything left at the end. But I did learn how to extract more out of myself, to run closer to my physical and psychological limit for longer. Eventually, I began to understand how to persuade my body to continue doing something it thought it could not: to believe it always had a bit more to give.

*

By the end of September 1980, I had completed the Three Peaks on three occasions, improving from what now seemed a pedestrian nine hours to a more respectable 5h 37min. I had achieved my second crossing of the Welsh 3000ers in 11h 23min but knew I could do much better. Up to this point, I had improved by incorporating more jogging into my long walks, but I had never trained on a daily, or even weekly basis. It was time to start.

I completed my first-ever training run on 15th September 1980, aged twenty-eight, and duly entered it in my new logbook, complete with accurate time and distance. In my impatience to improve as quickly as possible, and believing that more must surely be better, I recorded three runs that first day. With no thoughts of possible injury, I recorded three runs the following day and three on each of the subsequent days, always recording my times and intermediate split times at convenient places. I became obsessed with trying to shave a few seconds off each run or each split. I was trying to achieve a level of fitness in a few weeks that would normally take years.

After two months I was, inevitably, forced to take a break. My log was now showing several consecutive entries of 'injured'. After a period of kicking my heels until I recovered, I resumed my training, albeit more cautiously. By a gradual increase in weekly mileage and in the length and speed of my longest run, I was able to run further and faster. It was impossible to completely eliminate time out with injury, so I tried to minimise its impact by reducing the mileage or taking a short rest before any injury became chronic. I was naïve but single-minded and incredibly determined. In the absence of a planned strategy, these attributes and a certain amount of good luck in mostly avoiding injury allowed me to continue like this for many years.

In common with many runners during the eighties, I was drawn into the marathon-running boom. On 10th May 1981 I stood on the start line of the Nike People's Marathon, my debut. I had been training regularly for eight months; I had gleaned valuable tips on training and preparation from reading *Running* magazine. Most marathon schedules advocated a longest training run of eighteen miles, five weeks prior to the marathon. The final five weeks would be a tapering of weekly mileage to allow a recovery period, hopefully without losing fitness. This final stage could be adapted to suit personal circumstances – that is, one's levels of fitness and ambition and the incidence of injury. Given that my personal circumstances consisted of naivety and single-mindedness, a final long run of twenty-four miles and a nine-day taper seemed quite sensible. Three days before the marathon, I was having second thoughts: maybe I hadn't done enough. But I did resist the temptation to increase my mileage or to squeeze in another twenty-four-miler.

Being my first marathon, the experience was quite a novelty, but the race was uneventful and on a tedious course. I was pleased to finish in 3h 22min. If only I had found all my subsequent marathons that easy! A further two marathons completed before the end of the year, in 3h 13min and 3h 11min, gave me hope that one day I might achieve sub-three hours.

CHAPTER 2:

A Dream Comes True

As 1981 drew to a close, I joined the Long Distance Walkers Association (LDWA) with the intention of entering their long events and progressing to take part in their annual 100-miler. Entries from runners were neither encouraged nor discouraged, but there was always a small contingent at the front. I enjoyed being part of that 'small contingent' on several occasions. These events were always very friendly and well organised, with a detailed route description available in advance.

In April 1982 I camped in the Llanberis Pass with the intention of improving my time for the Welsh 3000ers. I now knew the route quite well; apart from my two previous crossings, I had also run many of the sections in training, so it was satisfying to complete the traverse in 7h 56min.

Although I had now completed several long runs and become much fitter, I still hadn't competed in an A Class fell race. I was keen to make amends, so only four days after the 3000ers, I lined up at the start of the Kinder Downfall Race in England's Peak District. Chatting to a very fit-looking fellow competitor at the check-in, I mentioned that this was my first fell race and I just hoped I didn't come last. He soon put my mind at rest. 'No,' he said, 'that won't happen. Nobody comes last. I've never seen anybody come last.'

I came 127th out of 232, which was OK. Curious, I went to watch the prize-giving. As my acquaintance from the check-in duly accepted the winner's trophy, I understood why he had never seen anybody come last.

My running had gone very well up to this point in the year, with plenty of injury-free training and racing. I had also completed that year's Fellsman Hike, alongside Alan Payne and Kevin Smith, in 17h 48min. Although slightly slower than my first, I found it a lot easier. Maybe I hadn't tried hard enough!

My chance reading of an article in *Climber and Rambler* magazine stirred my interest in something new. I'd never heard of the Bob Graham Round, and I didn't know anybody who had done it, but I was fascinated. The article explained that the 'round' is an established test piece for fell runners, the object being to visit the tops of forty-two designated peaks in the Lake District in under twenty-four hours. I didn't know anything at all about it, but that didn't stop me wondering. Could I do that?

The magazine article explained that the Bob Graham Round started and finished at the Moot Hall, Keswick, and the route could be run either clockwise or anticlockwise. The forty-two peaks included the four highest in the Lake District: Scafell Pike, Scafell, Helvellyn and Skiddaw. The terrain ranges from tussock grass, bogs and scree slopes to rock scrambling, where the use of hands as well as feet is required. This scrambling section is called Broad Stand and is the shortest route between Scafell and Scafell Pike; it is avoidable, but only by a longer, more time-consuming detour. In the interests of speed and safety, many contenders choose to enlist the help of a climber friend to pre-rig a rope. The round is split by four road crossings which provide convenient support points, allowing the contenders access to food and equipment. It is accepted practice for each contender to be accompanied on each section by support runners, whose job it is to carry supplies and help with navigation. A team of two or three support runners on each section is generally considered optimal. A successful contender is eligible to join the Bob Graham 24 Hour Club if they are 'accompanied at all times by at least one witness'.

So began several months of planning and undertaking training runs on each of the five sections to determine the most efficient route between peaks. On 28th August 1982, a mere six months after reading the article, I set off from Moot Hall at 3.30 a.m. My support runners numbered only three – Dave Chamberlain, Graham Barnes and Bill Naylor – with Gill driving and organising roadside support. Only three support runners for five sections would rather overburden my friends, so to ease the load I elected to run the Wasdale to Dunmail Raise section solo. This is a long and difficult section, crossing some of the roughest and highest terrain in the Lake District, including the descent of the notorious

Broad Stand. My rock-climbing experience stood me in good stead here and allowed me to make the passage safely without the need for a rope. What we lacked in numbers, we made up for in careful planning and a collective determination. My arrival at Moot Hall in 21h 44min was a memorable occasion; I had completed what was considered the blue riband achievement for long-distance fell runners. However, I had not been accompanied on the entire round, so I was ineligible to join the Bob Graham 24 Hour Club. I was aware of this criterion before I started, but the forecast of bad weather had caused me to change my start time. This meant one of my support runners could not be present. Primarily, I had sought the experience of the challenge, not the joining of a club; nevertheless, my euphoria was tinged with just a little disappointment. I had unfinished business.

The following year, 1983, proved to be my best year so far and started with a solo winter circuit of the Yorkshire Three Peaks, for which I recorded a time of 4h 57min. To achieve this in only a little over half the time I'd taken for my first circuit was surprising, especially given the poor conditions. That same winter, the full snow cover on my fourth crossing of the Welsh 3000ers in a best time of 6h 59min provided an unforgettable day – crystal-blue sky, ice on Crib Goch and racing across frozen snowfields on the Glyders. No ice axe in hand, no crampons on boots; from then on it was studded running shoes and a bum bag for me. One week later, I entered the Three Peaks Race for the first time and finished in exactly four hours, another unexpectedly fast time. A personal best (PB) time of 2h 43min, an improvement of twenty-eight minutes, provided my first sub-three-hour marathon at Wolverhampton. The seventh place I achieved on the Fellsman Hike one month later – in a time of 13h 17min, my best by four and a half hours – would have seemed impossible only twelve months previously.

Breaking three hours for the tough Windermere Marathon in October meant that I'd run my third sub-three-hour marathon this year, and placing third with Dave Chamberlain on the KIMM (a two-day mountain marathon for teams of two) Strathyre score class brought a fantastic year to a close.

I had raced and trained hard, competing in thirty organised events or races, including short 'fun runs', A Class fell races and LDWA events, but I was now acutely aware that further improvements would not come without an increase in training. Through January and February of the following year I averaged seventy miles per week. I didn't realise at the time that such a weekly average would soon become commonplace; indeed, I would sometimes count it as a 'recovery' week.

My log for the early part of 1984 shows a mixture of fell and road races of all distances between three and thirty-six miles, with a noticeable number of training runs marked as 'PB' in red ink. Ten miles on the road in sub-sixty minutes became the norm, as did sub-seventy-five minutes for the half-marathon. The longest runs were either LDWA events or training runs.

As I jogged through the streets of Ingleton at the start of the 1984 Fellsman Hike, I couldn't possibly have guessed what was in store. I was still in the early stages of my ultrarunning career, but one principle I was now sure of was the importance of conserving energy during the early stages.

I started slowly, expending as little energy as possible; I wanted to cross the terrain carefully and efficiently. Gradually, over the big climbs of Ingleborough, Whernside, Gragareth and Blea Moor, I worked my way through the field to Great Knoutberry Hill and the halfway point. The marshal on top clipped my tally and informed me that I was about ten minutes behind the leader. This good and unexpected news spurred me on to gain another two or three places over the next ten miles of hilly moorland. I was running well; I had a sense I was gaining ground on the leader.

The Middle Tongue checkpoint is at forty-two miles. 'You're in second place,' said the marshal. I could hardly believe what was happening on this, of all races – the Fellsman Hike, a race on which I had struggled so much at my first attempt. I soon caught sight of a distant figure, the leader. It was Stan Bradshaw, a very fit and experienced man who I believed was a far better runner than myself. But surprisingly, instead of watching him gradually pull away from me, I was slowly but surely catching him up.

For safety reasons, the organisers insist that runners form into groups of at least four during the hours of darkness; 'grouping up' times are stipulated for each checkpoint and must be strictly adhered to. As we approached the Cray checkpoint in the late evening, darkness was nearly upon us. I knew that Stan and I would probably fail to get through the checkpoint before the cut-off time. We would then be required to wait for the next two runners before continuing through the night as a group of four and then on to the finish. Our 'waiting time' would be deducted from our final time, so whoever got to Cray first would have the most time in hand, but there would only be a minute or two between us. Suddenly, I was aware of a belated but exciting race strategy: if I could overtake Stan before we got to the checkpoint, I might just get through before the cut-off time, and Stan may not. I would then be able to continue to the next checkpoint on my own, where I would wait to form a group. Stan himself would be required to wait at Cray to form a group, which would then include three slower runners.

I knew I was going to finish in the first two, and either outcome was far better than I had ever thought possible. Undeniably, I would rather finish first than second, but more important than my finishing position was the thrill of achieving such a successful run. To perform so well in a race in which I had struggled so badly only four years previously would prove the value of my increased training. But above all it would reinforce my self-belief.

I was determined to run as fast as possible to record the best time I could. Focussing on catching Stan allowed me to immerse, even indulge, myself in that quest.

To have walked for a few paces at the many steep rises and boggy hollows would have meant little time lost and much energy saved, but I continued to run. It came easily. Behind the sore feet, the aching quadriceps and the tentacles of cramp creeping up my calf muscles, I found an inner strength.

The time I saved was minimal, the ground I gained on Stan almost unnoticeable. But the gains, if small, were real. For the first time, I was racing for the lead. I was extending myself physically and mentally; it felt like cruising along the gritstone flakes of the 'Sloth'. My sweat-soaked body was strong and alert, responsive and willing to answer my calls for speed and fluidity. Stan's distant figure gradually became closer and clearer. I can't remember what we said to each other when I caught up; Stan was probably polite and congratulatory, whereas I probably mumbled something about finishing together, while actually thinking the opposite.

The marshal clipped my tally at the Cray checkpoint with one minute to spare. Setting off across the moor towards Buckden Pike, I looked back; there was no sign of Stan. He had failed to beat the cut-off time. My strategy had worked, but for a moment I felt envious; Stan could now have a rest while he waited for his group to form. But my turn to rest came in another six miles, at the Park Rash checkpoint. I enjoyed chatting to the marshals and resting as I waited fifteen minutes for Stan and his group. I had time to reflect on my recent glimpse of the physical state to which I had aspired. I wondered if these momentary encounters were directly related to the amount of training I could cope with, or whether they would always be spontaneous, elusive and alluring, a transient vision of a state which ultimately may never be permanently obtainable.

A dream came true. I won the Fellsman Hike for the first time. My time of 11h 45min was my best by one and a half hours. I could hardly believe that six years previously I had hobbled into the school hall to watch in awe as the front runners were presented with their trophies. Now it was my turn to be presented with the coveted winner's trophy, the unique Fellsman Axe.

*

The 1986 Wolverhampton marathon was my fourteenth, and it was the most memorable, for two diverse reasons. I ran a PB of 2h 37min, only to discover later that it was a short course. The other notable occurrence, which in retrospect seems amusing, was being 'taken short'. I could see that finding somewhere to make the necessary pit stop was going to be problematic; Wolverhampton is very urbanised and well populated, with fields and hedgerows scarce. I needed a cunning plan. The abundance of pubs could provide the obvious solution, but to just blunder into any old pub and search around for the gents would be too time-consuming. I had to do better than that, especially as my PB hung in the balance.

Many of the pubs were of the old traditional style with a big double door at the front, a small door to the bar on one side and a corresponding door to the lounge on the other side. The lounge and the bar each had a small annexe with a frosted-glass window. I knew what was in there, and now I had a plan. Unfortunately, the typical pub car park in those days was huge, a similar size to an athletics track; nowadays, the land would probably be sold for housing. The next pub along the road had the same layout, with the unexpected bonus of a small car park, which I thought must be worth a few seconds. Breaking ranks, I shot across the car park and through the door to the bar. It was full of smoke and packed with lunchtime drinkers. Making a beeline for the estimated location of the gents, I almost ran into the dominoes table. Mission accomplished, and apologising to the dominoes players while niftily ducking to avoid a dart, I made an equally slick exit and was back in the race, PB intact.

The following month, Paul Mitchell and I finished in joint fourth place on the Fellsman Hike, recording a time of 13h 30min. Paul and I had a good run – we hadn't wasted any time or made any route-finding errors – yet were 1h 45min slower than my time of two years previously. I had become accustomed to improving year after year, so this felt like a slight setback. Up to this point, I'd believed I could still improve indefinitely, but now I wondered whether this was a sign that I had reached a plateau, or even the limit of my capabilities.

The second running of the West Highland Way Race was scheduled for 21st June 1986, four weeks later – a linear off-road route of ninety-five miles, starting at Fort William and finishing at Milngavie, a few miles north of Glasgow.

The prospect of undertaking my longest-ever run on a route I didn't know, without support, should have caused me some misgivings. Looking back, I realise I didn't even consider what the consequences might be of running out of food or water – let alone losing my way, falling and being incapacitated. It was an irresistible challenge. I posted my entry form, dreaming only of adventure and success.

The day before the race, I hitch-hiked from the finish at Milngavie to the start at Fort William, stashing food and drink at strategic places ready for the race the following day. It also seemed prudent to leave a torch in the last stash. To help me remember the exact locations, I tied small pieces of red tape to nearby walls or bushes. My expectation of enjoying a good night's sleep in a guest house near the race start didn't materialise; the raging all-night party in the room next door unexpectedly provided my first experience of an early start without sleep.

At 3 a.m. the small field of runners set off from the Nevis Bank Hotel. The main street through Fort William was packed with pairs of highly inebriated revellers, arms draped over each other's shoulders. As the drunken duos weaved their erratic courses they sometimes paused before taking three backward steps while emitting a loud but unintelligible wailing noise, punctuated occasionally by a 'Yee-haw' or a 'Yip-yip'. The spectacle resembled a grotesque version of the Gay Gordons. Despite the obvious possibility of two pairs on opposite tacks colliding, I only witnessed a couple of near misses. I wondered if they possessed a bat-like sixth sense, only activated after imbibing at least eight pints of McEwan's 80 Shillings.

We were soon clear of the mayhem and making our way south towards the Devil's Staircase and Rannoch Moor. General Wade's military road was easy underfoot; not so the path alongside Loch Lomond, which was a tangled mass of roots and mud. I was pleased not to make any route-finding errors and to discover that all my stashes were in place. Duncan Watson, the race organiser, met me at the finish and informed me I had won by a comfortable margin, in a time of 18h 47min, and that 'quite a few' had dropped out. Upon receiving the race report some days later, I learnt I was first out of only three finishers, with a winning margin of 15h 18min. The short report simply said, 'Most runners got lost by Loch Lomond.' I guessed the two runners behind me, David Kerr and Jack Newbigging, were firmly in that category. It seemed I had won because I was the only one of the three finishers not to get lost.

Five weeks later, Graham Eccles and I jogged out of Keswick, our intention being to make an anticlockwise circuit of the Bob Graham Round. I had something of a score to settle: I wanted to complete the round again, but this time I wanted my membership to be ratified. We had a simple plan: we would run the entire route together, effectively being each other's verification runner. Graham's wife, Kerry, had agreed to join Gill to form our road support crew. On 26th July 1986, Graham and I completed the round in 20h 50min and were duly accepted as members of the Bob Graham 24 Hour Club – membership numbers 439 and 440, respectively. As we had both recorded the same time, we were awarded our membership numbers in alphabetical order. I've no problem with that, but just for the record (and not wishing to be too pedantic), I touched Moot Hall first. I will let it go.

*

As pub crawls go, the 'Tan–Cat' – a walk from the Tan Hill Inn, North Yorkshire, to the Cat and Fiddle in Derbyshire – must be the hardest. The 120 miles separating the two highest pubs in England are some of the roughest miles to be found anywhere. The route makes its way south via Great Shunner Fell, Buckden Pike, Great Whernside, Jackson's Ridge, Blackstone Edge, Black Hill, Bleaklow and Kinder to finish at the Cat and Fiddle, near Buxton.

The idea for this marathon walk came from Fred Heardman of the Rucksack Club, who devised it as a way to celebrate the club's golden jubilee. The Rucksack Club was formed in 1902 and quickly gained a reputation for long and fast walking tours in the Derbyshire Peak District. To most people, a 'walking tour' would mean a multi-day excursion, either backpacking or stopping overnight at youth hostels. To the Rucksack Club it meant the same, with one significant difference: there would not be any overnight accommodation. The chosen route would be undertaken non-stop, as quickly as possible.

During its first fifty years, the club flourished, producing rock climbers and mountaineers of the very highest calibre. In particular, the club's dedicated band of long-distance walkers and runners became legendary. The very tough forty-mile Derwent Watershed, now known as the High Peak Marathon, was inaugurated by the Rucksack Club in 1918. The marathon is open to teams of four, and the club duly won the first six races. The now classic Marsden to Edale is another Rucksack Club creation, still enjoyed as a club walk on an annual basis. The esoteric technique of 'bogtrotting' was developed to facilitate the crossing of bogs, slowly enough to conserve energy but quickly enough to prevent sinking into the mire. This is an exceptionally fine balance to strike, where a slight misjudgement can have very messy consequences. The preferable physical attributes of big feet and a lightweight body are the envy of many a bogtrotter.

The Tan–Cat provided a highly demanding undertaking, but a club which had achieved so much and set such high standards would expect nothing less. The mile after mile of bog and rough moorland – much of it trackless, and including 20,000 feet of ascent – was a fitting test for the elite of the club's bogtrotters. The inaugural run was achieved in 54h 10min by Vin Desmond in 1952, and this was lowered to 38h 10min by John Richardson in 1970. In 1979 Mike Cudahy reduced the time to 32h 20min, and on 11th May 1985 he lowered it again to an extremely fast 26h 36min.

Guy Collinson, Howard Sawyer and myself set off from Tan Hill at 4 a.m. on 9th August 1986. Some fourteen hours later, dragging myself out of the ditch, I looked around and checked the map. It showed we were on Jackson's Ridge. I was confused; we were following a ditch, not a ridge. I supposed the map could be wrong. Many times I had been hopelessly lost and blamed my predicament squarely on the inaccuracy of the map.

'Do you think we're right, Howard?'

'Yep, this is it. Jackson's Ridge.'

Unconvinced, I sought a second opinion. 'Guy, what do you think?'

'Yeah, that's what it says on the map.'

Either we were completely lost and my two friends were staging a rather unconvincing cover-up, or I was being subjected to a ridiculous, if somewhat unimaginative, prank. I may have been tired, but I could still tell the difference between a ditch and a ridge. Keeping my thoughts to myself, I checked the map again. After ten minutes alternating between scrutinising the map and tripping over in the heather, I determined that the ditch was, in fact, a county boundary – somewhat confusingly called 'Jackson's Ridge'. We were about halfway through our 'pub crawl' and thoroughly convinced the route's reputation was well deserved. It was tough.

Darkness fell as we followed the Pennine Way over Blackstone Edge. It was a moonless night. Everything was black: the sky, the peat and the rocks. The name seemed fitting. Fortunately, the track was easy to follow, and the first glimmers of daylight complemented our failing torches as we arrived at Crowden. We had covered ninety-five miles in twenty-five hours. We were not going to break any records, but that had never been our intention. However, both the elapsed time and the mileage were significant, if only to me. My longest previous run had been the ninety-five-mile West Highland Way, and the longest time I had ever run for was 20h 50min on the Bob Graham Round. I was entering new territory, both physically and psychologically. Suddenly I felt very tired. My feet were sore; my legs were so stiff they were hurting. I felt apprehensive.

Frank Yates and Max Wood were waiting at Crowden. They had provided road support for the entire distance but now, unwittingly, they presented a temptation. Despite their encouragement – that we were doing well and we were 'nearly there' – I considered quitting. This was becoming not only the longest but also the toughest run I had ever done. Guy had decided a few miles back to call it a day, but Howard looked as strong as when he started and was keen to get to grips with the last twenty-five miles; he would not have any trouble finishing on his own. If I stopped, I would put an immediate end to the tiredness and discomfort. My stiff legs and sore feet would soon recover and be forgotten, but the disappointment and sense of failure would be with me for ever. I didn't realise it at the time, but once I overcame the temptation to give up, I eventually would not need to persuade my body to keep going; I would be unable to stop. Failure would become unacceptable. At last, we could see the outline of the Cat and Fiddle on the skyline. We had taken 34h 44min. What a pub crawl!

*

The year 1987 felt like it could be a turning point. I had become much fitter and a lot more confident. Despite finding the recent Tan–Cat run tough, especially towards the end, I accepted the difficulty as part of a learning process. I was sure it was a stepping stone. I believed that at some point in the future, I could achieve the ultimate physical state and the ultimate run.

The year started well, with a winter crossing of the seventy-mile Colne–Rowsley, again with Guy and Howard. My two companions had made an unsuccessful attempt on the Tan–Cat the previous February. Guy's reply to my question 'Why did you try it in winter?' was simply, 'To make it harder. The only trouble was, it was too hard.' So I believe this run was by way of compensation. They expected to find it easy; after all, it was fifty miles shorter.

The walk was first accomplished in 1926 by Fred Heardman, in the company of John Firth Burton and Harold Gerrard – three of the Rucksack Club's leading bogtrotters. Nowadays, Colne and Rowsley may seem slightly obscure places to have started and finished a walk, but when personal transport was uncommon and rail links were plentiful, they were in fact convenient choices. Starting from Colne railway station, the trio crossed the high Pennine country of Boulsworth Hill, Black Hameldon, Black Hill, Holme Moss, and on to Britland and Withens Edges. They then visited the wonderfully remote Outer Edge and Margery Hill. High Neb, on Stanage Edge, marked the start of a classic tour of the Eastern gritstone escarpments. The edges of Burbage, Froggatt, Curbar and Baslow were also traversed, before the route followed field paths through Chatsworth Park and Beeley to finish at the Peacock Inn, Rowsley.

Since Fred's inaugural traverse, Rucksack Club members have been exclusively responsible for improvements in the Colne–Rowsley record. In 1963 John Richardson and Dennis Weir recorded a time of 18h 55min; Mike Cudahy and Geoff Bell recorded 16h 0min in 1980, and that same year Dennis Weir improved this further to 12h 35min. The current record of 11h 44min 30sec was achieved by Mike Cudahy on 25th July 1982.

We jogged out of Colne at midnight on 10th January 1987. I had prepared a schedule for seventeen hours, based partially on timed reconnaissance runs but also on my increasing experience. I believed it preferable, on an ultra, to utilise all the available daylight, therefore minimising the time spent running in the dark. If my schedule proved to be accurate, we would finish at 5 p.m., thus avoiding a second night. Conditions were good. The bitterly cold northerly wind had frozen most of the bogs; only a few of the deepest refused to succumb and had to be 'trotted' over. Graham Barnes and Richard Ezard would be meeting us at road crossings with hot drinks and food. Providing road support on an ultra is a thankless job.

Keeping track of food, drink, spare clothing, running shoes, torches and batteries, plus a myriad of other items, requires organisation and diligence. In winter, the addition of wind, rain, darkness and the possibility of challenging driving conditions makes this an extremely difficult task.

The weather deteriorated as we reached the White House, the twenty-mile point. The wet mist had frozen onto our waterproofs, breaking off like eggshells as we jogged up to the support car. It was 4 a.m. and conditions were inhospitable, to say the least. Graham and Richard welcomed us with hot soup, but they were soon colder than we were, having vacated their warm car to attend to us. Due to the cold, our torch batteries had been failing very quickly, so we collected replacements before we departed for Blackstone Edge and White Moss. Head torches, lithium batteries and LED bulbs were not yet in general use, but a hand torch did have an unexpected advantage: to compensate for the inevitable rapid deterioration of alkaline batteries, the torch could be held close to the ground to improve vision.

White Moss features some of the wettest and deepest bogs on the Pennines. In contrast to its name, it is a black, semi-liquid wilderness. On a wet winter night, it can provide a bogtrotting experience of the highest order. Mercifully, on this occasion it was well frozen and therefore dry, if a little slippery. As we left Black Hill, Guy must have been disappointed by the dry crossing we'd had so far, and demonstrated an uncanny ability to detect the only unfrozen bog we had encountered. As he uttered an unprintable word, sometimes used to describe certain parts of the male anatomy, I noticed his torch was getting closer to the ground. I could tell by the way he nuanced the word – not so much a highly charged exclamation, more a resigned acceptance of his fate – that he was sinking.

Having extricated the literally half-frozen Guy from the black, oozing pit, we continued towards Holme Moss. As we jogged across the moor, I noticed he had adopted a rather peculiar lopsided gait. Due to his recent experiment with cryobiology, his trousers and their contents were frozen solid. Conscious that for Guy's sake we ought to reach the car and his dry clothes as soon as possible, I reassured my companions that we would not have any trouble locating the TV mast close to the next support point.

I confidently announced it would be 'lit up like a Christmas tree'. I was wrong. It wasn't; it was pitch black. The mist was now thicker and the wind stronger, and Guy was becoming cold. Suddenly, we were puzzled to see a massive steel spike sticking out of the ground. Relief: it was a cable support for the mast. I thought, 'If they'd put the ruddy lights on it'd be helpful.' We took a welcome break at the car while Graham and Richard poured hot water on Guy to thaw out his trousers. What a night he'd had!

It was now daylight, and we were over halfway. We felt we had cracked it. Picking up the pace, we made light work of Britland and Withens Edges. The Derwent Watershed route from Howden Edge over Margery Hill to Moscar was fortunately well frozen and visibility good. After enjoying sausage butties for breakfast, we started the long traverse of the gritstone edges, many of which I had climbed on; Stanage, in particular, brought back memories of my first rock-climbing trip. As we ran along the top of Froggatt Edge, the sky cleared and the temperature plummeted, causing the condensation inside my cagoule to freeze; I could open the cuff and shake out the ice. A pleasant run through Chatsworth Park brought us to the finish at Rowsley in 17h 6min. It had been a tough and adventurous run which put into perspective how extreme a winter Tan–Cat must be.

I felt no need for a recovery period so, with thoughts of recording a fast time on this year's Fellsman Hike, I resumed training the following day. I was now finding it quite easy to run several consecutive high-mileage training weeks, interspersed with long events. In early March, after recording over 1,000 miles in a ten-week period, I completed the thirty-three-mile Haworth Hobble in 4h 36min with Pete Skelton. After that, times of 2h 44min for the Wolverhampton Marathon and 3h 44min for my twelfth circuit of the Three Peaks preceded one or two short fell races up to early May.

I did indeed record a fast time on the Fellsman Hike: 11h 2min, my best by forty-three minutes. But I wasn't on my own, finishing equally with Stan Bradshaw (my friendly adversary from 1984), Alan Jones and local runner Harry Pinkerton.

The next weekend, I had entered the LDWA Snowdonia 100. I didn't really expect a good run after such a short recovery period, but thought it would be good stamina training and an indication of how well I had recovered from the Fellsman. From the start, I ran with Mike Cudahy. Mike already held the records for both the Pennine Way and Wainwright's Coast to Coast, so I believed him to be above my station in both fitness and experience.

It was obvious from the start that he knew the route; he had taken the trouble to check it thoroughly, essential if one has ambitions to record a fast time. I believe I inadvertently caused us to lose some time overnight; we were climbing the Roman steps, an obvious and easy path up onto the Rhinogs. 'Do you think we're on the correct path, Mike?' I said.

'Well, now you mention it, I'm not sure,' he said.

After a quick discussion and a look at the map, we convinced ourselves we were indeed on the wrong path. The Roman steps were over to our right, just a short yomp across some rough terrain. After an hour of struggling through waist-deep heather and armchair-sized boulders and nearly falling over a fifty-foot cliff, we came to another conclusion: we had been on the Roman steps in the first place. As dawn broke, we could see in front of us the distant figure of David Rosen running down the valley. During our foray into the wilderness, as we tried to find a path which we had not actually lost, he had overtaken us.

We had now fallen from equal first to equal second. We set off in pursuit, determined to make up lost time and reinstate our position. When we eventually caught David up, his first words were a very gracious 'Well done, lads. Good recovery.' As soon as we were out of earshot, I turned to Mike and whispered a very ungracious 'Come on, Mike. I bet we can drop him.'

We ran the remainder of the route together, finishing equal first in 21h 35min. I could not help but feel a bit of a fraud as I had relied unfairly on Mike's knowledge of the route. I had even questioned it needlessly, causing us to lose time. But he brushed aside my apologies, saying he had enjoyed my company; we had a good run and an adventure.

I subsequently wrote to Mike to enquire whether his Pennine Way record of 2d 21h 34min still stood, and to ask if he had used any of Wainwright's alternatives. He was extremely helpful and informed me that his record did still stand – but it was fifty-four minutes, not thirty-four, which should make it much easier to crack. Mike assured me that he, like all previous record holders, had followed the route as described in the current edition of Wainwright's *Pennine Way Companion*. He was quite happy for me to use alternatives, but only if they were longer or harder options. He also informed me he had taken one and a half hours' sleep and that it was 'a long way'.

CHAPTER 3:

Tested to Destruction

After thirty seconds of careful consideration, I announced, 'I'll do it next year.' It was July 1987, and Gill and I were on holiday at Portpatrick on the west coast of Scotland. We had noticed a footpath sign saying 'Southern Upland Way, Cockburnspath 212 miles'. The prospect of undertaking a run of that length was irresistible. I wish I could say that I had made a critical analysis of my achievements and balanced them against my intention, but I cannot; it was purely impulsive. Before the end of the day, I had purchased the Ordnance Survey map and guidebook, then spent the remainder of our holiday talking excitedly about the route. The Southern Upland Way would dominate my thoughts for months to come.

On weighing up my chances, I could see that my list of 'cons', although short, was significant. Firstly, I would be attempting to run almost twice as far as my previous longest run, the 120-mile Tan–Cat. The second was equally important: I would be attempting to endure two nights without sleep. I had never experienced any adverse effects from one night without sleep, but two sleepless nights presented the prospect of an unpredictable and challenging experience. My list of 'pros' was longer. I had now completed quite a respectable list of ultras, and a speedy recovery from the Snowdonia 100 reinforced my self-belief. I easily persuaded myself that my list of 'pros' outweighed the 'cons'.

My study of the map seemed to indicate quite a lot of easy terrain with many miles of minor lanes. Checking with a map wheel also showed ninety miles of forest track. This was in sharp contrast to the many miles of tussock grass and bog on the Tan–Cat.

These factors, combined with my determination to train hard over the coming winter, convinced me I wouldn't find the Southern Upland Way any harder than the Tan–Cat; I hoped I might even find it easier. I believed it would be a valuable intermediate goal between the Tan–Cat and an attempt on the Pennine Way record in 1989, a useful box to tick.

The remainder of 1987 went well, and my training felt enjoyable and rewarding. I continued to train well through the autumn, and by January 1988 I was often recording best times on my runs to work through Cannock Chase. My route consisted of a mixture of lanes and forest tracks, similar terrain to the Southern Upland Way; this fuelled my expectation for a successful run. I started the year with a few short and medium-distance races, on both road and fell. In March I recorded a PB of 2h 13min for the Milford 21, my local trail race, before very nearly recording a PB of 3h 27min on my thirteenth circuit of the Yorkshire Three Peaks. A final outing on the Fairfield Horseshoe fell race brought me to the middle of May and within one week of my main preparation run, the LDWA White Peak 100. At this point I had averaged 120 miles per week.

The LDWA provides all entrants with a detailed route description prior to the event, information which allows reconnaissance to be undertaken in advance. Knowing the route can undoubtedly save time and effort and be conducive to a fast and error-free run. However, such information can be a two-edged sword: if the route has been thoroughly rehearsed, this can encourage an overenthusiastic start, and burning up too much energy too early could have disastrous consequences. I decided to use the route description shrewdly and elected not to reconnoitre the first thirty miles. This would force me, on the day of the event, to navigate carefully and therefore run conservatively for the first five hours. I did check the remainder of the route, paying particular attention to the miles I expected to be covering during the hours of darkness.

The event started on 28th May on a fine, dry morning. The underfoot conditions were good: dry and firm, but not 'as hard as concrete'. Passing through the first checkpoint at eight miles, I was in 147th position, but confident that my strategy was correct. By checkpoint four – the twenty-eight-mile point – I was in first equal position with John Leather, and it felt satisfying to know I'd had the brakes on and was ready to speed up. Satisfying also to know that from then on I could relax, knowing I wouldn't make any route-finding errors. Gradually, I pulled away and then increased my lead as I ran through the beautiful limestone country, a landscape which, as the name suggests, always seems light and bright. At the halfway point, I was thirty minutes clear of the second man; at seventy-five miles, as darkness fell, I found myself nearly two hours in front.

The sky cleared and a full moon rose. In the brilliant moonlight my torch seemed superfluous, so I switched it off. I could see my shadow running next to me. The dew-soaked grass cooled my feet and a light frost sparkled on the stiles. Passing the Roaches, I looked up at the 'Sloth'. The lower part of the climb was bathed in silvery light, while the overhang was in shadow, black and sombre – even more menacing than usual. I still felt strong as I ran continuously for the two uphill miles from Upper Hulme to the Mermaid Inn at the ninety-seven-mile point. The misty and cold 4 a.m. finish at Warslow ended a most enjoyable hundred miles and a memorable night of running.

I'd had such a good run, I could hardly believe what I had achieved: recording 17h 58min to finish in first place, out all night and running all the big hills. Afterwards, I kept thinking about cruising up those hills in the dark, calm and in control. I'd worked hard and it certainly hadn't been effortless, but I was fully rewarded. I had achieved a level of fitness which ten years ago had only been a dream.

I could hardly wait to get started on the Southern Upland Way. I felt supremely confident and there was no doubt in my mind. I was going to produce the best performance of my career.

I didn't work out a time schedule, but a simple calculation based on my White Peak 100 time produced a finishing time of thirty-eight hours. This did seem a bit ambitious, given that it was more than twice as far, but I had found the White Peak well within my capabilities. I visualised myself speeding along the easy terrain of the Southern Upland Way, taking advantage of my new level of fitness and confidence.

To break the 270-mile Pennine Way record the following year, I would need to run the 212 miles of the Southern Upland way at an equivalent pace and then be capable of running another fifty-eight miles without slowing down. The Pennine Way record time of 69h 54min equated to

55h 45min for the Southern Upland Way. I rechecked my calculations. Thirty-eight hours definitely was ambitious, so I compromised; there didn't seem to be any reason why I shouldn't finish the 212 miles in under forty-eight hours.

*

I felt relaxed and confident as I jogged out of Portpatrick in the morning sun. It was 9.30 a.m. on 2nd July 1988. Gill, Clive Russell and Richard Ezard would be supporting me all the way to Cockburnspath. Our plan was for me to run the first day on my own; Clive would then accompany me through the first night and Richard the second night. Apart from that, all three would run sections whenever it suited them. We were looking forward to a pleasant, low-key, sociable couple of days.

I was blissfully ignorant of what was to come. I didn't realise this would prove to be the most difficult run I had ever done. We were, fortunately, unaware that during the next two days, our collective resolve, patience and friendship would be tested to their limits. If I had known at the beginning what I was to endure, I would not have started.

Castle Kennedy was our first support point; it was at fourteen miles, but it felt a lot shorter.

'You're not going a bit too fast, are you?' said Gill.

'No,' I replied. 'That was never fourteen miles. I'm hardly trying. I must have measured it wrong on the map.'

As I set off on the next section, I knew I hadn't made a mistake – it was fourteen miles – but I was convinced I had been expending energy at a very conservative rate. Apart from the first two miles of clifftop path, the remainder of the section was on quiet lanes and good tracks; the terrain had lent itself to easy progress. Although I had to admit to myself that fourteen miles in two hours did seem rather fast, it certainly didn't feel like it. I wondered if thirty-eight hours was, in fact, possible.

The terrain was similar for the next thirty miles to Glentrool, but with longer sections of enclosed forest track which, thankfully, were interspersed with occasional pastoral and mountain views. In particular, the distant view of the Galloway hills from the summit of Craigairie Fell was welcome.

The support team met me at convenient road crossings, where I would often find them lounging in the sun. The day had a relaxed, easy-going atmosphere. I felt quietly confident.

The Caldons campsite in Glentrool was our next support point, and it brought back memories. Two years previously, Gill and I had competed in the KIMM, and the event start was at the nearby Goat Park.

I had been suffering bouts of mild nausea, although I hadn't been physically sick, so I decided to try a change of food and drink. But swapping from peanut butter and jam sandwiches to chopped bananas and cream made things worse. Feeling nauseous, although unpleasant, wasn't really a problem – whereas being sick, as well as being distressing, made things very inefficient. The potential for wasting time trebled: stopping to eat, stopping to be sick, and stopping again to eat.

Having now run forty-five miles in 6h 37min, my average speed was 6.6mph. Brushing aside Gill's continued concerns that maybe I had started too fast, I said, 'Before I go, I'll have a quick look at my foot.' A small hot spot was developing. I applied a generous smear of Vaseline, a tried and tested remedy.

'Is it OK?' she enquired.

'It's nothing,' I replied. 'It'll be fine. I'll get going.'

The next twenty miles, to St John's Town of Dalry, was a mixture of lanes and forest tracks with the occasional stretch of boggy moorland. Soon after setting off, the track climbed quite significantly, so I decided to conserve some energy and walk for a while. I had done a lot of running, and a shorter stride length would be welcome for a few minutes. When I reached the top, the view of Loch Trool far below confirmed just how big the climb had been. As the track started to descend, I noticed a slight reluctance to resume running. Walking for a short while to enjoy the change of pace and the views, I felt a recurrence of the soreness on my right foot. Although not unduly worried about the odd hot spot, I decided to collect a small tub of Vaseline at the next support point to carry with me.

After a long but steady climb from the eastern end of Loch Trool, the track eventually left the forest and levelled out, giving way to easy running. At least, it should have been easy. I didn't feel quite as fluent as I had earlier, but it had been a hot day; I was probably a bit dehydrated. The next time I met the support crew, I would take in plenty of fluid and have a look at my foot. The mountain scenery was now impressive, with some of the most intriguingly named mountains to be found anywhere. Curleywee to the south, the Rig of Jarkness and Mullwharchar to the north. Beyond stood Merrick, at 843m the highest point in southern Scotland and the centrepiece of the rough and remote Range of the Awful Hand.

Good views of Loch Dee appeared on the left, but not for long. The track soon crossed the Black Water of Dee to plunge into another long section of forest. A short run along the side of Clatteringshaws Loch provided some relief from the increasingly tedious stony tracks.

My expectations of fast, easy progress over the early sections of the Southern Upland Way had been met — even exceeded — but now I was slowing down and my confidence was fading. Approaching Shield Rig, I was thankfully again out of the woods and onto the open fellside. My spirits lifted still further as I crossed the open south-western slopes of the Rhinns of Kells. But on the pleasant lanes near Knocksheen, I noticed that the hot spot on the ball of my right foot was worse and I also seemed to have a small stone in my left shoe. Stopping to carry out an inspection, I discovered I now had two problems. The hot spot had become a blister, but to make matters even worse, the 'small stone' was in fact another blister. They were only small, but they were enough to cause me concern. I had only run sixty miles, so inevitably the discovery further dented my confidence. I would have a proper look at them when I arrived at Dalry, and work out what to do. While I'd got my shoes off, I took the opportunity to loosen my laces, as both shoes now seemed too tight. Standing up, I noticed a slight but ominous stiffness in the top part of my thighs.

On my arrival at Dalry, I found the support team in good spirits. 'I'm glad to see you've had the good sense to slow down a bit,' said Gill, jokingly.

I slumped in the camping chair and stared at my feet. It wasn't good sense that had caused me to slow down — I didn't really have any choice — but I couldn't bring myself to admit I was finding the run disappointingly tough. Gill had assumed that after ten hours of almost non-stop running with little food, I would be ravenous; she had prepared a feast of doughnuts, fruit, rice pudding and tea. Although my body must have required sustenance, I didn't have any appetite, so I did feel guilty as I made only a half-hearted attempt to eat. Up to this point I had run sixty-five miles at an average speed of 6.3mph, a small reduction from the 7mph I had averaged for the first fourteen miles. Although this was to be expected, I was disappointed to find I had only averaged 5mph for the most recent eight miles.

The stiffness in my legs had become worse, and was especially noticeable while negotiating stiles. It also made the process of inspecting and applying first aid to my feet quite awkward. Clive offered to help and, as he talked enthusiastically about running with me through the upcoming night, demonstrated his previously unsuspected chiropody skills.

The next seven miles to Stroanpatrick crossed some pleasant open country, fortunately with fewer forest tracks. Faint and boggy paths took me through isolated farms and gave views of the distant Cairnsmore of Carsphairn range. As I approached my first night, I tried to use these few miles to dispel my increasingly negative thoughts and regain some optimism. With Clive looking after my feet, maybe the blisters wouldn't get any worse. But my hope that the stiffness in my legs would be alleviated by softer terrain was dispelled by the guidebook comments: 'From here the general firmness underfoot improves markedly for the rest of the Way'.

No matter how much I tried to regain my enthusiasm, I couldn't escape the fact that I was finding the run considerably more difficult than I had expected. I was convinced my early pace had been steady, but then I began to wonder whether perceived effort was not the same as actual effort. I had to admit that I might have started too fast, and the many miles on dry, hard surfaces had contributed to stiffness and blisters. I still had a lot to learn about pace judgement.

I couldn't believe this was happening. I wasn't even a third of the way to Cockburnspath, and I was struggling. I had made a big mistake, which made me introspective and depressed. I soon convinced myself that given the level of effort I was now being forced to expend and the amount of discomfort I was enduring, I would not be capable of completing the run. Clive was planning to join me at Stroanpatrick for the overnight run via Polskeoch bothy to Sanquhar and on to Wanlockhead, the 100-mile point – but there didn't seem any point in forcing myself through this first night, only to abandon the run the following day.

I decided to announce that I was terminating the run and save us all the trouble of going through the night. My disappointment was almost overwhelming.

Clive was waiting when I arrived at Stroanpatrick: a rolled-up map in one hand, a water bottle in the other, his rucksack packed with waterproofs, spare clothing, food and drink.

I sipped a cup of tea.

'How's it going?' he said.

'I want to say something,' I replied.

Gill probably guessed from my tone what it was. I hesitated and looked down at my feet. My mind was in turmoil, battling between this treadmill of effort and the crushing disappointment of failure. But if failure was a certainty, as it surely must be, why prolong the inevitable?

I still don't know how I managed to say what came next. 'Clive,' I said, 'can you put a tub of Vaseline in the rucksack?'

'It's in.' he replied. 'Are you ready?'

The twenty-mile stretch to Sanquhar is one of the remotest sections of the route, with only the halfway bothy to provide sanctuary in the event of bad weather. In daylight, the high-level traverse would afford good views and be a pleasure, but today, with the light fading and my body low on reserves, it felt committing. I was apprehensive, and glad I wasn't on my own. We left Stroanpatrick at 9.24 p.m. as Gill and Richard set off for Wanlockhead and their overnight stay in a guest house.

In Clive's company, I felt at ease; his quiet, assured demeanour conveyed confidence, and I felt I could cope with the difficulties more easily. Although I was undoubtedly tired and my feet still hurt, the discomfort now seemed more bearable. I was glad I hadn't quit at Stroanpatrick. The time to admit defeat would undoubtedly come, but not just yet. I couldn't bring myself to terminate the run until I was convinced that failure was unavoidable.

My next opportunity to retire would be at Wanlockhead, still some twenty miles distant. I could quit there and consider the 100 miles I had completed to be a very demanding training run on which I had struggled and learnt some valuable lessons.

As darkness fell, the track entered yet another uniform section of forest which led up to Manquhill Hill. More open country soon followed to the trig point on Benbrack, at 580m the highest point on the route so far. In daylight we would have enjoyed the view behind us to the Rhinns of Kells and ahead to the Lowther Hills.

I was being careful with my footing, trying not to stumble in shoes that now definitely felt too small. Suddenly, while crossing an area of tussock grass, I stubbed my toe and sent shock waves through my stiff thighs. I tripped and shrieked in pain, then lay in the grass for a few moments while the pain subsided, thankful that I was spared the cramp spasm that can often result from sudden trips and falls. When I stood up, there was no sign of Clive. I was just about to bellow his name at the top of my voice, thinking he hadn't noticed my fall, when he switched his torch on; he was sitting in the grass next to me.

After crossing Black Hill, we entered another short stretch of forest before arriving at Polskeoch bothy. At midnight we opened the door to find two backpackers in residence. They were interested in my undertaking and impressed with my progress. Their comments that I looked fit and must be going very well, although gracious, were obviously misplaced. After Clive and I had enjoyed a sit down and a chat, we stood up to leave, and the true state of my physical condition must have become obvious to them. I could hardly believe how much I'd stiffened up in ten minutes.

Leaving the bothy on the tarmac lane made my feet sting, but the Way soon turned off the road onto softer terrain. Another ten miles of remote country brought us to Sanquhar, but despite the slightly easier underfoot conditions, I had tripped and stumbled a few more times. Darkness was partly the cause, but also the stiffness in my legs was making me less agile.

The next eight miles to Wanlockhead would be difficult, but the remaining 120 miles to Cockburnspath seemed like a physical impossibility. I was incapable of completing the route. I couldn't do it. It seemed futile to continue.

My decision made, all I had to do was suggest to Clive that we rest here until morning then phone the guest house and ask Gill and Richard to come and pick us up. But I did feel a pang of guilt at expecting them to come and collect us. If I was going to abandon it, I should at least get to the support car. Anyway, it would be preferable to waiting here in the dark, getting cold.

After a short break for some food, Clive stood up, looked at the map and said, 'We have a big climb to do now.' I didn't say anything; I couldn't. Standing up, I winced and wished I had some bigger shoes. He was right; it was huge – a thousand feet up onto the moors via Bogg Farm and Cogshead. I could see the first glimmers of daylight. With them came improved vision, which meant more accurate foot placements and a slight reduction in effort.

We stopped on top of Glengaber Hill to put the torches away. Although it was now daylight, the sun was still below the horizon, but the clear eastern sky promised another fine day. As we ran down to the Wanlock Water, I felt relieved that I would soon be finished. But my relief was tinged with sadness and more disappointment than I would ever have imagined.

Jogging the last three miles to Wanlockhead gave me time to consider what I was going to say to Gill and Richard. I was sure they would encourage me to continue, but my mind was made up. It was time to admit defeat. However, the more I thought about announcing my retirement, the more upsetting the prospect became. I felt tears well up – tears of disappointment and tears of frustration at my inadequacy.

When we arrived at the car, Richard passed me a drink, and I could see Gill waving from the guest house window. They were both positive and enthusiastic. I don't know how they found the strength to offer that support and encouragement when it must have been obvious I would never make it to Cockburnspath.

Although I had planned to run solo for the next twenty miles to Beattock, I now didn't relish the prospect. When Gill pulled marital rank and decreed that I would not be running any more sections on my own, I felt relieved.

The prospect of completing the remaining 112 miles, including another night out, seemed impossible, but at the same time the thought of failure was abhorrent, even intolerable. I didn't know what to do. My body was telling me I couldn't do it, so there was no point in continuing, but my mind just couldn't accept failure. I felt despondent and miserable. I was sure I couldn't carry on, but I knew I was unable to concede, at least not voluntarily.

I began to notice a slight change in my mood: my indecision was being replaced not by a renewed determination, but by a feeling of inevitability. My physical discomfort was increasing – I knew that if I continued, I might be tested to destruction – but I felt less distressed at the prospect. I had to accept my fate.

It was a beautiful clear morning as I set off for Beattock. I felt very tired and I was running into a headwind, but I now felt a calm acceptance of my situation. I didn't know what my fate would be, but that no longer seemed important. I would continue jogging and walking, making my way eastwards, until I became incapable. I would then accept defeat.

Writing this now, thirty-three years later, I have forgotten many details. There are long sections I cannot remember at all. In retrospect, I can see that the blank sections in my memory become longer and the landmarks and incidents I remember become fewer. I do wonder if this fading of memory is a sort of subconscious denial; perhaps I don't really want to remember. Or is it possible my mind learnt to blot out much of the discomfort at the time, to allow my body to absorb the increasing tiredness more easily?

The twenty miles to Beattock are split by two road crossings, providing three contrasting sections. The first six miles to the Dalveen Pass is the high-level traverse of the Lowther Hills. Despite the effort required for the initial 1,000-foot climb, I felt more at ease now I'd reconciled myself to a new and unanticipated mindset.

The route doesn't actually visit the summit of Lowther Hill, as this is occupied by the 'giant golf ball' radio station. The highest point of the Lowthers is Green Lowther, which stands a little way off route but is accessible, according to the guidebook, 'by a short ridge walk along a tarmac track'. This 'short walk' is in fact one mile each way. I decided to give it a miss. The Lowthers would have provided a few enjoyable miles of high country if it hadn't been for the clutter of radio equipment. According to my schedule, after completing the Lowthers I met the support car at Nether Fingland at 6.45 a.m. and again near the Daer Reservoir, but I have no memory of either meeting.

Reaching Beattock felt significant. At 122 miles, I was over halfway, but it was also a very convenient and tempting place to abandon the run; the A74 would provide an easy route south and home.

Gill and the two lads knew I was struggling and had been for a long time. They must have known my chances of success were poor. They could easily have encouraged me to accept I had made mistakes and to concede defeat. Instead of having me battle on towards inevitable failure, they might have suggested I write this escapade off to experience and return for another attempt. But the proposal was never mooted and, I now realise, never would have been.

I could tell that my increasingly morose introspection was affecting us all. They must have been troubled by my grim stubbornness and reluctance to enter into conversation, but never once did I detect an underlying atmosphere of impatience or see a glance of exasperation.

Whatever the outcome, I had undoubtedly learnt a lot. Accurate judgement of my early pace and keeping hydrated were both critical lessons, and a spare pair of larger shoes would have saved much discomfort.

We had also learnt a lot about support; I wasn't the only one who was exhausted. Unquestionably, a larger and more experienced support team would have eased the burden – another mistake I would not repeat.

After Clive yet again demonstrated his chiropody skills and provided some inviting but unwanted food, Gill ran with me for a couple of miles. I didn't need to say how hard I was finding it; she was well aware of that and had been for many hours. Even in a moment of close emotional honesty, neither of us could bring ourselves to openly confront the apparent futility of my continuing with something which was obviously going to fail.

Richard joined me for the sixteen miles over Ettrick Head to Scabcleuch, the 135-mile point. I was now running and walking in approximately equal amounts; soon I wouldn't be able to run at all. It was now mid-afternoon on the second day and, despite my slowing pace, the miles were drifting by. Each one seemed to take a long time, but time itself, strangely, seemed to pass quickly.

The next twenty-seven miles to Yair Bridge hold few memories for me except for a mixture of stiff-legged jogging and walking. However, my slow pace meant that Clive could read the map and guidebook more easily. We would spend a short time memorising the route before jogging and walking for a mile or two. It was on this section that we encountered two walkers; they were the only two people I met on the entire 212 miles, apart from in towns and villages and the two in the bothy. An indication of how little attention this remote and beautiful area receives.

I do have a vivid memory of my arrival at the ancient Tibbie Shiels Inn, where Gill presented me with an enormous chip butty. As I munched my way along the side of St. Mary's Loch, I managed to increase my pace, but by the time Richard and I arrived at Dryhope, I had reverted to a slow, exhausted plod. The sudden onset of nausea was the first episode since Glentrool and made the thought of any more food unappetising. Although I was never actually sick, the awful feeling dogged me for the remainder of the route.

I have no memory at all of the long climb to Blake Muir or the next six miles to Traquair. I dread to think what the possible consequences might have been had I been on my own.

The Way leaves Traquair on the evocatively named Cross Borders Drove Road. As darkness fell, it seemed fitting that we were following in the footsteps of grim marching armies, monks and drovers from centuries past. The ascent to Minch Moor was long but easy underfoot. I have vague memories of walking and jogging behind Richard. His torch beam was casting flickering shadows of his feet, sometimes fast, sometimes slow as he changed pace to suit the terrain.

As we approached the Three Brethren, as if to prove that I didn't need to walk at all, I ran a steep uphill in a sudden burst. Exhausted from the effort, I then reverted to a slow walk. To say this was a pointless waste of energy and had proved nothing wasn't quite true; I was underlining my intention, if only to myself, to complete this exercise as quickly as I possibly could. I was also proving the validity of the 'tortoise and the hare' fable, as Richard soon caught me up.

A calculation of pace at Yair Bridge showed I had covered 162 miles at an average speed of 4.5mph, but the average for the last ten miles was only 3.7mph – a far cry from the 7mph I had started at. It was now 10 p.m. and I was preparing for my first experience of a second night without sleep. Only five weeks ago I had achieved my best-ever ultrarun. The White Peak 100 had been the perfect 'textbook' ultra. Today, apart from the first fourteen, every mile had been increasingly hard won. I had expected to arrive at this point tired and a bit apprehensive, but quietly confident; instead, I was exhausted, injured and on the verge of failure. I was paying a heavy price. It was only afterwards that I realised the price had bought something of worth: it had bought a new and valuable experience. I had searched my body for every last grain of strength. All my previous physical and mental boundaries had been transcended, and my perception of the meaning of 'effort' had changed forever.

My newfound state of calm resignation and acceptance of the task ahead meant I was no longer daunted by the remaining fifty miles, nor was I unduly concerned at the prospect of the upcoming second night. I was attempting to achieve a balance between the increasing deterioration of my physical state and the patient fortitude still required to complete the run. But it felt like a very fine line to tread; my mental and physical equilibrium was being tested. Mind and body would be entering unknown territory.

In an attempt to find some much-needed relief for my tortured feet, I removed the insoles from my shoes, which did have the desired effect of creating a bit more room. It also had the unwelcome effect of allowing me to feel every pebble on the track.

The next sixteen miles took six hours, at an average speed of 2.6mph. My memory is of a black, endless night, relieved occasionally by lying down on the track to allow Richard to massage my legs. The massage itself was painful but gave some short respite from the stiffness. After one such stop, somewhere between Melrose and Lauder, I was astounded to see a horse and rider galloping across a field to our right. We were jogging and walking downhill on a bridleway; the rider, with black hood and cloak flowing, was obviously intent on intercepting us. In the corner of a field we negotiated a small maze of sheep pens and stone sheds, and I expected to be confronted by the menacing spectre at any moment. But there was nothing. On exiting the maze, I looked across the field and back along the bridleway; nothing.

At last, there came a misty and almost imperceptible change from night to day. The path traversed a long, narrow field. The mist was so thick we almost walked into a massive boulder. I was too tired to wonder why a large boulder would be in the middle of the path. However, closer inspection revealed it had a tail at one end and a protrusion with a copper ring through it at the other, and it was emitting a faint but potentially aggressive snoring sound. I was sure there must be a law against keeping a bull on a public right of way, but I had a vague recollection that its right to be there might depend upon its age and breed.

Richard had recently read JRR Tolkien's *The Hobbit*, so couldn't resist drawing a comparison with Smaug the Magnificent. Not wishing to offend Smaug the dragon by questioning his date of birth and family history, we tiptoed past.

Suddenly, we heard a loud grunt. Smaug was awake and lurching to his feet.

As I was now incapable of running, we gained the gate at the far end of the field by 100 yards of brisk backward walking which, oddly, seemed to relieve my stiffness and was probably slightly quicker than walking forward. Smaug must have decided he had better things to do, and made his way towards some more 'boulders' which we hadn't noticed in the heat of the moment.

We arrived at Lauder at 5.24 a.m. The strain of lowering myself slowly into the camping chair was too much for my now almost inflexible thighs to bear, the last few inches being an uncontrolled and painful slump.

Lauder was at 180 miles, which left only about thirty-two miles to the finish at Cockburnspath. The concept of 'only' is, of course, relative. At the beginning, 'only' thirty-two miles would 'only' take about five hours. Now, sitting in my chair wondering whether I was even capable of standing up, thirty-two miles seemed like an impossible task. My progress had been reduced to a shambling, limping shuffle, and my body was almost finished. The calm acceptance which I had felt briefly was waning. I wanted an end to the effort, the blisters and the nausea. But still I could not concede. The end would only come when I reached Cockburnspath.

Gill, Clive and Richard continued with their encouragement, assuring me that if I could keep going and if I could sustain the constant emotional equilibrium between pain and patience, I should be finished in another ten hours.

'Ten hours!' The words echoed through my consciousness like a tolling bell. 'Ten hours!' My mind balked. I know they meant it to be an encouragement, but to me it sounded like a sentence to ten years' hard labour. I was sure they must have made a mistake.

They had. Those last thirty-two miles were to take me twelve hours, almost to the minute.

The fourteen miles over the Lammermuir Hills to Longformacus via the two enormous cairns of Twin Law were the last miles of high country. The remaining eighteen miles became low-lying, mostly arable land with many picturesque villages and, at last, my first view of the east coast at Pease Bay. After a hot and only partially remembered six hours, eventually I turned away from my coastward direction and swung inland to the Mercat Cross. Cockburnspath is a pleasant enough village, but not an inspiring place to finish, especially considering the close proximity of the beautiful Cove Harbour.

I had finished in 55h 55min – 5h 40min faster than the previous best time recorded by Mike Cudahy in 1986. I didn't realise this at the time, and only became aware of Mike's run on reading the traumatic account in his book *Wild Trails to Far Horizons*.

Although I had eventually completed the Southern Upland Way in record time, I failed to negotiate the final hurdle. My legs were so stiff that Richard wasted no time in carrying me up the stairs in the guest house, the final supreme act of a selfless supporter. Unfortunately, I was in too much discomfort to sleep; even bearing the weight of a thin cotton sheet was too painful for my legs to tolerate.

My expectations of this being 'the best performance of my career' and 'a useful box to tick' now seemed absurd assumptions, based more on dreams and optimism than on reality. The stiffness in my thighs was worse than on my first Fellsman Hike eight years ago. The Pennine Way would surely be impossible. I felt like a complete beginner, back to square one. I had been tested to destruction.

CHAPTER 4:

Battered and Bruised, but Not Beaten

The Southern Upland Way had left me battered and bruised, both physically and mentally. I was demoralised, so before I commenced training for the Pennine Way, I had to be sure what the reason was for my poor performance.

I couldn't accept that it was a lack of fitness, especially after my highly successful run on the White Peak 100. The extreme stiffness I had suffered might have been due to the many miles of hard surfaces, but it seemed unlikely; I had run hundreds of miles on the similar terrain of Cannock Chase, and I expected that to be an advantage. Despite my refusal to believe it at the time and my reluctance to believe it even now, I had to accept that starting too fast must have been the reason. If I wanted to succeed on the Pennine Way, it would be critical to avoid making the same mistake again. At the same time, my Southern Upland Way performance indicated other areas in which I might improve.

It had been a mistake to run just on 'feel'; I should have prepared a schedule. There would come a time when I could tune in to my body and trust my instincts, but I wasn't there yet. At this stage in my development, especially at the start of such a long and important run, using discipline and patience would be a more prudent approach than relying on 'feel'. I decided to prepare a schedule for the entire 270 miles of the Pennine Way and, importantly, planned a conservatively paced start. Improving my level of fitness by increasing my training load would complement a steady start and allow me to feel genuinely comfortable. The 'slow start' approach I had employed on the White Peak 100 had worked well, so no matter how slow it felt, I would exercise restraint and self-control. This approach became key to my ultrarunning strategy. To fail on the Pennine

Way would be disappointing, but if poor preparation in training or impatience in execution were the reasons, it would be inexcusable. An accurate schedule leading to better pace judgement, extensive knowledge of the route and a large support team were all important. However, achieving an even higher level of fitness would be my insurance policy.

After a few weeks spent mostly cycling, the stiffness subsided and eventually disappeared. My feet returned to their normal size and I felt physically recovered. My ambition to break the Pennine Way record was not diminished but strengthened.

I started training in September 1988 and gradually increased my weekly mileage. I split my training into blocks of four weeks, increasing my mileage progressively for the first three weeks before an easier 'recovery week'. Each successive block comprised weeks of a higher mileage than the previous block.

It was at this point that Gill encouraged me to join a training group supervised by George Taylor, a teacher at the school where she worked. George was an athletics coach with Cannock and Stafford AC and he believed that, in order to be successful at long-distance running, it was necessary to develop a high cruising speed. The faster you could run over short distances, the faster you would be able to cruise long distances. This was simple but good advice which served me well on future ultras. George organised a weekly training session designed to increase speed. An 'interval' session includes high-intensity periods of fast running interspersed with short jogging sections to allow partial recovery before the next increase in effort. Interval training often uses landmarks such as lamp posts or junctions to signify the start and finish of the high-intensity periods, but George's group would run at night, in the headlights of his car on quiet country lanes. A hoot of the horn was the signal to speed up or slow down, and the timings were always random. Sounds simple, and it was – for George, sitting in the car. The lengths of the fast and slow sections always varied and were unpredictable. The hoots to accelerate always seemed to come at the start of a long uphill, and the signal to ease off was sometimes so long in coming, I often wondered if the horn had broken. The sessions were remorseless. We would often return to base having completed between ten and fifteen miles at an average speed in excess of 10mph, including the jog recoveries.

By Christmas, I had averaged 100 miles per week for sixteen weeks, including a maximum week of 130 miles. I felt I had significantly improved my strength and stamina, while also remaining injury free, and that the best way to prepare for the strain of running 270 miles was by learning to absorb ever more training miles. To this end, I planned to achieve my maximum mileage by the end of February.

I had a short break at Christmas, then despite poor weather and short daylight hours I started training with a vengeance. I knew I was getting fitter, but I was also becoming obsessive. The more running I did, the stronger I felt and the more I wanted to run. I was enjoying training hard, exploring my limits. I wondered if one day I would reach that magical state where I could run without perceived effort.

On weekdays during January and February, I ran to work and back – seven miles there and ten miles home. My job as a meter reader entailed walking for six hours every day, and with little time to recover between the two runs, my legs often felt tired and heavy. On Tuesdays I would run three times; pretty tough, especially as the third run was the interval session. At weekends I undertook long runs on either the Pennine Way or my local long-distance footpath, the Staffordshire Way. On rostered days off from work (three days each month) or 'rest days' as they were called, I embarked upon long road runs of between fifteen and twenty-five miles. My colleagues found it highly amusing that I should want to run twenty-five miles on my 'rest day'. The object of these runs was to improve my speed-endurance; that is, the ability to run close to my limit for as long as possible. Aches and pains came and went but whenever they started to become worse or insistent, I would cycle for a few days, hoping to maintain fitness and stave off a chronic injury.

At the end of January, on the spur of the moment, I decided to undertake a fifty-mile run. I had become aware of the Three Rivers Walk, a tour of the rivers Dane, Manifold and Dove. The route was inaugurated in 1956 by RE (Larry) Lambe of the Rucksack Club. He started at 9.17 a.m. on 25th August from Rushton Spencer and followed the Dane to Dane

Head, before turning south along the Manifold to Ilam Hall. From here, he followed the Dove to its source near Dove Head Farm on the A53 Buxton Road. The August weather was atrocious, with some riverside paths being impassable, forcing him to make detours. In the early hours of the following morning, Larry stopped at Spider Cave in Wolfscote Dale to meet friends – his only support point. He was three and a half hours late and surprised to find they were still waiting. Using a primus stove, they soon reheated the stew they had brought. His watch had become waterlogged some weeks before but, wanting to keep check of time, he carried an alarm clock in a plastic bag. At 4.35 a.m. he checked his clock, changed his boots for 'rubbers' and resumed the walk. Larry completed the entire walk alone, and his finishing time of 25h 35min bears testament to the poor conditions he endured.

I started out from Rushton Spencer at 8 a.m. on 4th February. The weather was dry and windy, but conditions were muddy underfoot. Gill, Richard and Tony Ezard supported me, and I finished in 7h 36min. Thankfully, I didn't have to contend with any floods or carry an alarm clock. Allowing not a single day to recover, I resumed my training.

Most of my route to work lay across Cannock Chase, a large forestry area; in the dark, cold and mud, it sometimes felt adventurous. Often, I disturbed a dog at an isolated farm, its barking and howling making my imagination run riot. I was convinced that one day it would break its leash and chase after me, triggering an impromptu speed session. One morning, in deep snow, I changed my route to cross an area of disused mines. As I descended the steep side of a spoil heap, the whole slope collapsed. I must be the only person ever to have been avalanched on Cannock Chase on their way to work. My biggest fright was almost running into a stag. It was a particularly dark morning as I ran through a deep cutting. I must have been downwind from the animal, and we only became aware of each other's presence when we were about two yards apart. The stag bolted up the bank in a storm of flying pebbles and sand, causing my heart rate to reach a level normally only achieved during the Tuesday interval sessions.

By the end of February, I had improved my ranking in the interval session. My long weekend runs had increased to between thirty-five and forty miles on both Saturday and Sunday, and I started to really look forward to the speed-endurance runs on the road. Recording split times at landmarks added interest and provided an incentive to complete the course more quickly next time. These speed-endurance runs coupled with regular interval sessions soon began to produce an overall increase in my running speed. I'd also increased my mileage, averaging 130 miles per week, with the maximum completed in a seven-day period being 170 miles. At the time, I wondered if I was going too far – perhaps I didn't need to do that much – but I'd promised myself I would train to my limit and could not bring myself to ease down. I was always treading a fine line between fitness and injury. When I thought about how much I'd suffered during the Southern Upland Way and how much further the Pennine Way was, my conviction to train as hard as possible was strengthened. If I failed, it would not be because I wasn't fit enough.

I was ready to start the next stage of my preparation by early March, and I was looking forward to it because it would involve a change of strategy. I had greatly improved my tolerance for physical effort and was now strong enough to absorb a level of training of which I had never thought myself capable. My plan now was to do less running overall and to do most of my midweek mileage on the road. I would still run every day, but I hoped this small change would have the effect of further lifting my speed. It would also be a welcome change from slogging across Cannock Chase in the dark and mud every day. Walking daily at work for six hours would still contribute that all-important base level of endurance.

Embarking on a series of medium-distance ultras at approximately monthly intervals was the next part of my plan. As well as the obvious training benefit, I hoped I would become better at pace judgement. Experimenting with food, drink, shoes and clothing would also be useful. Most importantly, I hoped to improve my performance on each consecutive ultra, culminating in the ninety-five-mile West Highland Way race on 24th June. I visualised myself having a storming run, the best and fastest run I had ever achieved. But then, I had visualised something similar once before.

My first objective, on the 4th March, was the Dales Way, which runs east to west from Ilkley to Bo'ness. At eighty-one miles and not especially hilly, it would be ideal as my first long preparation run. I planned an ambitious schedule for 13h 46min – equal to the current record, which had been set by Dennis Beresford in August 1983. I wasn't expecting to break this record, as I knew Dennis was a very fit and experienced runner. I also expected the many miles of riverside path to be wet and muddy so early in the year. Gill, Richard and Clive would be my support team, with Guy Collinson joining me at the halfway point. Two days prior to the run, a forecast of strong westerly winds persuaded me to change the direction of my run: I would start from Bo'ness and perhaps get an eighty-mile tailwind.

Starting in the dark from Bo'ness, Richard and I soon took a wrong turn, even though Gill and I had walked the route two years previously. Being fifteen minutes behind schedule within the first few miles was an inauspicious start, but I wasn't really expecting a fast run. The amount of mud exceeded my worst fears; many passing boots had churned the narrow path between river and fence into a quagmire.

As I approached the forty-mile point at Far Gearstones, I noticed that the squelching and sucking noises made by my left shoe had changed tone. Closer inspection showed the outer sole about to part company with the mid-sole – which it soon did, quickly followed by the mid-sole itself. With the upper twisted backward nine inches above my ankle, I jogged up to the car.

'Never seen shoes like those before. What type are they?' asked Guy.

'New Balance Trail Busters,' I said.

'Well, they're certainly bust,' was his predictable reply.

Now halfway to Ilkley and only eighteen minutes behind schedule, I felt I might actually have a chance of breaking the record. An easy path into Ilkley and a small, planned buffer in the schedule got me over the line in 13h 34min. What a surprise; it was a lot quicker than I had expected, and this felt like a good omen. However, my new record didn't last very long: an extremely determined Dennis returned two months later to record the astonishing time of 12h 44min.

After a one-week recovery followed by four weeks of steady running, I was refreshed and ready for my next long run. On 8th April I started out on the ninety-two-mile Staffordshire Way. The route from Mow Cop to Kinver Edge is complicated, following field paths, forestry areas and canal towpaths; it reportedly includes 350 stiles. During my long winter training runs I had reconnoitred the entire route, except for just a few miles at the beginning. For this short but crucial section, I enlisted the help of fellow Macclesfield Harriers John Amies and John Axson. These two local runners were experts on the route and got me off to a good, error-free pre-dawn start. Gill and Richard Ezard were sharing the driving, with Richard also running some sections. Mike Chandler and Alan Roberts, fellow participants in George's interval sessions, joined in to find out 'what this ultra stuff is all about'. Richard Day was another clubmate, from Mercia Fellrunners, who had local knowledge of the central section of the route. Heavy overnight rain after a wet week ensured the first half of the route, when not waterlogged, was 'sticky', to say the least. But then Staffordshire mud is reputed to be the stickiest mud anywhere.

Abbots Bromley, at forty-four miles, was almost halfway – and was home to my speed mentor, George Taylor, who kindly turned out to see me through. Here I took my first stop, just two minutes, during which I picked up a drink and had a quick chat with George. I had been running for a little over seven hours, so my rough prediction of completing in sixteen hours did seem possible. The record was held by John Britton, who five years previously had completed the trail in 17h 57min. John hadn't done a complete reconnaissance, and undertook the run at the end of June when vegetation was high, so to complete the route in such a fast time really was a remarkable feat. In his post-run report, John made clear his belief that rest during an ultra has a value. He felt that regular stops were important to boost morale, provide a sense of wellbeing and thus contribute to a quicker overall time.

John's strategy was the opposite of the one I had been pursuing over recent years. I was convinced that stopping for a rest (as opposed to stopping to eat or drink) might make me feel better for a short while, but I would soon feel just as tired as before. So my intention had become to stop as little as possible or not at all, sometimes employing the rather extreme technique of 'rolling support'. This means the runner doesn't stop but receives food and drink on the move from his support runner.

A few more miles and I was crossing the familiar terrain of Cannock Chase, which was thankfully a lot drier. Thereafter, conditions underfoot continued to improve. A look at my schedule and a few optimistic calculations led me to think I might be able to break sixteen hours, but it wasn't to be. I finished in 16h 10min, including sixteen minutes' stopping time, compared with John's 17h 57min, which included 1h 52 min stopping time. I've often wondered whether John's theory was in fact correct. Was it possible to produce a faster time by incorporating small amounts of 'recovery rest', or would it be faster not to stop at all?

About this time, I received an invitation to join the British Ultra Squad on condition that I could complete a 100km road race in under eight hours. As a member of the national team, I would have the opportunity to compete in national, European and world championships, an exciting but daunting prospect. The next 100km on the UK calendar was in Solihull, and being on the 23rd April would fit nicely into my training plan. Having competed in many road races, including fourteen marathons, I was no stranger to the tarmac, but 100km on the roads around Solihull did feel like an awfully long way. Nevertheless, I was pleased to finish in first place with a time of 7h 45min, which confirmed my place on the squad.

I now had a real sense that my training plan was working; the many, many miles had been worthwhile. Completing successful ultraruns in record times was most satisfying and felt like just reward for the ceaseless determination and effort.

The next three months leading up to the Pennine Way brought a period of mixed fortunes and mixed emotions. I enjoyed two of my best performances, bringing me closer to that elusive pinnacle of physical excellence of which I dreamt. But I also suffered an injury which, in its initial stages, made me doubt I would even start the Pennine Way. The time needed for recovery and the unavoidable reduction in training led to a period of self-doubt, which was only banished by my unexpectedly fast time in the West Highland Way Race.

Only two weeks after the Solihull 100km, I was first over the line on the Leek Moors Marathon, a thirty-mile off-road race, finishing in a record time of 4h 53min. Within two days, I felt not only recovered, but sharp and eager for another long run. One week later, I jogged up Ingleborough at the beginning of my seventh Fellsman Hike – and 10h 32min later, I jogged into the finish in first place, having beaten my previous fastest time by thirty minutes. I knew I'd worked hard to get to this level of fitness, but I was still surprised at how quickly I could now recover between runs. My level of fitness and, importantly, my speed of recovery were underlined the following week when, without taking a break, I ran 157 miles in training, including consecutive twenty- and thirty-milers.

The LDWA Brecon Beacons hundred-miler at the end of May was to be my next target, but during a training run with Clive and Richard on the Cheviots, I was suddenly hit with a pain in my gluteus maximus. It felt as though my right buttock was being savaged by a large, unseen dog. The pain was excruciating; I could hardly walk, let alone run. As I limped along in dejected silence, Clive suggested I should make my way to the nearest road, while he and Richard went to collect the car. Aborting the training run was disappointing but unavoidable. I hoped, after all the improvements I'd made, that my Pennine Way attempt wasn't now in jeopardy. We agreed a rendezvous point and I began the long and painful walk down to the road.

Occasionally, on an easy section of ground, I would attempt to resume running, as if to convince myself that I really was injured, not just suffering a muscle spasm. After some experimentation with stride length and angle of footfall, I discovered I could avoid the worst of the pain by modifying my gait. Unfortunately, this involved adopting a rather peculiar half-height goose-step. A full-height goose-step was just about pain free, but uncomfortable; half height was easier, and the pain bearable. After a little practice, I found I only needed to employ this technique on the injured side. So the sequence would be: normal step left, half goose-step right, normal step left, half goose-step right, and so on. My first proper attempt at running a substantial section of easy terrain came to an abrupt halt when, without warning, the pain suddenly erupted, causing a rapid and involuntary return to full goose-step mode on both sides. Even if this rather bizarre style had proved to be pain free, I wouldn't have felt inclined to make such a ridiculous spectacle of myself to bemused hillwalkers.

I had to face the fact that I was paying the price for an ambitious and rigorous training regime. It really brought home to me how very fine was the line between supreme fitness and injury. On returning home, I withdrew my entry for the '100' and took stock. The ninety-five-mile West Highland Way race on 24th June would be my next and final preparation run and, with that date being only five weeks away, I would have to balance recovery from the injury with maintaining fitness. Obviously, I would need to stop running for a while, but for how long? Not allowing enough recovery time before restarting training would only prolong the injury. I decided to rest for two weeks; after that, if the injury still persisted, I really would have a problem. Two weeks without running felt like an eternity, but after a few cycle rides and a couple of physiotherapy sessions, the walking at work started to feel easier. On tentatively restarting training, I was relieved to be pain free. After two more easy weeks of short runs and cycling, I felt I had, thankfully, recovered. One more week of complete rest and I was able to breathe a sigh of relief.

*

At last, I stood at the start of the West Highland Way Race. I wanted to win, but more importantly, I had some pressing questions to ask of my body. I'd had no recurrence of the injury and felt well rested – perhaps too well rested. After several easy weeks, I did wonder whether I had lost some of my hard-earned fitness. Would the injury return? I sincerely hoped not; I didn't relish the prospect of goose-stepping all the way to Fort William. A key goal in my preparation had been to complete the ninety-five miles of the West Highland Way at a pace significantly faster than I intended to run for the first 100 miles of the Pennine Way. I knew I should be able to do that, because I was fitter than I'd ever been. At least, I had been, five weeks ago.

Racing along in the leading group, the pace was fast, but I was holding back. I knew I could run faster. Haunted by thoughts of an injury recurrence but fuelled by adrenalin and a desire to speed up, I forced myself to be patient. At about halfway, with my self-control waning, worries about a return of the injury receding and my confidence growing, I increased pace. Pulling away from the group, I sensed tension and indecision among my fellow runners. Some must have thought that the increase would be too fast for them, so would maintain their current pace; others may have thought they were running far too fast anyway. But I was convinced one or two would rise to the challenge and come with me. However, the dire consequences of overcooking it at this stage must have persuaded them to bide their time. I went on alone, trusting it was not I who was making the misjudgement.

I soon established a substantial lead; I was running better than I'd dared hope. I had trained hard, and the enforced rest had unexpectedly worked in my favour. I had got it right. I was flying.

Gill met me at Altnafeadh, the seventy-eight-mile point, and I wolfed down copious amounts of food and drink. It felt like I was burning calories as fast as I could consume them. I had become a supremely efficient running machine.

'There's someone catching you up,' Gill said.

I spun around; I could see a lone runner in the distance.

She tried to reassure me. 'But he's probably not in the race – he'll be doing something else.'

Just then, a car pulled up. It was Dave Wallace's support team. Dave had won the race the previous year and had been part of the leading group when I pulled away. Eventually, on the Devil's Staircase, at eighty miles, he caught me up; he had trusted his instincts and was now reaping the rewards. After I'd held him off for a few miles, we traded the lead a couple of times before he finally pulled away on the hilly road section near Lundavra, only five miles from the finish. I watched Dave gradually but inexorably increase his lead, but I wasn't disappointed. I had paid attention to my training and preparation and exploited my skill set, with a measured and patient first half followed by a second half where I pushed myself to the red line. I was still running very well when Dave overtook me; it wasn't as though I had slowed down.

Dave judged his race to perfection to finish first in 15h 26min, a hugely impressive performance and one of the best ultraruns I have ever witnessed. I was extremely pleased with my race; it was one of my very best. My finishing time of 15h 32min was quicker than I had hoped for, and represented an average speed of 6mph; I was planning to average 5mph for the first 100 miles of the Pennine Way. The following day, I had no injuries and no stiffness. I was ready.

CHAPTER 5:

The Pennine Way

The suffering and disappointment of the Southern Upland Way were still clear in my mind. But I was in no doubt that the experience contributed to making me stronger and more resilient. Mistaking euphoria for fitness, as I did during the early stages of the Southern Upland Way, was something I would not do again. It had been a painful but valuable lesson.

Before an important run, I had sometimes wondered whether I really had logged sufficient miles or completed enough single long runs. I had often doubted my ability to succeed – but not this time. Apart from a relatively brief period of injury, everything had gone according to plan. My training, particularly over the last ten months, had been extremely successful. Not only had I achieved most of my intermediate goals, but the results had been far better than I had hoped for. I had become accustomed to a huge volume of training, and my speed of recovery was now astonishing.

One week after the West Highland Way Race, I felt recovered, but in a quandary. Accepted practice would be to taper my weekly mileage for the last four weeks up to the Pennine Way, but I felt strong enough to continue at the same level or even increase my mileage. Fortunately, common sense prevailed. I knew my chances of success would be reduced by doing more, rather than less. The last thing I wanted was to feel tired at the start. By significantly reducing my training, I would at least feel fresh when I started out. Resting would make more sense than running. If I wasn't fit enough now, then I never would be.

The reduction in my training coincided precisely with a significant and unexpected pain in my left knee. I did wonder if my body was complaining about not doing enough running, but I resisted the temptation to increase my mileage and booked a physio session instead. The knee pain was a good reason to rest, but after all I'd done over the months and years, I found it impossible to be idle, so I followed a programme of mostly short runs but also a couple of steady twenty-milers and a few bike rides. Although I didn't run to work through this period, I was still walking each day for my job. However, despite the reduction in training, the pain refused to go away. Perhaps I should have stopped training completely – it probably wouldn't have made much difference to my fitness and stamina – but I didn't. I began to have doubts about even starting the Pennine Way, but I still had four weeks in which to recover. Apart from the injury and its incredibly bad timing, I was very satisfied with my physical condition, and most of my logistical arrangements were in place. I felt no need to improve my fitness, but this final month would be a good time to make any last-minute adjustments to my overall plan.

Whether to start the attempt at Edale in the south or Kirk Yetholm in the north had been an interesting question to answer. Five of the previous eight record runs had been completed in the north-to-south direction; the other three, including the then current record of 2d 21h 54min set by Mike Cudahy in 1984, were completed from south to north. I decided to start at Kirk Yetholm and thereby complete the longest and most remote part of the route, over the Cheviots, first. To negotiate this twenty-nine-mile section at the end, without road support and when I was tired, could be dangerous and demoralising. I remembered how tired and vulnerable I had felt at the end of the Southern Upland Way. It would also be logistically easier to arrange support on a Sunday afternoon at the southern end of the route because many of my supporters lived closer to that part. Finally, when I was tiring towards the end, I would be running on terrain which had a friendly and familiar feel because I had crossed it many times before. There was also the bonus of a quick and easy trip home from Edale once I had finished. The only advantage I could see in running from south to north was the possibility of a south-westerly air stream; this could provide an immensely helpful tailwind, especially in bad weather. But I didn't relish the thought of running in bad weather at all, regardless of the wind direction. It wouldn't be very enjoyable and, crucially, I would be far less likely to break the record. So I would start in the north, and in the event of an unsuitable weather forecast, I would cancel the attempt.

An enthusiastic and optimistic support team is essential for a successful run. The nucleus of my team would be Gill, Clive and Richard. Over recent years, these three had become my most experienced and trusted supporters, and their help and encouragement had been vital to my completion of the Southern Upland Way. We had all been tested, but we had won through, and I couldn't contemplate starting the Pennine Way without their help. Frank Yates, as well as being timekeeper for the attempt, was also an accomplished runner and an experienced supporter of many ultras. These four would share the duties of driving, preparing food and running sections with me.

A team doing roadside support is required to conjure up an array of appetising food and drink, in any weather, at any time of day or night. Over a three-day period, this is a difficult task to achieve, requiring imagination and resourcefulness. The team only gets a snapshot of the runner at each meeting point, at intervals of between one and three hours. The physical and psychological changes in the condition of the runner can be dramatic, ranging from running well, up on schedule and full of joy to walking, limping and talking about abandoning the attempt.

Gill, Clive and Richard had learnt to employ a simple strategy to help keep me focussed, even under the most trying circumstances. No matter how tired, injured or disheartened I became, they would never suggest even the possibility of terminating the attempt; the subject was taboo. This approach could be just as testing for them as it was for me. None of us wanted to be responsible for planting a seed of doubt which could germinate and flourish and possibly lead to failure, so I was the only one who even had the right to broach the subject. On the rare occasions when I did mention quitting, they would dismiss the suggestion out of hand, insisting I was only going through a low point which would pass. They would suggest that by the time I reached the next support point, climbed the next hill or even completed the next fifty miles, I would feel a lot better. This was often, but not always true.

On each section of the route, I would also require at least one support runner to accompany me, to carry food and drink and help with navigation. I contacted everyone who had made even a tentative offer of help in the previous twelve months; I was relieved to find that no one had forgotten and that they were waiting for me to get in touch, and I soon had a full complement of support runners. My already high level of self-belief was heightened still further, knowing that I would be supported by companions who were experts in all aspects of ultra-trail running. Their collective skills of running on the fells at night, navigating and providing moral support were considerable; many also had a detailed knowledge of the Pennine Way. Most were already friends or acquaintances, but some were friends of friends, keen to offer their help and expertise and to be part of my record attempt. I could not have wished for a better support team; I just hoped I wouldn't let them down.

For logistical and safety reasons it was essential that the support car and runners always knew my whereabouts. Everyone had to be in the right place at the right time. I compiled a list of forty-four points where the route crossed the road, complete with grid references, intermediate mileages and cumulative mileage. These locations were then annotated on two sets of 1:50,000 Ordnance Survey maps: one set for use in the support car, the other to be carried by the support runners. I used the intermediate mileages to calculate a time schedule, which showed an estimated time for each section and an estimated time of arrival at each road crossing. The final column on the schedule was for recording my actual times, which was to be the job of the road support team. Gerald and Betty Woolley, my in-laws, had kindly agreed to act as overall coordinators for the duration of the run, and to be available twenty-four hours a day. The road support team would call them at regular intervals to report my progress, and runners who were due to meet me could make contact with HQ to obtain an accurate update. In 1989, making contact wasn't always easy. Firstly, it required finding a telephone box. Although these very visible red boxes were marked on Ordnance Survey maps, they had often disappeared or were not in working order.

Compiling a list of locations and mileages was quite straightforward, but estimating my time of arrival at those locations was more complicated. A run of 100 miles was now well within my capabilities; I could complete the distance in approximately twenty hours at a constant speed of 5mph. But the Pennine Way was 270 miles, and I would be running for two entire nights without sleep, so I expected to slow down. I decided to incorporate a gradual reduction in pace into the schedule. Allowing for a decrease of 0.25mph for every twenty-five miles would, I calculated, provide a reasonably accurate estimate of my actual rate of progress.

On several occasions I had run through a complete night without any adverse effects. But I had found my second night on the Southern Upland Way so difficult that I was sure a third night without sleep would be impossible. The only way to avoid that eventuality was to start at dawn on the first day and finish before nightfall on the third day. I decided to start at 3 a.m. and calculate a schedule based on an average speed of 4.25mph; this would allow me to finish at 6.30 p.m. on the third day, in a time of 2d 15h 40min, breaking the record by 6h 14min. If I hadn't finished by half past six, I would still have about four hours of daylight remaining, plus an additional 2h 14min in hand to break the record.

Of course, I wasn't the first person to run the Pennine Way in record time. In 1958 Arthur Puckrin, a talented and prolific ultrarunner, recorded a time of 6d 7h 25min running solo from south to north – a remarkable feat, considering the route was barely marked on the ground, requiring him to navigate mostly by map and compass.

Twelve years then elapsed before Ted Dance and Dennis Weir, both members of the Rucksack Club, completed the route in 4d 23h 20min, travelling from north to south. Their run prompted a succession of attempts and a gradual lowering of the fastest time. In 1971 Bill Bird did it in 4d 8h 8min, again running from north to south, and in 1972 Alan Heaton and Mick Meath improved that time by three hours to 4d 5h 10min on a north-to-south traverse. Two years later, in 1974, Joss Naylor, running from north to south, completed the route over twenty-four hours faster, in the impressive time of 3d 4h 36min. One year after that, Pete Dawes came tantalisingly close to the three-day barrier; also running from north to south, he recorded a time of 3d 1h 48 min.

In 1979 Brian Harney arrived in Edale a mere forty-two minutes over the magic three days. I wonder what he was thinking as he crossed the bogs of Bleaklow and Kinder, so close to the end. Five years later, on 3rd June 1984, Mike Cudahy, also a Rucksack Club Member, raced down off the Cheviot through the rain and mist to touch the Border Inn a mere 2d 21h 54min after leaving Edale. This was Mike's eighth attempt, but like he said, 'After only thirty years of steady training I had become the first person to run the Pennine Way in under three days.'

*

As we drove up the M6 on the Friday night before the attempt, we could see the Pennines on our right. I looked at Cross Fell – the 'summit' of the Pennine Way, as Mike Cudahy called it. I would be there tomorrow night with Pete Simpson, my support runner for that section. Pete is an ultrarunner and mountaineer of the highest order; I would be more than happy to trust his skill and judgement on that remote and committing section.

We met Frank at the Border Hotel in Kirk Yetholm on a beautiful warm evening. After checking in to our rooms, we watched a lone walker finish his marathon journey. Although limping, he was in high spirits and rightly proud of his achievement. 'What! You're going to run it?' he exclaimed, on hearing of my intentions. 'Finish on Sunday? You must be mad!' He then shook his head and burst into a fit of slightly sardonic laughter.

I was unsure whether to laugh with him out of politeness, or to explain that our definitions of 'mad' were probably completely different. Thinking that trying to justify my 'madness' would be a pointless exercise that would only prompt more head shaking, I decided to hold my tongue and go for a short jog up the road.

It was nice to be on my own for a while, to relax and collect my thoughts. After a few hundred yards I stopped and looked at my knee; if only it didn't hurt, I would feel invincible. I tried to focus on my preparation, which had been thorough – even obsessive. My single-minded ambition had allowed me to sustain a relentless training programme and I had adopted a meticulous but pragmatic approach when calculating the schedule. No matter how many times I thought through my preparation, my conclusion was always the same – I'd done everything possible – but worrying about my knee was nurturing a seed of doubt.

On my return to the Border Hotel, the walker was sitting outside. We exchanged greetings, but I wasn't sure what to make of his slow shake of the head and wry smile. I could only assume that he either didn't believe I was serious or thought that if I was, I had failed to appreciate the enormity of the challenge. If only he knew how wrong he was!

Gill and I spent a pleasant evening chatting with Clive, Richard and Frank while watching several other walkers arrive who, we assumed, had also walked from Edale. When I stood up to go to the bar, the pain was absent but, expecting it to resume, I instinctively limped. On returning to the table, I found that my momentary change in gait hadn't gone unnoticed.

'Is your knee hurting?' Gill said.

'I'm not sure,' I replied.

'Well, if you're not sure, it can't be, can it?'

'What's wrong?' Frank asked.

'Nothing,' replied Gill. 'He thinks his knee is hurting, but it's not!'

Looking round in surprise at Gill's unsympathetic response, I caught the eye of the walker. As he raised his glass and mouthed a silent 'Cheers', I thought I could detect a hint of superiority. I wondered what he was thinking; probably that we were both limping, but at least he had finished.

To sleep well on the night before an important run and to wake refreshed was a luxury which so far had eluded me, and this occasion was to be no different. I knew that 'trying' to sleep was never successful and an early start meant worrying about oversleeping. But I wasn't concerned; I hadn't slept at all on the night before the West Highland Way Race, which was one of my best runs. Simply keeping my eyes closed and relaxing had been adequate. On the other hand, a good night's sleep and a late leisurely start before the Southern Upland Way had preceded probably the worst run I have ever had, thus proving to me that sleep the night before an ultra is no guarantee of a successful run and may even be unnecessary. But the Pennine Way and Southern Upland Way are long enough to require two nights without sleep, so no sleep before the run means, effectively, three full nights without sleep. A worrying prospect.

*

Eventually the alarm sounded. It was 2.30 a.m. on 25th July 1989. Gill whispered, 'Good luck. Don't worry, it'll be OK.'

Richard was outside packing his rucksack ready to accompany me over the Cheviot, Frank and Clive were taking photographs, and suddenly it was 3 a.m. Relief – I was on my way at last.

As we jogged along the lane towards Burnhead, I told Richard I was planning to walk for short sections 'to give my knee a chance to warm up', although it actually felt fine. Dawn broke as we passed below Black Hag to the sound of gunfire from the nearby firing range – the first of three consecutive dawns I would be witnessing.

Considering this first section is twenty-nine hilly miles, there is surprisingly little water. During our reconnaissance run, a soldier – who, incredibly, had parked his Land Rover on top of the Schil – had generously refilled our bottles. Today the ground was even drier so, playing safe, I allowed Richard to carry enough for both of us. We were soon on the Cheviot, and the usually very boggy peat surrounding the summit trig point was now dusty dry. On one particularly wet winter run, I'd found a glove sticking up out of the quagmire, fingers curved as if clutching at the air, pleading for a helping hand. But it was only a glove, I think! There was a hat next to it, but I didn't see the possible connection at the time.

The firm underfoot conditions, although very welcome, would prove to be a double-edged sword before I was finished.

Because I'd calculated my schedule on the assumption that my speed would decrease, this first section should, in theory, require the fastest pace. So, although we got into our stride traversing Windy Gyle, I didn't really expect to be on time at Byrness. For a fleeting moment I did feel the temptation to hurry, just to have the satisfaction of being on schedule at the first support point, but quickly dismissed the idea; I now knew the value of patience. Richard and I arrived at Byrness at 8.23 a.m., completing the first twenty-nine miles in a time of 5h 23min, against the schedule time of 5h 18min. My estimated finishing time of 2d 15h 40min was an ambitious 6h 24min inside the record, so to be five minutes late at this point was quite acceptable, even expected.

Frank had everything ready for my first pit stop. His organisation and enthusiastic banter were to become a welcome feature over the next three days. After a seven-minute break, he shouldered the small rucksack to run with me over the next nine miles. He commented that he didn't expect me to be walking any of the uphills at this early stage. Although I was well capable of running even the steepest hills, I had learnt some hard lessons. A fast start could be counterproductive, whereas I was sure an extra hour or two spent over the first 100 miles could stave off far greater time losses over the last 100. I had a long way to go. I needed to make progress as smoothly and efficiently as possible; the time would undoubtedly come for making a huge effort.

We lost the route slightly in the forest. I'd only been over this section once before, and my memory wasn't as reliable as the map. I was keen to retrace our steps for about a mile to regain the route, but Frank persuaded me to cut through the forest as the correct path was parallel and only a few yards away. This was against my instinct; I had found on a previous and memorable occasion that a path which was 'just over there' was nothing of the sort. Fortunately, Frank's instinct was correct, and we were soon back on route, our little detour costing a mere few minutes. Gill and Clive met us with the car at the next road, then both took turns, along with Richard, to run with me to Caw Gap, where we met Ian Leighton. Ian was a friend of Pete's and it was the first time I had made his acquaintance. He kept me entertained with accounts of his multi-day Scottish runs and told me that he cycled 100 miles per week and only ran at weekends to avoid injury. Ian was to stay with the support team for the next eighty miles, running with me for fifty of those. In his company the miles passed easily and enjoyably.

Richard joined us for the run over Wain Rigg to Kellah Burn. As we crossed the dried-up Glencune Burn, we recalled a reconnaissance run the day after the 1988 KIMM when he fell waist-deep into a bog of particularly fine consistency. The shock of the cold water took his breath away and rendered him speechless, but I made up for that by laughing enough for both of us.

I arrived at Alston having completed eighty-seven miles, and was still only five minutes behind schedule. However, I found it impossible to pass through the town without partaking of a superb fish-and-chip supper.

Although the resulting eighteen-minute stop was the longest so far, I did keep it to a minimum by eating the fish and chips with my feet stuck out in front for Clive to change my shoes and socks. This did feel highly efficient, if a little decadent. As Ian and I prepared to leave, Pete Simpson arrived to check on progress. Pete would be joining me at Garrigill to accompany me over the high and featureless plateau of Cross Fell. Gill, Clive and Richard now left us to drive to their digs at Thwaite; I would see them again at the Tan Hill Inn tomorrow morning, sixty miles south.

Before they left, Gill asked, 'How's your knee?'

Being reluctant to admit that I'd forgotten all about it, I just said, 'It's OK, I think.'

'See you tomorrow,' she said.

Ian and I jogged the four riverside miles to Garrigill at a steady 5mph. We arrived to find Frank preparing food and Pete packing the rucksack ready for the night ahead. It had been twelve months since Pete had first promised his help, and he was of course true to his word. He knew the importance of accurate route-finding on record attempts. Pete had covered the next sixteen miles to Dufton many times before.

As we set off for Cross Fell, Ian and Pete were weighed down like packhorses with spare clothes, food, map, torches, spare batteries and water. Pete was a bit surprised at the large size of my torch, not to mention the weight, but I'd paid £25 for this 'state of the art' Maglite, so I was determined to use it.

The track starts steeply, so to conserve energy I elected to walk the first mile or so and start running where it levelled out. Meanwhile, back at Garrigill, Frank, when packing the car, thought we'd forgotten the map. In his haste to drive up the track after us, he had failed to shut the boot properly, so all our gear slid out of the tailgate. Our idle chatter was interrupted by Frank shouting and waving his arms half a mile behind us. His fears were unfounded, however, as the map was safely stowed in Pete's rucksack. The fact that it stayed there for the remainder of the night was testimony to Pete's familiarity with the route. Reassured, Frank then hurried back to the car to retrieve the trail of equipment and avoid being reported for fly-tipping by a vigilant local.

As darkness fell and the temperature dropped, we stopped to put on more clothes, and I relieved Pete of my enormous torch. He was glad to hear that I hadn't bought the largest torch in the Maglite range. The even bigger six-cell version is so powerful its beam could possibly present a hazard to traffic on the motorway or low flying aircraft.

I took a short breather in Greg's Hut while Pete and Ian searched the rucksack for food we thought we might have forgotten. Fortunately, our fears again proved unfounded. Pete was now navigating very confidently; with the occasional reference to his compass, he took us over Cross Fell's windswept plateau without error. My mind flashed back to the drive up the M6 yesterday. Only yesterday; it felt like a lifetime away.

As we skirted the perimeter fence of the radio station on Great Dun Fell, it reminded me of a solo recce run I'd done. At the time, I had thought the next half-mile of the route would be tricky to navigate at night. But Pete's navigation was perfect, and we were soon running over Knock Fell, and on past the massive cairn of Knock Old Man. As I jogged along behind Pete and Ian, I could hear them joking with each other like two friends who knew each other well and enjoyed each other's sense of humour. Pete once did a winter Tan–Cat with Ian completing most of it and Frank providing support. If any route needs friends with a sense of humour, that one does.

At 1.30 a.m. we jogged along Dufton's deserted main street towards the waiting Frank, who (of course) had everything ready: pasta and soup, Lucozade, tea, clean socks, Vaseline and my chair. My feet were becoming sore, and I decided to take a spare pair of shoes on the next twelve-mile section. Although Dufton is only 108 miles from the start and not even halfway, the discomfort in my feet didn't trouble me unduly. It didn't occur to me that if they were hurting at this stage, then the pain was likely to become worse and my chances of success must be decreasing with every passing mile. I didn't grit my teeth in determination or become despondent; I just accepted it as part of the experience. Furthermore, although I had to deal with this discomfort for the remainder of the run, I'm sure it didn't diminish my sense of achievement. It may even have enhanced it by providing an additional hurdle to overcome.

After an eleven-minute stop for some welcome food, Pete jammed the spare shoes into his already bulging rucksack and we were on our way again. Putting my weight back on my feet made them sting, but the sensation soon subsided on the walk up the long track to High Cup Nick. In daylight there are many wild flowers and mosses to be seen, but in darkness the massive natural amphitheatre of basalt crags and pinnacles has a wild and sombre atmosphere.

As we ran along the pleasant moorland path towards the Maize Beck crossing, we discussed the 'flood route'. This is a short detour to a footbridge which can be used when the beck is in spate. There was certainly no need to use it today, but we had both checked its location, just in case. It was a relief to pass through the isolated farm of Birkdale, unheard by the dogs with which I'd had an altercation on a previous occasion. Encountering a pack of loose dogs in a dark farmyard at 4 a.m. was not something I relished.

The two hours before dawn are always a trying time; the body is at its lowest ebb and wants to shut down and sleep. But I could sense the approaching daylight and felt a desire to pick up speed. It wasn't quite light enough to see well, so I had to quell my impatience and settle for a sort of cruise control. The descent of the rocky steps at the side of Cauldron Snout holds one of the strongest memories for me. It was difficult to tell how close we were to the edge of the ravine, but despite the low water conditions, the noise of falling water seemed deafening. As we reached the bottom in the half-light of dawn, the atmosphere was damp and refreshing. I stopped for a bite to eat while Pete packed the torches away. Lying on my front on the cold-dew soaked grass, feet in the air, provided thirty seconds of heaven, a relief for my burning feet. I had employed this resting technique numerous times over the years. It was also quite a convenient position to adopt for map reading and eating, but drinking was more problematic.

I once said to Gill, 'Why is it always my feet that get sore?'

'Because they are the only things that touch the ground,' was her obvious reply.

Frank and Ian were waiting near Widdybank Farm with more soup and pasta. Ian then joined us for the next nine miles along the beautiful River

Tees. Full daylight now, and with it came new strength and optimism. I felt my body gradually ease back into top gear; we fair raced along the rock-hard riverside path to Middleton-in-Teesdale. My legs were starting to stiffen slightly, but I had now completed 129 miles, with the last nine being on an awfully hard surface at a speed of 6mph. I hoped I wasn't heading for a repeat of the Southern Upland Way.

The climb up Harter Fell was just what I needed. The change in gradient and stride length loosened my leg muscles completely. Oddly, this was the only stiffness I experienced on the entire run. Reconnaissance runs by Pete and myself now paid dividends as we negotiated the moors of Mickleton and Cotherstone without error.

Reaching the A66 was a significant point on the run; I was now about four miles over halfway in 28h 38min, equivalent to a total time of 2d 7h 30min. That time was obviously unattainable as it would not be possible to run two equal halves, but then I didn't expect to. Based on my schedule for 2d 15h 40min, I was 1h 48min down; projecting ahead, this produced a finishing time of 2d 17h 28min.

At this stage I didn't know whether I would succumb to the effects of sleep deprivation and be forced to take a long stop. Even if I wasn't actually forced to stop and sleep, I might start to lose time to the extent that the record would slowly but surely slip from my grasp. Under those circumstances, I wasn't sure I would be able to apply the massive effort the final stages would inevitably require. My desire to complete the run would then be truly tested. To set a record for the Pennine Way was, of course, my intention – but to manage without sleep and to always be in control would be another step towards my goal of physical excellence.

I was pleased to find my new pacers waiting at the A66. I already knew Guy, Howard and Andy Brear; Neville Hawkins was a friend of theirs I had not previously met. These four would be running with me for the next thirty-nine miles, via the Tan Hill Inn to Thwaite and then Horton in Ribblesdale.

The section that lay ahead can be a bit demoralising: the next support point at the Tan Hill Inn is visible from the outset, but at nearly seven miles away it's just a small speck on the horizon.

After crossing a few fields and mixed terrain, we started the only part of the Pennine Way that I'd been apprehensive of: Sleightholme Moor. The moor itself is only three miles across and gains a modest 400 feet in elevation, but it's a tough three miles. The last time I made the crossing, the ground was very wet and boggy, so although the conditions were much better today, I didn't really expect to meet my schedule time. Guy and Howard are both expert moorland runners, a skill honed from many years of training and racing on the Pennines. They were adept at setting an efficient pace, speeding up or slowing down to accommodate slight changes in the terrain; this assistance, and their passing me a drink of water or offering a word of encouragement at just the right time, were all conducive to an extremely satisfying run.

Eventually, the small speck became a large speck and, at last, a building. Soon I could make out Gill and other figures coming to meet me. I was glad to see her. As I approached, I could see she was expectant, wondering whether the fifty-eight miles since she had seen me last had taken a heavy toll. Guy told her, 'He ran all that – he's going well.' She burst into laughter, as if a cloud of doubt had been lifted. I felt elated, the sun was high, and Gill's presence lifted my spirits immeasurably. I was full of optimism and could barely wait to start the next section. I had initially written off the schedule time for the usually boggy Sleightholme section as unrealistic but, due to the dry underfoot conditions, I completed the seven miles in 1h 34min, just one minute inside the schedule time.

Despite my increasingly uncomfortable feet and the probable, but not yet noticeable, effects of sleep deprivation, I was running well. I sat on the camping chair, gulping down food, arms in the air for Gill to change my shirt, feet stuck out in front for Clive's attention and for Richard to change my shoes. I didn't quite burn any rubber as I left Tan Hill, but I was over halfway and feeling good. The last time I'd been here with Guy, Howard and Frank, we were setting off for the Cat and Fiddle, 120 miles away. Incredibly, our time for that run was 1h 19min slower than I subsequently ran the remaining 124 miles to Edale.

After crossing the River Swale near the junction with the Coast-to-Coast Walk, we came to my favourite section: the superb contouring path along Kisdon Hill with its unparalleled views of Swaledale. The dale is full of small fields and drystone walls, and every field seems to have its own barn; it's surely one of the most picturesque dales in Yorkshire. The boulder-strewn path was awkward to run, but eventually it gave way to an easier diagonal descent across fields to Thwaite. My support team had set themselves up outside the Kearton Guest House, where Gill, Clive and Richard had spent the night. A repeat of the Tan Hill pit stop provided the other guests with some amusement while they took their morning coffee.

Today was the 22nd of July, the hottest day of the entire summer, with a top temperature of 34°C; indeed, the three days I spent on the Pennine Way were subsequently recorded as the three hottest days of 1989! The walled track up Great Shunner Fell was like a furnace, the sun beating down and the ground baked hard as concrete. Running on the valley side of the track, I could take advantage of a slight breeze that wafted through the broken wall. As we neared the top and crossed the bone-dry peat bogs, the lads encouraged me, saying I was going well and was bound to make it. Of course, none of us could possibly know at this stage whether I would be successful, but total confidence and optimism from your whole team is essential. It was good to reach the top of Great Shunner Fell, which was surprisingly busy; in the distance I could even see children playing football.

It was a relief to start the descent towards Hardraw. The increase in pace created a little more draught, but I was now very tired. I thought about the children playing football; it did seem a rather odd sight on top of a 2,000-foot mountain. I was just about ask the others if they had also seen them when the thought occurred to me that maybe the children were not actually there. Perhaps I had imagined it. I could have been hallucinating. If my companions had, in fact, seen them, all well and good (unless we were all hallucinating, then not so good). If they hadn't, then perhaps they weren't looking, or I was more tired than I thought. Feeling confused, I decided not to ask.

It felt a long, long way down Shunner and it was extremely hot, so it was nice to see Gill and Clive coming out to meet me. As we ran down the last bit of stony lane, my feet were really hurting. By the time we reached Hardraw, I was feeling quite jaded. To my horror, I could see the support car parked off route.

'Why has he parked over there?' I snapped, and immediately regretted it.

Gill looked surprised; after all, it was only fifty yards away. What was another fifty yards on top of 270 miles?

I was now extremely hot, sticky and uncomfortable. Gill had insisted I pack a long-sleeved cotton work shirt for use on occasions like this. The flat grass fields as we ran towards Hawes were easier on my feet. The shirt, open and flowing in the wind, was a revelation – cool and comfortable – and my spirits were raised when Andy and Steve Taylor joined us on the climb up towards the Cam Road. It was wonderful jogging along the side of Dodd Fell, chatting away the miles, with Guy and Howard passing me water. Another stop at Kidhow Gate and then on to Horton, saying our goodbyes to Andy and Steve at the Dales Way junction. I was now running on the side of the track, as the grass was more comfortable on my feet than the hard stony surface. At last, we could see Horton in the distance. Guy ran on with the message, 'Socks, Vaseline, sun cream and his footman.'

It was a nice surprise to find Gill's brother Derek and his wife, Lorraine, at the support point. I'd done the Lakes Karrimor with Derek. He'd suffered bad feet then; now it was my turn to suffer. It was so hot I had to move the camping chair into the shade of a nearby van. I think they were impressed when, within seconds of me sitting down, Clive sprang into action, whipped off my shoes and applied Vaseline and Scholl moleskin. My right heel had been troubling me for some time; it was OK on the uphills but very painful on the downhills. This injury had an ominous feel, because it wasn't really sore but bruised and tender. The combination of physical exertion and extreme heat didn't seem to have affected my appetite, so, while Clive performed yet another repair job, I shovelled down copious amounts of fruit and rice pudding.

Perhaps it was the thought of the next two climbs, Pen-y-ghent and Fountains Fell, that tempted me to stop for all of eighteen minutes before Andy and Neville took me up Pen-y-ghent. I was satisfied to run the flats and walk the steep sections. The sun was lower now but, despite this, it seemed even hotter; I could feel the heat radiating from the ground. Thankfully, where the track was next to the wall it was possible to enjoy intermittent shade. Eventually, the path left the sanctuary of the wall and became a recently resurfaced, glaring white ribbon of limestone. I felt awfully slow and the climb seemed never-ending, but eventually we stood on top and looked back down to Horton behind us and Dale Head in front. I later checked my time for this climb up Pen-y-ghent against the Three Peaks Race results and found to my amazement that I wouldn't have been last, despite having run 178 miles. Fountains Fell rose ahead, another big climb coming up soon.

The descent to Dale Head was the most painful yet. I'm sure shoes full of razor blades would have felt more comfortable. I was starting to get depressed about my feet and began to wonder whether I really would make it all the way to Edale. Clive was doing the best he could for me, but I was approaching the point where nothing more could be done. About halfway down Fountains Fell, I could see three runners coming up.

'They must be coming to meet you,' said Andy.

Although I was not due to meet Dennis Beresford, Tom Robertshaw and Peter Geldard until Malham, they'd come out early to see how I was.

After much friendly encouragement, they left us to drive to Malham and prepare for my second and obviously crucial night. The next ten hours could make or break the attempt. If I survived the night without needing to sleep and without route-finding errors, and if I was still running in the morning, then surely I was on my way to a new Pennine Way record. If, on the other hand, I was unable to stay awake or couldn't bear the increasing pain in my feet, the possibility of breaking the record would evaporate. The thought of not breaking the record — or worse, abandoning the run after all this effort — was more than I could bear. I couldn't accept the disappointment of failure. I knew I would find a way to succeed; I had to.

Clive and Mike Shaw now joined the three of us for the five-mile run to Malham. We made the mistake of not taking torches, and darkness fell before we reached the top of the cove. I was just about to swear at myself for being so negligent when Clive handed me a torch. He probably wanted to make sure I didn't fall over the edge of the cove and waste all the effort he'd put into repairing my feet. The potentially leg-breaking limestone clints and grikes above the cove are tricky to negotiate in daylight, so they would have been a nightmare in the pitch dark without the torch. This was a significant point on the run; I had now done most of the big hills along the way and I was going into my second night, something I had only experienced once before.

There was quite a group of us at Malham – five retiring runners and three new runners, four cars with four drivers – with one common objective: that of getting me to Edale. I felt tired and grateful, almost overwhelmed with emotion.

Gill, Clive and Frank left to enjoy a couple of hours' rest at Tom's house at East Marton. Prior to the event, none of us had known Tom and his wife, but their friendliness and generosity were very welcome.

I set off into the darkness with Tom and Peter. Although I had not met these two lads before, their friendliness and confidence soon put me at ease. The route along the line of the Aire Valley crosses many miles of fields, farmyards, riverside paths and lanes. I had done this part of the route before, but running alone I would have lost time, being forced to use a map to stay on route. After a short while, I became aware I was with two runners who were absolute experts on the route. They knew which side of the path was easiest to run on, where the tallest thistles were and where the grass was shortest. One ran a few yards in front to give us our general direction, and the other ran just to my side, illuminating the ground in front. When we came to a stile, they ensured both sides were well lit for me. Tom and Peter encouraged and treated me with the utmost consideration and patience. We approached Gargrave amid lightning and distant thunder, and I stopped to put on waterproofs. There wasn't really any need, as the storm had just missed us, but it wouldn't have helped me to get a soaking. We jogged into Gargrave to meet Dennis; I had now completed 200 miles in 45h 37min. Behind the tiredness, I knew I had an inner resilience. Deep inside, I was still strong. When it got light, my feet would feel a bit better; I would make better foot placements and fewer stumbles. My dream was still alive. I knew I wouldn't give in.

After another few miles, Dennis and I started the run onto Pinhaw Beacon. As we were leaving the car, we saw a procession of people walking down the hill towards us who appeared to be wearing long cloaks. I must admit, it worried me slightly; I thought they might be members of a secret sect or a black magic circle. It was 2.40 a.m. and it felt quite sinister. Surely no normal people would be up here at this time of night? We were here, of course, but that was different – we had a sensible reason. As Dennis and I set off, I asked Gill to get in the car and leave, but looking back I saw they had reached the car before it had left. It was a great comfort to know that Clive, Tom and Peter were with her.

Dennis and I jogged up Pinhaw Beacon to be greeted by the sight of a cloaked figure sitting on top of the trig point.

'Crikey,' I said to Dennis, 'what do you make of that?'

'Aye,' said Dennis. 'It'll be right.'

If I'd been on my own, I'd have turned round and gone back, Pennine Way record or no Pennine Way record.

But it takes more than a sinister figure in a cloak sat on Pinhaw trig point in the middle of the night to frighten Dennis Beresford. With nerves of steel, he jogged straight up to the trig point and said, 'How do'.

The figure replied, 'You meet some strange folk up here.'

'Not as strange as this one,' said Dennis. 'He's come from Kirk Yetholm.'

What a relief; we had stumbled into a group of innocent stargazers.

As we approached Cowling, we crossed countless fields and stiles. I lost track of where we were, but Dennis's knowledge of the terrain was flawless. I was now going through that difficult pre-dawn period, the physical and mental low point on all long runs. Suddenly, I stumbled and almost fell over. Stopping to regain my balance, I realised the stumble had woken me up; I had fallen asleep on my feet for just a few microseconds. Dennis talked to me constantly, telling me about other Pennine Way attempts on which he had helped, boosting my confidence immeasurably when he said I was running better than any previous record contender he had ever witnessed. His boundless energy and optimism were exactly what I needed during this difficult period.

The next five miles were the most memorable of the entire run. Dawn broke as we climbed Ickornshaw Moor – another big hill, another cloudless, perfect dawn. I was starting to feel exposed to the elements, as though it wasn't natural for a human being to be outside, labouring without cover or sleep, for such a long period. It was a strange sensation, as though the normal 'sleep, work, rest' routine of life no longer existed; I felt I could just go on jogging, walking and travelling forever. I emerged from my thoughts to find that despite my sore feet, the cumulative tiredness and the steep gradient, I was running uphill easily. I wasn't 'trying'. I was experiencing an effortless control and a physical and mental fulfilment like never before. However, to believe this was just reward for the many miles of training was an oversimplification. I sensed it was far deeper than that. Had I, at last, achieved the ultimate physical and mental state I had dreamt of for so long? If so, my previous assumption that this heightened state could only be experienced in the absence of physical discomfort had been turned on its head. I wondered whether the opposite was, in fact, true. Perhaps to immerse body and mind in an almost overwhelming level of effort would prompt a deep inner searching of the self. Access to this mysterious but powerful inner self may make possible the acquisition of the 'Zen' (or in western parlance, 'flow') state. Anyway, I couldn't possibly have achieved it. Or could I? As we started our descent, the realisation that I may, just for a few moments, have achieved 'an effortless and serene application of energy' was brought to a sudden halt by the return of stinging feet.

A time check at the support car near Ponden Reservoir (226 miles) showed that, although I was more than two hours behind my schedule for 2d 15h 40min, I wasn't losing any more time. We were all optimistic; the consensus was that if I could maintain this level of effort and not suffer any major setbacks, I would break the record.

Top Withens was another long climb, taken a bit more steadily than Ickornshaw. As we descended the other side towards Walshaw Dean Reservoir, Dennis and I discussed the Dales Way record. In March I had improved Dennis's time by a mere twelve minutes. He knew I lived in Staffordshire, so had always assumed I was born there; when he discovered I was a Yorkshireman, the same as himself, he seemed relieved and said, 'I couldn't understand how someone from Staffordshire could break the Dales Way record, but that explains it.' Dennis ran on ahead to the Widdop Road to organise food and a change of clothes for me. On arrival, pleased with his discovery, he announced, 'I've found out what makes him tick; he's a Yorkshireman.' I've often wondered whether, if Dennis had known beforehand that I was a Yorkshireman, he would have tried so hard to reclaim the record – or if he would even have tried at all. Anyway, I'm sure his Dales Way record will stand for a very long time.

Arriving at Widdop Road, I was surprised to find the support team wrapped up in balaclavas or towels, as protection not against the weather but against the midges. I enjoyed a very refreshing wash and change of clothes, albeit interspersed with much swatting and slapping. I set off in good spirits with Dennis and Tom towards Colden – only to stop suddenly, crouching on the floor and clutching my foot in agony as another blister burst.

The monument on Stoodley Pike dominated the landscape ahead and appeared quite close, but it did seem to take us a long time to get there. My recent euphoric experience had been a sublime and, I hoped, a seminal moment, but it had passed all too soon. Now I was becoming impatient. I wanted to get finished.

At last we were jogging along the escarpment towards the White House. Frank was now back with us, rested and full of his usual optimism. As we approached the road, John Amies and Anne Stentiford came out to meet us, along with John Axson and Geoff Pettengell; they were my final team of runners for the last thirty-four miles to Edale. I must have looked in reasonable condition when we arrived at the road, because John Axson later told me that when he saw the group of us approaching, he didn't realise I was with them, as he didn't expect me to be going so well.

My feet were now a real problem; my right foot, in particular, seemed to have increased in size. The only way to make running downhill bearable was to cut a hole in the toe of the shoe. It wasn't obvious to me at the time, but all I needed was a right shoe that was at least two sizes larger. After my Southern Upland Way experience, I should have been prepared for this. As runners and supporters swapped notes, my still-healthy appetite allowed me to eat more rice pudding and melon. Reluctantly I said goodbye to Dennis, Tom and Peter. These three lads, members of Clayton-le-Moors Harriers, had given me tremendous support over the last forty-three miles, and I was sorry to see them go.

Although the route over the Dark Peak is straightforward, my new team, like all the others, had been out and checked it to make sure that on the day they would be, as John put it, 'word perfect'. Blackstone Edge was, as expected, dry and firm, not its normal glutinous mire. The last time I'd been across here had been in January, at the end of a long solo training run. Wallowing deep in liquid mud on a black starless night had been disconcerting, the thought of sinking completely always on my mind. When I arrived back at my starting point, I found a police car parked alongside.

'I saw your torch. Are you OK? Where have you been?' the officer enquired.

'I've been for a run on the Pennine Way,' I said.

'What for?'

That was a question that would have required a rather lengthy answer — which might not, in fact, have made much sense to him. So I avoided it by making polite excuses about getting cold and wanting to get changed.

I was pleased when Brian Hickling joined us at Standedge Cutting, as I hadn't seen him for some years. He was the organiser of the thirty-six-mile Peakland Heritage Event, in the Peak District. As well as entering as a regular competitor, I had also completed the course on many occasions in training. The continuous running offered by the limestone dales and gritstone tracks suited my running style perfectly. Just before we left, Pete Simpson and his wife, Rosie, arrived to check on my progress. Pete resisted the temptation to join in again, having spent all of Friday night — the eve of his wedding anniversary — with me.

Suddenly, Frank said, 'Pete, what size are your shoes?'

'Size ten,' he replied.

'Mike's are a size eight. Would you mind if he borrowed one?'

Pete readily agreed, of course, but may have been pushing thoughts of shoes with holes cut in them to one side.

Running across Black Moss and White Moss was like running in the desert. The peat surface pulverised into dust; I'd never seen it so dry. Brian ran in front to determine the best line, and John ran fifty yards behind him, fine-tuning the route. This allowed me take the easiest course through some difficult terrain. Geoff was at my side, passing me water every few minutes.

After a three-minute stop at the A635 road crossing, we set off for Black Hill. The path was indistinct, and we soon lost it in the maze of peat hags and groughs. Brian angled off to the left and soon had us back on route. I stopped a couple of times to try to alleviate the pain in my right heel. A plastic heel cup given to me by Anne had failed to make any real difference and was soon consigned to the rucksack. However, thanks to Pete's shoe, the toes on my right foot definitely felt better.

Now my frustration with the awkward foot placements took over and I stormed up Black Hill, running all the way to the trig point. Not so much an 'effortless and serene application of energy', more of a single-minded impatience. The rocky path above Laddow Rocks was very difficult for me to run. After knocking my heel badly, I would stop and clasp my foot until the pain subsided. Arriving at Crowden, I was pleased to find we'd made up some time. I was extremely tired, but the combination of a slower scheduled pace and my unexpected ability still to run uphill fuelled the fire.

John and Anne took over for the last two sections across the moors of Bleaklow and Kinder. The climb up onto Bleaklow's summit was accomplished more easily than I had been expecting. It was still very hot, so with dehydration a real and dangerous possibility, Anne wisely passed me the water bottle every few minutes. John suggested I cool my feet in a nearby stream, but I was reluctant; I didn't want to risk making the discomfort worse. However, I regularly ran for miles on the fells in winter with wet feet, without any adverse effects. Eventually I tried the stream, and the effect was just delightful. I immediately wished I'd done it sooner.

Soon after leaving Bleaklow Head, I stopped for something to eat. I suspected John and Anne were watching me discreetly. I had now been running for over sixty hours without sleep, and they must have known my condition was potentially critical. I was treading a knife edge, and it would be possible to slip into an abyss of exhaustion. We continued to descend to the Snake Road, the last road crossing before Edale. I could hardly believe I was still running.

My ambition to break the Pennine Way record had started as a dream. Three days ago, at Kirk Yetholm, that dream had felt in jeopardy with the possible recurrence of the knee injury. Thankfully, the pain disappeared as unexpectedly as it had begun. At dawn this morning, a record time had seemed a strong possibility. If I could avoid any serious mishaps and carefully manage my last reserves of energy, I should arrive at Edale in the fastest time ever recorded.

Frank and Clive joined the three of us for the last eight miles. Blinking away tears, I tried to conceal my emotion from my friends. I'm sure they understood – especially Clive, who had helped me through so much on the Southern Upland Way and had seen me off from Kirk Yetholm. Running intermittently up Mill Hill, chatting with the others, I felt incredibly proud of myself, but also relieved to be nearly finished. As we climbed slowly up the rocks towards Kinder, my legs felt tired and heavy. Clive walked behind, encouraging me in his quiet, unobtrusive way, talking me through the effort, imparting a determined but calm patience. Soon we spotted a pair of Union Jack shorts running towards us, containing the shirtless and suntanned figure of Martin Stone. What better place to make his acquaintance than here at the end of a record run?

Eventually, we reached Kinder Downfall – only four miles to go. I was nearly there, but then it seemed to take an age to get to the top of Grindsbrook Clough. I knew I was going to break the record, but to my surprise I started to feel impatient. After 266 miles, my patience and self-control were ebbing away.

The final descent of Grindsbrook was purgatory. The path negotiates a steep rocky scramble before entering a narrow, boulder-strewn gully. I hadn't bargained for such discomfort. Every step had to be carefully executed to avoid banging my heel and inducing a searing pain shooting from my heel to my knee. But it was impossible not to stumble, and the more I stumbled, the more impatient I became. I just wanted to get to the Nags Head and stop the clock.

I had dreamt of this moment so many times: running smoothly into Edale, tired but in control, with the record safely in my grasp. But not injured. That was not part of the dream.

Unbeknown to me, Gill intended to ask each of my supporters to sign my copy of Alfred Wainwright's *A Pennine Way Companion*. She would then present it to me on my arrival at Edale as a memento and a record of everyone who had run even the shortest section. Thinking it may be tempting fate to acquire the signatures before I had finished, Clive had suggested that everyone should sign his copy. If I failed in my attempt, Clive would keep his copy and I would never know. The chapter aptly titled 'The Brotherhood of the Pennine Way' was duly signed by all twenty-one support runners, as well as Gerald and Betty, and is now one of my most treasured possessions.

As I approached the finish across the easier terrain of open grassy fields, I could see figures waiting for me. My mum and dad; Gerald and Betty also, their job as telephone coordinators now redundant.

In addition to Gill, Clive, Frank and my support runners from the last leg, we were joined by support runners from previous sections. Indeed, some friends who had not run were also present to add their voices to the many congratulations.

The relief of stopping was fantastic. At last I could take my shoes off and need go no further. I now realised my dream had always ended with the stopping of the watch. Perhaps that really was the end of the dream; I had realised my ambition.

But the experience wasn't yet over. After three days of continuous movement – running, walking, eating and clock-watching – suddenly there was nothing. Three days of complete and unwavering focus had been replaced by a cessation of effort of any kind. But that physical and mental void was being replaced by something else, no less important and, to me, just as difficult to deal with.

I wanted to make a heartfelt speech of gratitude and humility to thank everyone sincerely. But I felt an upsurge of emotion so strong, I hardly dared speak for fear of bursting into tears. I had enjoyed friendship and support of the highest order, but many years later I still doubt that I thanked everyone enough. I just hope they can all forgive me and that they remember the occasion with as much pride as I do.

I had been tested to my absolute limits, overcoming discomfort, injury and sleep deprivation, but my endeavours had brought the ultimate reward. I had succeeded. My time of 2d 17h 20min was 4h 34min faster than the previous best time – but I do not measure my success entirely by that margin of victory. My real success was to briefly enter a state where time and distance, and even pain and injury, had no meaning. I had at last achieved, just for a few precious moments, perfect physical and mental harmony.

CHAPTER 6:

Round and Round and Round

Completion of the Pennine Way left me feeling I had achieved what I considered to be the ultimate record, but not necessarily the ultimate run. I knew I could have gone farther, certainly into another night – not very quickly and maybe not without sleep, but I could have carried on. I still needed to experience the ultimate effort. I had to know just how far I really could go, to see what was round the corner of that third night.

Once the enjoyment of breaking the record had subsided, I mulled over a few possibilities for 1990. Eventually, I hit upon an idea that suited me ideally: the Three British Rounds.

These, consecutively, would surely provide the ultimate test. At 183 miles and 83,000 feet of ascent, I would be in no doubt as to just where my limits lay. It seemed such an obvious challenge that it was surprising it hadn't been tried before. After all, the Three British Peaks are often done, running, cycling, sailing, etc., so I would look upon it as an extended version of that: Ben Nevis, Scafell Pike and Snowdon – plus 110 tops.

First, though, I needed to recover from the Pennine Way. This involved a few weeks of 'active rest' – easy running and cycling. In September I began entering fell and road races before resuming George's interval sessions in October. By now I was fully recovered, increasing my weekly mileage and recording regular PBs. A series of 100-mile-plus weeks brought me up to the High Peak Marathon.

This Rucksack Club classic is organised early in March. It starts at Edale in the Peak District and covers forty miles of rough moorland and bog. Just to make sure it's as difficult and unpleasant as possible, the race is completed mostly during the hours of darkness. Some of the bogs are rumoured to be 'bottomless', and attempts to negotiate a bog of particularly fine consistency could end in complete submersion. For safety reasons the organisers insist that competitors enter as teams of four and stay together for the duration of the event. My average-sized feet combined with below-average body weight gave me hope that I had a reduced risk of drowning in the liquid peat. However, my heart sank on meeting my three teammates at the pre-race check in. They were big blokes. I hardly dared to look at their feet; they would need flippers to survive this, and the rule of four meant that if one sank, we must all retire. What if they all sank? I would be in breach of the rules and disqualified if I finished on my own. Underfoot conditions were dreadful, with snow, ice and slush in abundance.

It's difficult to convey the sheer purgatory of wading through calf-deep slush and being thankful for the underlying support of a layer of ice . . . until it breaks. From calf-deep, the slush suddenly becomes thigh-deep, while the shins scrape through the jagged ice. My teammates and I finished the forty miles in 11h 48 min. For all except the first couple of miles, my feet were completely numb and, as I discovered on thawing out, badly bruised.

The following week, still suffering from bruised feet, I entered the Milford 21, and this was quickly followed by the Edale Skyline and the Manx Mountain Marathon. My hope that my feet would recover in time for the Fellsman in the middle of May and a planned Bob Graham two weeks later proved wishful thinking. They didn't.

The 1990 Fellsman was very memorable, and not just because of my bruised feet. Something fascinating happened: I had another encounter with that elusive state of 'effortless and serene application of energy'. The event was plagued by high winds, lashing rain and low cloud. Visibility was poor, making careful navigation crucial. The tents at the checkpoints were waterlogged and battered. At the halfway point, I was in tenth place and so exhausted I was convinced I had some sort of illness. I was looking for a reason to quit.

Gill was following the race by car and met me at the Fleet Moss checkpoint, almost forty miles into the race. I was just about to announce my retirement when she said, 'You're in sixth place – they're coming in from all directions.'

In an instant, I realised I still had a chance. I knew the route well. No longer feeling tired or ill, I raced across the quagmire of Fleet Moss and up Buckden Pike, reaching the top in second place. I was first to the top of Great Whernside before enjoying a storming run across the bogs and tussock grass to the road head at Yarnbury and a final sprint down the lane to finish at Threshfield in 11h 19min, seven minutes clear of Joe Kyle and Tony Ratcliffe.

Whatever happened there? I had been transformed from feeling as though I couldn't carry on to having one of my best runs. I hadn't eaten or drunk anything that was likely to have made such a profound difference; the only thing that had changed was my view of what was happening, and that changed my entire physical state. What a revelation – all I needed to do was alter my perception of the situation and I would run effortlessly whenever I wanted! Needless to say, whenever I deliberately tried, it never worked; it only ever happened in the absence of conscious effort.

As my attempt on the Three Rounds drew near, the challenge took on an ominous aspect, and the 83,000 feet became more daunting by the day.

Gill told me to keep it in perspective. 'Lots of people have done this sort of thing before.'

Not that I knew any. Well, it was too late to change my mind now; everything was organised, the pacers ready and waiting. Anyway, I'd opened my big mouth, and now I had to step up to the mark. I searched in vain for some physical reason why I couldn't start, but I had to admit I was fully fit. At last I convinced myself it wouldn't be any harder than the Pennine Way; the 83,000 feet of ascent would be offset by the fact that it was ninety miles shorter. If only I'd known how wrong I was.

The Ramsey Round

At 1 a.m. on Friday 13th July, the moment arrived. On Thursday I'd enjoyed the company of my support team, but I'd only been able to pick at my meal and had not been able to sleep at all.

As I jogged, alone, along the lane and up through the mist-shrouded forest, I had time to weigh up my chances. On the minus side, my bruised feet had refused to recover (I vowed I would never do the High Peak Marathon again – but, of course, I did). On the plus side, I had found a solo Bob Graham Round fairly easy – in 20h 5min, two weeks after the Fellsman – so I knew I had the stamina and probably the correct mental attitude. It felt exciting to take on something that had not been tried before. I also knew there were some who thought it could not be done.

I was running solo for the first seven hours, and the Mamores were dark, misty and lonely. If the weather forecast was correct, the mist would clear by lunchtime. Descending Stob Bàn, the mist parted just long enough to reveal the lights of a town far below.

'Fort William!' I shouted out loud. 'It can't be!'

With relief, I realised it was, of course, Kinlochleven. I ran with caution downhill through the mist, compass in one hand, torch in the other. I wasn't looking at a map but using detailed notes and bearings that I'd established on training runs, and this worked very well. Soon I passed the place where I'd lost part of my torch while helping Pete Simpson on his round in June. Following him down the steep rocky descent of Stob Bàn at night without a torch was frightening; I've never been so glad to see the dawn in my life.

Alex Macrae had all my food laid out when I reached An Gearanach. He had been there some time and must have been frozen. It was nice to take a five-minute breather on this rocky perch. After making the awkward contour of Stob Coire a'Chàirn, I was soon climbing Na Gruagaichean, almost treading on a family of ptarmigan as they scuttled around my feet. On Binnein Mór I faced what is probably the most important route choice on this section. The north ridge looked longer but also easier than the one to the north-east, so with my compass set at north, I set off down. Disappointingly, the small path soon disappeared into boulders and rough ground, but it was too late to change my mind.

Suddenly, I was out of the mist and, as if by magic, onto short grass all the way to the lochan. Passing this on its west side was also good going. The gamble had paid off; I was on Binnein Beag in thirty-five minutes against a schedule time of forty. The isolated aspect of Binnein Beag makes it look quite intimidating but, in what seemed no time at all, I was up and down and running along the superb descending path towards Sgùrr Eilde Mór, the last hill of the Mamores.

John Amies and Clive Russell were waiting at Loch Eilde Mór with welcome food and hot tea. Having just run over the eleven Munros of the Mamores ridge solo, partly in darkness and mist, I was feeling very pleased with myself. I was seventeen minutes up on schedule and, with so much potential for mishap, relieved to get the attempt off to a good start.

I was apprehensive about the punishment 83,000 feet of ascent would inflict on my already bruised feet – so clean socks, Vaseline and soft road shoes seemed sensible preparation for the next eight stony miles to the foot of Beinn na Lap. As I set off with John, I noticed for the first time a slight but ominous twinge behind my right knee. While Clive returned to Kinlochleven to set up a twenty-four-hour telephone check with Gerald Woolley, John and I gained steadily on the schedule over Beinn na Lap and the next two Munros. After the complex top of Stob Coire Sgriodain, we dropped off steeply to the railway alongside Loch Treig.

Loch Treig dam is the only support point near a road head on the Ramsay Round. At thirty-seven miles, fourteen Munros and twelve hours into the circuit, it is well over halfway. However, the second part of the round includes most of the long climbs; this, combined with its rougher terrain, probably makes the Ramsay about two hours longer than the Bob Graham. Clive had all my gear ready and after ten minutes I was off, in shorts at last.

I enjoyed feeling the wind and sun on my legs as I set off up Stob a'Choire Mheadhoin accompanied by Brian Dodson and Nigel Rose. I'd not met them before, but their friendliness and obvious expertise made me feel at ease. They took me up a cunning route on small trods and tracks. Jogging and walking, we arrived on this majestic top another eight minutes up on schedule. We were due to meet Pete Simpson and Ian Leighton in the Lairig Leacach, but as we approached we could not see them and I began to feel anxious. Then with impeccable timing we all coincided just after crossing the burn.

The long climb up Stob Bàn took its toll, but sixteen Munros and forty-four miles were bound to have an effect. I told myself not to worry; it was nothing I hadn't experienced before and wouldn't experience again. With ninety-seven tops and 139 miles still to go, I must be patient and, as Dennis Beresford said to me so often during the Pennine Way, 'just keep putting it away'. The weather was now perfect, and the switchback ridge of the Grey Corries stretching before us under a crystal-clear sky made for a truly memorable traverse. Ben Nevis appeared quite close, but the rough going over the nine and a half miles and 6,500 feet of ascent leading to it would take five hours.

I glanced at the Mamores, which looked impressive. I felt a good deal of satisfaction in having traversed them in the dark solitude of the night, taking full responsibility for my decisions. As we climbed Sgùrr Chòinnich Mór I remembered my last visit here, caught in a white-out without ice axe or crampons. I'd crept down steep snow slopes, fearing at any moment that I would start an uncontrollable slide. Now the boulder ridge was dry and the wind refreshing to working muscles and a concentrating mind. Soon we were meeting Alex with more food before the major ascent of Aonach Beag.

The climb up to the Aonachs was gigantic, and the 1,650 feet of ascent seemed to take forever. But in due course we made it up onto Carn Mór Dearg and the traverse of its famous arête; airy, spectacular and very enjoyable. Our inevitably slow progress seemed not to matter as it was such a great place to be and marked the end of a great day. After a photograph on the summit of Ben Nevis, I changed into soft shoes for the long, stony descent to the Nevis youth hostel. As I followed Pete, I reflected on how odd it was that instead of relaxing and sleeping, I would be climbing Skiddaw in a few hours' time – the first top on the Bob Graham Round – with Graham Eccles and Geoff Fletcher.

Soon we crossed the footbridge to finish this first and toughest round in 21h 14min. It was such a shame that Gill wasn't there; it was the first time I'd completed a major run without her. But I knew it was going to get harder and she would be there when I really needed her. Within six minutes I'd changed and said a hurried thanks to Pete and Alex. Ian ran up to the car just in time to pass my feeder bottle through the window before we drove off.

My plan was to eat and then sleep, so – probably a bit prematurely – I started gulping down pasta and soup. It had been quite cool on the Ben, but now I was boiling over; my thermostat couldn't cope. The pasta was on its way back up, but luckily there was a plastic bag to hand. Unluckily, it contained some spare gear. Perhaps I should have used the food flask and recycled it later. Eventually I managed to eat, but only some tinned oranges. The eating plan didn't seem to be working too well. I wrapped a blanket around myself and tried to sleep. It was a four-and-a-half-hour drive, and I slept for perhaps an hour – probably less.

The Bob Graham Round

At Keswick Moot Hall, at 2.45 a.m., Geoff and Graham were surprised to see me jump out of the car ready to go. My legs felt a bit stiff on the climb up to Skiddaw, but a steady walk put us on top in 1h 30min, fourteen minutes up on schedule. After Great Calva and a refreshing, foot-cooling splash through the River Caldew, I enjoyed weaving down the rocky ridge of Halls Fell, always an exciting run.

At Threlkeld I spent time urgently attending to a lump of hard skin on my heel. Then, with Andy Brear and Howard Sawyer, I was off over the Dodds on what was now a beautiful morning. Compared with Scotland, the terrain seemed more like a run in the park. However, I was definitely tiring, and I knew things were going to become much harder.

Descending Seat Sandal towards Dunmail Raise, I was astonished to see six cars and Pete's motorbike waiting for me. Gill was by the stile, expectant, wondering how I was. From now on I would have her strength and optimism to help me. I left for Steel Fell on schedule and in good spirits. With Clive and John, I was on top in twenty-five minutes and continued to pick up time over the Langdale Pikes to Rossett Pike, where Frank Yates appeared with a large lump of succulent melon. Rejuvenated, we took the diagonal line to Bowfell and soon met up with Andy and Howard on Scafell Pike. Beyond Mickledore, we all headed for Broad Stand, the quickest way to Scafell and a route I'd enjoyed climbing many times.

After some foot aid at Wasdale, I set off up Yewbarrow with Colin Brooke. I had gained 1h 16min on my original schedule of 25h 18min, so a sub-twenty-four-hour round seemed possible. It was the day of the Wasdale Fell Race, and some of the long-distance specialists had waited to see me arrive. Martin Stone accompanied me part of the way, while Colin made light work of the heavy rucksack. Although the sack was jammed full, he always seemed to have whatever I needed at the top. It was now 6.45 p.m., but the heat was intense, radiating off the boulders and burning the backs of my legs. It was one of those occasions in ultrarunning when the atmosphere and the environment are so intense as to be unforgettable, yet so difficult to describe. Perhaps the mind is more receptive to moments like these, when the body is tired, or maybe it just wants a distraction and clings to it when it finds one.

On Great Gable, the sun was setting and the wind was cold. Graham and Geoff met us there, and I was glad of their help to put on extra clothes as my balance didn't feel too good on the steep ground. By Green Gable, it was dark, and with the darkness came a wave of fatigue. I couldn't seem to coordinate properly; my system wanted to shut down. Every stone I stepped on was a loose one, every tussock turned my ankle. Stumbling down to John's van at Honister, my enthusiasm was evaporating. I wanted to stop but knew that with a big effort a sub-twenty-four-hour Bob Graham was just possible. That would be a real thrill, something to be proud of. I could almost justify stopping at the Moot Hall. Almost! The problem was, I'd set out to complete all three rounds. I'd said I was going to do it. I knew deep inside that when I got to Keswick I would get in the car and go down to Wales. If the Paddy Buckley Round was going to be the biggest struggle of my life, then so be it.

Dale Head, Hindscarth and Robinson went surprisingly easily, and we made the road at Newlands Church with one hour left. At the end of a Bob Graham, these last undulating four miles usually take about forty-five minutes; today, I knew it would be a close-run thing for me. I channelled every last bit of energy and determination into a final effort, pushing hard all the way. Never once did I allow myself to ease off. My thoughts kept turning to the Moot Hall. If I finished inside twenty-four hours, a part of me wouldn't want to go any farther. But Gill and I didn't even discuss stopping the attempt; we both knew I would go to Wales, start the Paddy Buckley Round and see what happened. After all, that was one of the reasons I started out on this escapade: to go that bit further than last time, to find the ultimate experience, to achieve the ultimate run.

Richard Ezard and Gill drove me down to Plas-y-Brenin, with Gill navigating. I had too many aches and pains to sleep properly. Every time I slipped into a fitful doze, some physical discomfort would wake me up – either a painful muscle or an aching joint, but usually it was my feet pressing against the side of the car as we went round a corner. As we sped along the coast road towards Conway, the rising sun was a huge red ball sitting on the horizon behind us. A new day, a new experience to live through. Next time the sun rose, I would be up on the Glyders, I wondered how many aches and pains I would have then.

The Paddy Buckley Round

My feet were so sore and battered they would need some extra protection if they were to survive the next thirty-plus hours. I left Plas-y-Brenin wearing a pair of lightweight boots, one and a half sizes too big, with two pairs of insoles. Although a bit heavy, they did work quite well, giving underfoot cushioning and protecting my toes on the descents. The rubber rand and general strength made the stubbing of toes not as painful as it might have been.

My walk up Moel Siabod can only be described as slow, taking one hour exactly. As we jogged slowly along the ridge towards Clogwyn Bwlch-y-Maen, I felt I had to apologise to Geoff Pettengell and Mike Lawrence for going so slowly. As we picked off these minor tops, it became tempting to stop, just for a few seconds, or a minute, at each summit cairn. Eventually I conceded, on Allt-fawr, and took a five-minute break – pointless, really, as it was downhill all the way to the next support point at Bwlch Cwmorthin.

I was glad to see that Gill and Richard had walked up to meet me with food and drink. A paracetamol here helped to relieve devastated feet and an increasingly painful knee.

John Amies joined us as we set off for the Moelwyns. The day was warming up, so all three of my companions were carrying water bottles, and I was drinking every few minutes in an attempt to stave off dehydration. The potentially complex contour to Cnicht was straightforward today in good visibility, but the final pull to its top tested my strength. I was now running low on reserves – reserves that could not be replenished by food or rest. When I finished this epic, this 'ultimate' run – if, indeed, I could finish it – I would have nothing left. We soon jogged into Aberglaslyn, still ahead of a hoped-for three-and-a-half-day schedule.

John and Frank Thomas talked me up Moel Hebog, a long and desperately hard climb at this stage. A front of bad weather had moved in almost unnoticed; suddenly it was raining, and I felt cold. Such was my tiredness, I needed John's assistance with the zips and fastenings of my waterproofs. The normally enjoyable, airy and technical ridge to Y Garn was today wet, slippery and hateful. My spirits rose enormously when, at one point on the descent, John slipped onto his back. The combination of wet waterproofs and wet grass caused him to accelerate down the steep slope at an alarming rate. It was the funniest thing I'd seen for three days; fortunately, no harm was done.

At Rhyd-Ddu I took a twenty-six-minute break, the longest during the actual rounds so far. It was the lull before the storm. The storm was not to be a battle against wind and rain or hill and bog, but against physical and mental trauma at a level I'd never before experienced. In the comfort of John's van, Gill and I went through the ritual of her trying to find something I wanted to eat and me finding everything unappetising. The simple task of changing my clothes was difficult, painful and tiresome. At least the anti-pronation pad designed to stop my heel rolling seemed to be working well. We packed food, drink, warm clothing and plenty of torch power for the coming night.

With Anne Stentiford and Pete Simpson, I left Rhyd-Ddu at 7.37 p.m. in improving weather. My schedule times now looked ominously tight; although I was 1h 40min up on my three-and-a-half-day schedule, I was also 1h 19min down on my 29h 10min allowance for this round. I was slowly but surely losing time. The vague idea that I might be able to speed up was always in my mind – maybe I could do the Buckley Round in twenty-seven hours and therefore average twenty-four hours per round. Ever the optimist.

As we set off up the track, I felt quite reasonable, all things considered. Certainly, I was tired; this would be my fourth night without any real sleep. I knew it would require a massive effort, and my breaking point would be tested, but my spirits were good. In an odd sort of way, I was looking forward to this challenge. But despite my quiet confidence, I was not prepared for the sheer physical effort required to walk uphill, to put one foot in front of the other. I was not prepared for the mental application required just to keep going, to stay awake, to survive. My pace slowed all the time.

We arrived at Craig Wen in mist. It thickened as we approached Snowdon, and my senses also became dulled and confused. I was sinking into depths of tiredness I didn't know existed. There was no fear (yet); for the moment, I was happy to be in the company of Anne and Pete on the brink of what promised to be the ultimate experience, the ultimate run. Suddenly we stepped out of the mist; we stood only a few feet above the clouds, a raging silent sea lapping at our feet. Anne said it was as though we could jump off and float and swim on the clouds. It was the most incredible thing I've ever seen.

Night fell as we left Crib y Ddysgl. We descended into the boiling sea of cloud, into a swirling darkness that made my head swim. I was having difficulty focussing, and I was falling asleep, grinding to a standstill. Anne turned round; she must have sensed something was wrong. I was on the point of collapse.

Pete felt that a ten-minute rest would either make or break me. Not having much choice, I pulled my hood up and lay down thankfully on the side of the track. It was sheer bliss, an indescribable relief from the pain and effort. My two companions sat next to me and patiently waited; it was only afterwards I realised how much responsibility I had placed upon them.

High on the mountains, in the middle of the night, responsible for someone suffering extreme exhaustion, yet they were always calm and reassuring. I would have been extremely concerned in similar circumstances. Pete woke me after fifteen minutes; apparently, I'd been coughing and retching but also singing. The mind boggles. Heaven knows what it sounded like.

As we climbed Moel Cynghorion, Pete was about 100 yards in front, leading the way. I could sometimes see his silhouette outlined against the night sky, or the light from his torch when he turned round. Anne stayed close by, talking to me, encouraging me, a tangible link with reality in an increasingly frightening world. A black, dreamlike world of wind, grass and stones; a world of never-ending effort, seemingly without any light at the end of the tunnel. Time and distance no longer had any meaning. I had to keep going, I had to get to Gill at Llanberis, I had to complete my ultimate run. Stumbling down Moel Eilio, I knew that a proper sleep at Llanberis would be essential – indeed, unavoidable. For the first time the thought of stopping the attempt occurred to me. I didn't need to go through this torture; what was I trying to prove? But the thought of quitting was worse than the thought of climbing Elidir Fawr. I simply had not invested every last bit of mental application and every last ounce of physical strength from each muscle and each joint to quit now. The disappointment of failure would far outweigh the relief.

I must have been a dreadful person to be with that night. 'Forty-five minutes' sleep, and I'll be away within the hour,' I snapped at Gill as we arrived at Llanberis.

I don't know how she found the strength to wake me, but wake me she did, and she encouraged me to get ready and carry on. She could see I was dead on my feet, but would never ask me to stop. There were tears in our eyes. It was a very difficult time.

Clive Lane and Clive Russell accompanied me on the penultimate leg, over to Ogwen. The climb up the man-made incline through the slate spoil heaps was long but easy underfoot. As daylight came, I mused on my physical condition. The only thing that could stop me now was my body: either my inability to stay awake or the refusal of my legs to take another uphill step. The realisation that I was so committed I could not stop came as a slight shock. It dawned on me that my inner self, my very soul, would never admit defeat. If I came to a standstill, I could imagine myself saying, 'Well, I want to carry on, but this thing I'm inside won't go any farther. I must get a better one.'

By Mynedd Perfedd, I wasn't doing much running, and Y Garn signalled another bout of tiredness. But if I concentrated on the ground, my vision would clear and the stones and grass would come back into focus.

The nightmare of last night was being replaced by a morning of stunning beauty, the incredible cloud formations and Brocken spectres seeming in sharp contrast to my tortured body. Being anxious, Gill and John met me at Lyn Y Cwn with a spaghetti breakfast, which left me feeling much revived; the next big climb didn't seem too bad. After painful and laborious scrambles up the Glyders and Tryfan, we at last started the descent to the A5. Every step hurt my bruised feet; I tried to tread carefully, but my patience was wearing thin.

My arrival at Ogwen felt something of an anticlimax; we all knew I was going to finish. Anne and Pete walked with me up Pen yr Ole Wen, and my mood was one of quiet satisfaction, albeit somewhat travel-stained and tattered. I would just keep walking along, putting one foot in front of the other. Gradually we worked our way along the Carneddau, the uphills slow, the downhills painful, Anne and Pete passing me sweets and water. My mood of quiet satisfaction was being replaced by impatience. I just wanted to get to Plas-y-Brenin – the end. Every muscle, every fibre, was asking to stop; my eyes felt sunken, the skin on my face stretched tight. The spare end of my bumbag strap was a lot longer than when I started; I really didn't think I'd got any weight to lose.

Congratulations came on Pen Llithrig y Wrach, the last hill. Pete said it was an historic moment, but I didn't feel any emotion. I'd used all that up, along with everything else. I was just glad it was almost over, because I was almost finished. We found a good route down through the heather on small trods and tracks. My earlier thoughts of a sprint finish down the road had been abandoned. Slowly, the three of us walked down to Plas-y-Brenin, to the two Clives and my long-suffering wife, and stopped. After 3d 14h 20min, we had finished.

CHAPTER 7:

The Coast to Coast

St Bees, Cumbria, 19th July 1991. Hundreds of ghostly shapes screamed and dived around me. The seagulls were raucous and slightly intimidating. As I jogged along the sea wall towards the dark outline of St Bees Head, I wondered if they were angry with me, or whether they were always so bad-tempered before daybreak. The time was 3.30 a.m. exactly; it had to be exact because I wanted to avoid adjusting target times at each control point along the way.

After booking into our digs the previous evening, Clive Russell, Gill and I had walked down to the seafront to check how long it would take to get to the start of the route; a worthwhile exercise, as it took seven minutes longer than my original estimate. Thus, I could set off at precisely the scheduled start time. At least I would be on schedule at the beginning. Our landlady, Linda Moffat, was surprised to learn of my intention to leave at 3.10 a.m. in order to make a three-thirty start. I also suspect she was somewhat sceptical of my ability to run the 190 miles to Robin Hood's Bay by 9.30 p.m. the following day. She insisted I send her a postcard on my arrival.

In 1972 Alfred Wainwright achieved his long-standing ambition to devise a route from St Bees Head, on the west coast of the Lake District, to Robin Hood's Bay on Yorkshire's east coast. He published his book *A Coast to Coast Walk* in 1973, not intending his route to become an 'official' one. Inevitably, though, due to his amusing and eccentric style and the quality of the route, Wainwright's Coast to Coast became an extremely popular walk, and it soon came to the attention of the ultrarunning fraternity.

To the best of my knowledge, the first person to undertake it as a non-stop run was Mike Nicholson, who in May 1978 completed the 'walk' in 65h 30min, despite being unable to run the final forty-five miles due to a knee injury. Two years later, in August 1980, Pete Simpson and Frank Thomas, with the help of a small support team, recorded a time of 51h 11min; on this occasion, it was Frank who battled against injury. In 1985 Mike Cudahy set his sights on lowering the time even further. Mike set out from St Bees on 21st June with a target time of forty-six hours, supported by a small team of family and friends. He endured appalling weather conditions and completed the route in 46h 49min. It is interesting to note Mike's comments afterwards that 'the record must be considered soft; the experience of doing it, however, was not'. This comment took me back in an instant to the Southern Upland Way.

We spent a pleasant evening in the local hostelry, chatting about the route, the schedule, and the weather. Many times I have spent the night before a run worrying about an injury and its potential consequences. But not this time; I was injury free.

I had prepared a schedule for forty-two hours, which would require an average speed of 5mph. Inevitably, I would need to walk up the very steepest hills, and some stopping time would be unavoidable. How much time I spent walking and stopping would be key to achieving that average speed. I calculated my schedule, as I did for the Pennine Way, to take account of an inevitable decrease in pace. This should mean that even if I wasn't exactly on time, I should at least finish no more than an hour outside my forty-two-hour target. The slow pace I allowed for the last thirty miles would act as a buffer if I had lost time up to then, or else give me a psychological boost if I was ahead. I would endeavour to run as close to my physical limit as I dared, so planning only three ten-minute stops did seem a bit ambitious. Accurate pace judgement would be essential, the balance of speed and effort critical.

All previous record runs had followed the route as described in *A Coast to Coast Walk*. I did the same, always taking Wainwright's preferred routes where he described alternatives. There are four of those route choices in the Lake District. On reading his text, it becomes obvious which are his preferences; a close study of his line drawings shows that he only depicts mile markers on his preferred route, not on the alternatives.

As pre-run sleeps go, I did quite well – perhaps two or three hours. I have learnt that sleeping before a long run is not especially important. What is important is to rest, relax and keep my eyes closed. It is crucial to believe the alarm will sound on time; looking at the clock every fifteen minutes is a sure way to have a restless and sleepless night.

Despite believing I was relaxed, I must have been clock-watching, because I was up before the alarm sounded to tape my feet. I intended to travel light and run solo for the first fourteen miles to Ennerdale Bridge, carrying just photocopies of the map and relevant sections of the Wainwright book. As I approached the black outline of St Bees Head, the rain increased, forcing me to don waterproofs. I tried to summon faith in the weather forecast, which showed conditions improving. With a bit of luck, after a wet start I should get two fine days.

The breaking of a grey and drizzly dawn coincided, as expected, with the demise of my torch battery. Nice timing; there was no point in carrying a heavier torch or spare batteries. The plume from the nearby chemical works at Whitehaven indicated that the wind was, thankfully, blowing from the west. I could stand some bad weather, if it was short-lived and behind me. On through deserted farmyards, wet fields and green lanes, enjoying the smell of damp wild honeysuckle. The crossing of the main Whitehaven–Egremont road signalled the start of a short but uninspiring section through Moor Row and Cleator, where Wainwright suggests that it's 'better to look at the view ahead, to the green hill of Dent and the lofty mountains beyond'. The mist and rain were obscuring both. Reaching the top of Dent did feel significant – like a real hill, like the true start. There was a lightening in the sky, and I could feel a rising sense of impatience and optimism.

Peter Gent met me at Ennerdale Bridge with food and drink, ready to run with me as far as Rosthwaite. I was pleased to have someone with me who could describe every detail of the route ahead. We chatted away the lakeside miles, wading many streams swollen as a result of the previous night's heavy rain. On we went past Gillerthwaite and Black Sail youth hostels, followed by the climb up Loft Beck. As we reached the top, the rain ceased but a thick mist lingered, causing us to double-check our position with map and compass. Soon we were running confidently down towards Honister. The mist was clearing and the sun breaking through, and I gave an inward sigh of relief. As we crossed the road and made our way towards Rosthwaite, Peter informed me it was his first time over that section. He had actually memorised fifteen miles of the Wainwright book.

Dennis Beresford was waiting at Rosthwaite. Since I was thirty-nine minutes late, he had contacted our telephone coordinator, Gerald Woolley, to check whether anything had gone wrong. My scheduled pace through the Lakes had proved too demanding; I knew I was running well and not wasting any time. Beyond Richmond I was due to slow down, and the ground became easier, so I expected to be back on target for a forty-two-hour finish by the time I reached the North York Moors. We set off for Greenup Edge with me still wearing my waterproofs, even though it had stopped raining some time ago. This made me realise I was feeling anxious about being behind schedule. I reminded myself to relax and have faith in my fitness and my planning.

We were surprised how wet the ground was, especially on Greenup Edge, which had a lot of bogs and surface water. It was fabulous jogging over Calf Crag, Gibson Knott and Helm Crag, with the sun out and a decent breeze behind us. After a few seconds' break at Grasmere, Clive joined us for the next leg to Patterdale. Climbing Little Tongue, we passed three young lads, who started to give chase. We soon left them behind and I noticed they looked a bit red-faced – whether from exertion or embarrassment, it was difficult to tell; probably a bit of both. The path down to Patterdale became busy with walkers. At the road, Gill had experienced some difficulty finding a parking space, a now common occurrence in the Lakes. I grabbed a couple of doughnuts to eat on the move and Dennis had a quick change of trainers, as one had disintegrated. A time check here showed my thirty-nine-minute deficit had increased to fifty-six, over a mere nine miles. There was nothing I could about this, except run faster. However, the internal sense of pace and effort I had honed over the years made me feel that would not be right. I had to be patient and trust my instincts. A schedule is only a best estimate, after all, and racing up the next hill would probably do more harm than good. I still had quite a long way to go. Dennis, now clad in a pair of Clive's shoes, soon caught me up on the climb to Boredale Hause. Whereas Dent had felt like the start of the Lake District mountains, Kidsty Pike felt like the end of them.

We stopped on the summit for a moment to look back across the peaks behind us, then ahead towards the rolling limestone country of the Yorkshire Dales. The weather was now hot and, as we descended towards Haweswater, the ground became dry and hard. Running along the lakeside was easy, peaceful and tranquil. Despite the hot conditions, I was running well, really into my stride for the first time since leaving St Bees. Gradually, without me making a conscious effort, my speed increased. I was surprised when Dennis said he was finding the pace a little excessive. If one of the fittest and toughest runners I knew was feeling the strain, then maybe I was overcooking it at this relatively early stage.

On a marathon or road ultra, my stopwatch would tell me if I was running too fast; off road, running purely on 'feel', I had sometimes found it difficult to gauge my optimum pace. Notwithstanding one or two notable misjudgements, I now believed I could trust my instincts.

On tarmac, I knew within a few seconds per mile what my most efficient pace was for any distance up to 100km. Twenty-five seconds per kilometre slower than scheduled on a 100km race and it would feel easy; twenty-five seconds faster and 'the wheels could fall off'. The shorter the race, the narrower that fast cruising zone – maybe only five seconds per kilometre on a 10km race. My appreciation of the upper and lower levels of that zone had been gained from many miles of training and racing. During a long, fast training run, 'overcooking it' and being forced to slow down, although uncomfortable, wouldn't really matter, so I would experiment with trying to increase pace. Just at the point when my body wanted to slow down, I would force myself to speed up and then hold the faster pace for as long as possible. I could often maintain the higher speed for a surprisingly long time. Exploring the upper level of that zone (the anaerobic threshold) was part of the process of learning to run faster. Gradually, I improved my strength and speed endurance. But, more importantly, I learnt just how close I could go to the 'red line'. Inevitably, future races would present occasions to try it for real – a risky but thrilling strategy.

Running along the shoreside path beside Haweswater, the increased pace felt good. It felt right. Ultrarunning can feel demoralising when you're forced to run slowly due to exhaustion or injury. But it can also feel effortless. I was sure this was one of these latter occasions and also confident that I possessed a higher level of strength and stamina than ever before. However, with only fifty-three miles out of 190 completed, I was aware I could be misinterpreting my good feel. I hoped it wasn't simply adrenalin-fuelled excitement clouding my judgement. Too fast a start could do a lot of damage, both physically and mentally. Cramp, nausea or dehydration may pass, but the after-effects of overexerting early on can last a long while, causing ever more time to be lost. Pessimism and self-doubt could then become psychological hurdles.

It was obvious to both of us that I would either have to slow down or carry on alone. If I stayed with Dennis for the remainder of this leg, I would probably lose about ten minutes. Only ten minutes over 190 miles; I wondered if it might be worth it. But Dennis and I were on the same running wavelength. We both knew I wanted to break the record, and Dennis was there to help me. We did not need to discuss it. After sharing the remainder of the food with him, I set off alone, feeling a little guilty.

I was soon engrossed in running alone while trying to remember the route, which I had only been over once before. After my early restraint and patience, for the remainder of this section I felt really good. It was time to reap the rewards of several years spent improving my strength and stamina. After some hesitation, I started to enjoy speeding over the distance, convinced I was at the top of my game. The remaining miles to Shap Abbey felt short and effortless, the gradients always easy and my muscles strong. I cruised along riverside paths and across green meadows, enjoying every second. Occasionally, I thought about leaving Dennis, hoping the few minutes I'd saved would not cost me a friendship. He'd promised to meet me on the North York Moors the following day; I hoped he would be there.

At Shap, the support crew looked surprised and a bit alarmed when I arrived alone, but I suspect they guessed from my positive demeanour and the way I grabbed some food and ran straight through that all was fine. I left with John Amies and Clive, heading for Kirkby Stephen, a twenty-mile section for which I had scheduled 4h 12min. Soon after we set off, my legs began aching, the hills felt like real hills and my muscles were no longer so strong. I hoped I hadn't done exactly what I'd tried to avoid: set off too fast. The road section through Shap village felt tough; it's possible I was running faster because I was accompanied. Crossing the high limestone area towards Beacon Hill, I struggled to remember the route. We never needed to use the map, however, because a landmark or a view would trigger a mental picture of the next few miles.

The road junction before Beacon Hill is 69 miles from the start and was the first of three scheduled ten-minute stops. I enjoyed a welcome sit down, clean clothes and, as one foot was starting to feel slightly sore, a change from studded fell shoes to road shoes. I had been running for 13h 57min against a schedule time of thirteen hours. This included sixteen minutes' rest against a planned ten minutes. Despite being a bit behind my actual schedule, I was sure I couldn't have covered the ground any faster or taken less rest. I needed to have faith in my planning and believe that I would gradually come back on schedule.

From the road junction the original route went over Beacon Hill but, according to Wainwright, it was changed in 1981 due to there being no right of way. Wainwright suggests walkers go along the road through Orton, to rejoin the original route at Sunbiggin Tarn. A study of the OS map reveals that there are no rights of way shown for the first half-mile of the ascent of Beacon Hill (as far as NY641097), but there are gates and well-used paths on the ground. From here the map shows rights of way via NY640082, Acres, Sunbiggin and on to Sunbiggin Tarn. Because most of the route followed rights of way and the remainder was obviously well used, I went over Beacon Hill, as did Mike Cudahy when he set the existing record.

After the break I felt much revived and, having recovered from the minor bad patch, I eased back into top gear. Despite Clive's words of caution, I ran all the way up Beacon Hill. It was a magic moment; I felt I could do anything. In the beautiful evening light, all the colours seemed richer, more enhanced – even the smells seemed stronger. I wondered if an extreme level of prolonged effort could make one more receptive to such things; I had noticed a similar phenomenon on previous occasions. Physically, I was on a high. I felt in control and judged I was running well, as John and Clive seemed to be putting in a fair amount of effort.

In what seemed no time at all, we were at Sunbiggin Tarn – a super place, often noisy with sea birds. Clive decided to take a break here and lend a hand with driving duties. Just after leaving the tarn, I made the only navigational error on the entire run. I couldn't remember the route on the approach to Rayseat Pike and drifted off to the right, but I was soon back on course, having covered about half a mile extra. The path over the remains of Severals village is a bit vague; on my first reconnaissance run I lost the path, so I was glad I had made the effort to double-check.

At Smardale Bridge, we met two walkers who were making for their overnight stop at Kirkby Stephen. The young lady was looking sympathetically at her male companion who, apparently, could not walk any further. Kirkby Stephen was still five miles away, and we guessed that would take them until 11.30 p.m. Smardale Bridge is an idyllic spot, a lovely place to spend the night; at least, it is if you have a sleeping bag and a tent.

We overtook several walkers in ones and twos as we crossed the bone-dry fields towards Kirkby Stephen. They would soon be soaking in their baths and, later, enjoying a night in the local hostelry. Before they had breakfasted the following morning, I would have run through the sunset and the almost moonless night, through the cold early hours into a new day. I would probably be some sixty miles further east.

John and I met the support team at Hartley, just outside Kirkby Stephen. I had covered 84 miles in 17h 4min, of which nineteen minutes were stopping time. I had gained a few minutes and was now fifty-one minutes behind schedule. As Colin Brooke and I climbed towards Nine Standards Rigg, we were slightly concerned to see the top shrouded in mist. Neither of us had descended the other side recently, so we hoped it would clear before we reached the top. I began to regret not double-checking this high-level section over White Mossy Hill to Ney Gill. Even if the mist did not clear, I knew I shouldn't worry. Colin had supported me before; he was competent and reliable, and I would be OK. We visited the cairns of the Nine Standards first, then the trig point, as per Wainwright. I was surprised how boggy the summit was after the parched fields.

Experience has taught me that my physical state can fluctuate from deep lows to extreme highs during a long run. Sometimes this must be due to food and hydration – or lack of it. But a large part of it is due to my state of mind. If I was up on schedule and the weather was good, I would feel psychologically more positive. Nevertheless, a low point is a low point, for whatever reason. Experience has also taught me that, with patience, it will probably pass. However, throughout the course of an ultrarun, low points can become deeper and more difficult to deal with. As we started down the hill, I suddenly felt very cold, and put on all my spare clothes. Maybe I just needed some food, or maybe it was tiredness starting to creep up on me. With over 100 miles still to go, some doubts crept into my mind; if I was feeling tired at less than halfway, then perhaps I wasn't going to make it. I resolved to worry about that scenario when or if it happened. For the moment, I was OK.

*

Darkness fell as we jogged along the road into Keld. Although it was a clear night, the bright half-moon rose and set too early to be of any real advantage. I was feeling apprehensive about the next eight miles to Surrender Bridge. I knew Colin had not covered that section before, and it was several years since I had walked it with Gill. The thought of getting lost and losing even more time on the schedule was depressing. I cursed myself for not rechecking this short part of the route when I knew it would be run in the dark. Although most of the section was on good wide tracks, there were a couple of places where it would be easy to make a mistake: leaving Crackpot Hall to pick up the main path, and again finding a minor path on the left down to Blakethwaite smelt mine. These were easy enough in daylight, but each could be frustratingly difficult at night.

I took a few seconds' break at Keld to pick up a torch and have a bite to eat, then set off with Colin. A short time later we were at the ruined Crackpot Hall, where the path had disappeared in a maze of broken-down walls and head-high bracken. Just as the alarm bells started to ring, Colin confidently announced that the path must be just above us. After few minutes' bracken-bashing, we were on it. Great! It should be easy for a while now, but I was still feeling anxious about the minor left turn, which I knew would be coming up soon. As we ran, Colin was looking at the map and reading Wainwright's description. Suddenly he stopped. 'This is it' he said – and it was.

What a relief. I think I would have gone straight past it. Navigating unfamiliar terrain at night is a difficult skill to master, and accurate map reading and pace judgement are essential. For Colin to execute this task while under pressure and to get it right first time was very impressive. I was so grateful to him for getting me past these potential disaster points without error.

The long track run to Surrender Bridge seemed to go on forever. At every bend, my eyes were straining to see the lights of the support car. It's an easy track to run – too easy. I felt I had to run every step, or I would be wasting the runnable terrain. Eventually, I relented and allowed myself to walk the steepest uphill sections; the trouble was, there were hardly any. Beyond the Lake District, the Coast to Coast route has little obligatory walking, and a fit, determined runner could run themselves to a standstill. Eventually, I managed to relax and adopt the 'I'll get there when I get there' approach. My spirits rose when, rounding yet another bend, I thought I could see a light coming towards us; alas, it was only our torches reflecting in the window of an old piece of machinery. But at last Surrender Bridge appeared, and the support crew lights were an unmistakable and welcome sight. Pete Simpson was waiting; he has often supported me on overnight sections. His experience and optimism were long anticipated and much appreciated.

The eight miles from Keld to Surrender Bridge had felt a bit stressful, mainly because we had only limited knowledge of the route. Up to there, I had been running for twenty hours and covered 102 miles with only twenty-three minutes' rest; fortunately, the terrain had been mostly straightforward, with several miles on good tracks and not many junctions. Nightfall had coincided nicely with that easy terrain. The next twenty miles from Surrender Bridge to east of Richmond were altogether more complicated. Navigationally, this was the most difficult section of the route, with many field paths, farm tracks and turn-offs. Without prior reconnaissance, there was an extremely high potential for error.

It would have been possible to adjust my schedule to place this four-hour section during daylight, but that would have meant changing the start time and therefore the finish time. Starting four hours earlier, at 11.30 p.m., would have meant running through two nights; four hours later, and I would finish at 1.30 a.m., again running into a second night. I was convinced my strategy of starting just before daybreak on the first day and finishing just before dark on the second day was the best option.

It may seem obvious, but running at night is so much more difficult. On rough or rutted ground, foot placements can be harder to gauge, often leading to stubbing sore toes or aggravating blisters. The risk of tripping and falling is always present. Darkness makes it more difficult to do simple things like tying a shoelace, finding food in the rucksack or unfastening a gate. Everything also becomes more time-consuming. The combination of difficult terrain and tiredness can lead to impatience and frustration. It may only take one more issue such as a serious route-finding error, an unplanned sleep, bad weather, or a bout of cramp to tip the psychological balance towards giving up. No matter how difficult things became, I knew it was essential to believe that with daylight, colour and sun, everything would be easier. It is a hard and painful lesson to learn, and there is no substitute for experience to develop that belief.

After the anxiety of the previous leg, when I had to rely on Colin, it was a relief to feel confident, to know I had checked the next section and checked it well. It can be so easy to take a wrong turn along a hedgerow, or the wrong line across a meadow, then to compound the mistake by guessing, hoping that a shortcut you will get you back on route. In my experience, that rarely works. You really cannot know a night leg well enough.

After two minutes' rest, Pete and I set off, armed with an enlarged and laminated route description and a lot more confidence. Although I would always have a map with me, I often used notes, as shown below. It boosted my confidence to tick off landmarks.

Surrender Bridge to Reeth

Bear left straight away on wide path. Pass ruin on right. Path narrows. Up hill. Path now narrow and stony. Drop down to right to stream. Up to kink in wall. Keep left of large hawthorn bush. Stile in wall. Keep wall on right for 2 mins.

If I didn't see the 'large hawthorn bush', I would go back to the 'kink in the wall'. Surely much more satisfying than using a GPS or a tracking device.

We ran many miles on farm tracks and minor lanes, and our smooth progress confirmed the value of my thorough preparation. At 1 a.m. I was already looking forward to daybreak. It's a strange term, 'daybreak' – it sounds like a sudden change from dark to light, but it always seems a lengthy and frustrating process. Sunrise would be at 5.07 a.m. Allowing for forty-five minutes of dawn twilight, daybreak should be about 4.20 a.m. It felt appropriate to be running towards where the sky would lighten first; at least I didn't have to keep looking behind me. During the final hour before dawn, I was fixated on the eastern sky, wanting to believe it was getting light, willing daylight to come. Suddenly, I could see without my torch. It was strange to feel I had missed the actual moment when dark turned to light.

Eventually, Pete and I reached Streetlam at 129 miles, now forty-four minutes behind schedule, including a total of fifty minutes' rest. This was Pete's section finished. He had completed twenty-seven miles with me, mostly in the dark, and we had not put a foot wrong. While Pete and I were running this leg, Gill had been driving my support car, with Clive following in Pete's car. Gill related how they had been stopped by the police; a lady driving on her own at 3 a.m., being followed by a suspicious-looking male, had caught their attention. Meanwhile, that suspicious-looking male was preparing to accompany me for the next eleven miles to Ingleby Cross.

Undoubtedly, I had come an exceptionally long way since those early days on the Fellsman Hike. I had worked hard at my training, but I now understood I would never achieve the permanent state of physical perfection that had once been my dream. Nevertheless, I really wanted to make a good job of this run – not just to break the record, but to feel I had done everything right physically and logistically. I wanted to be certain I could not have done any better.

These thoughts came as I was tiring and beginning to develop a large blister. I was starting to struggle, and I wondered if I really could finish. I had never failed on anything, so the thought that I might not be physically capable of completing this appalled me. But deep inside I knew, ultimately, the desire to succeed would override all the pain and difficulty. I knew from deep experience that my mindset would be transformed, almost involuntarily, into a blind refusal to accept defeat. No matter how much pain I had to endure or how much mental effort I had to apply, I would never give in. I would not be able to.

While Clive attended to the blister on my right heel, I assured him that I, at least, did not consider him suspicious. As we headed for Ingleby Cross, I tried to analyse why I felt so tired; I was sure it could not have been lack of training or conditioning. As expected, I had taken a long time to recover after the Three Rounds the previous July. My log shows that, after two weeks' complete rest, the remainder of the year had been a mixture of running and cycling, the final five weeks up to Christmas 1990 being cycling only. Although my running average for this period had been less than thirty miles per week, I had resumed a track session through the summer, with Cannock and Stafford AC, switching to the interval session in October. I had also felt motivated enough to enter a few events – a half-marathon, the Otter 40, the OS Lakes Mountain Trial and the Glen Lyon Karrimor among them.

January 1991 had seen me fully recovered from the Three Rounds and determined to train well for stamina and speed, hopefully to achieve fast times on specific events. I had decided to alternate between high-mileage weeks and easy weeks, which would include a long event. In the high-mileage weeks I averaged ninety-two miles, usually running twice per day. Sometimes I did an interval session as well. A maximum week of 202 miles was perhaps a bit excessive, even obsessive. It comprised running fifteen miles to work, walking six hours at work, then running fifteen miles home for five days; Saturday, I ran twenty-five miles and Sunday, twenty-seven. Physically, it may not have been any more beneficial than running 100 miles. But I am sure it helped psychologically. It had reinforced my mental focus and resilience.

My hope that speed work, combined with high-mileage training, would help me achieve some of my best results was justified. It had been satisfying to record my best time of 10h 19min on the Fellsman Hike, achieving second place, eight minutes behind Tony Ratcliffe. This was one of my best runs, and to place second was certainly not a disappointment. Tony ran an excellent race, shadowing me for most of the way before choosing the right time to pull away and achieve a well-deserved first place.

Two weeks later I had finished first in the LDWA Lancastrian 100, in a time of 18h 48min, ahead of Brian Harney in second place. For safety reasons, the organisers require participants to form into groups overnight. Degrouping is then allowed at first light, and any 'waiting time' incurred is deducted from the finishing time. When we were degrouped, Brian and I were in equal first place, although I had more waiting time in hand to deduct. In the still, early morning I could hear Brian's footsteps, a few yards behind; I could also hear him retching and spitting. We were so close to the finish that even if he overtook me, he did not have enough time left to make up his deficit. He knew he couldn't win, but refused to ease off, determined to push himself to the limit. A masterclass in tenacity; no wonder he's a previous holder of the Pennine Way record.

At the end of June, I had been first over the line in the eighty-mile South Downs Way race in 9h 49min. Gill and I had walked the course only three months previously, finding it well marked on easy tracks – but not so easy that I could average 8mph for eighty miles. Even though I had become very fit and I'd had a good run, it couldn't be that easy. I have since discovered the race distance was actually seventy-three miles, my true average speed of 7.4 mph still proving it to be a fast course.

After the South Downs Way, I allowed myself three weeks' recovery, to be rested for the Coast to Coast. This might not have been enough, but several times previously I had run ultras with only one or two weeks' recovery. I was sure that neither too short a recovery time nor overtraining were the reasons for my present fatigue. I then realised what I had done. In my determination to have a fast run with minimal rest, I had been covering the ground much more quickly and at a more even pace than ever before. From St Bees to Patterdale (forty-six miles) I had averaged

5mph, by Shap (sixty-one miles) my average was 4.9mph, and at the last check at Streetlam (129 miles) it was 4.8mph. It was obvious to me now: I had been running at a relentless pace and I was now paying the price. In a way, I had become a victim of my own ambition. I had aspired to run as fast as I could, for as far as I could. Maybe I had reached my limit; maybe the wheels were about to fall off. If I were to maintain this level of effort for another sixty miles, I would have to draw on all my experience and stamina. I would have to remember all the hard-won lessons of suffering and injury management. I was in the shape of my life; simply completing this run in record time would not be good enough. I had to complete it as fast I possibly could. I just had to believe in myself.

Mike Cudahy was waiting at Ingleby Cross to accompany me for the next twenty miles to the Lion Inn. My feet had become very sore, and they were giving me a lot of discomfort on the downhills. I was constantly trying to lessen the pressure I was placing on them, trying to avoid stubbing my toes. The big blister was getting more painful. A couple of anti-inflammatory tablets made it a bit more comfortable, but I would just have to let it hurt. The final five miles to the Lion Inn were reasonably flat – a slight relief for my battered feet, but they were tedious miles, seeming to go on forever. Mike said he had found the same on his record run in 1985.

One hundred and sixty-five miles to the Lion Inn, and up on schedule for the first time. A sub-forty-two-hour crossing now seemed highly likely. I was pleased and relieved to see that Dennis had come to join me again. Dennis, Clive and Mike would take it in turns to run with me over the final thirty miles to Robin Hood's Bay. The details of the next twenty-four miles as far as Hawsker had faded since my reconnaissance runs, and I struggled to remember parts of it.

One of these reconnaissance runs had been undertaken in winter. My plan was to check the final thirteen miles to Robin Hood's Bay, meeting Gill at road crossings. It was February, very cold and wet, with a covering of snow for good measure. We planned to meet every two or three miles, so I was travelling light, with no waterproofs or additional clothing – and, of course, no mobile phone. Somewhere in the region of Little Beck, while negotiating complex, snow-covered paths, I lost my way. Becoming increasingly cold and frustrated, I made a hasty decision: I was off route anyway, so I decided to miss out the next meeting point and pick up the route further east. My reasoning was that Gill would drive to that point and, seeing there were no stud marks in the snow, assume I had missed it out. Of course, she did notice the absence of footprints but did not know whether this meant I had missed it out or that I hadn't passed through at all.

It was midday, and so began a long afternoon of second-guessing each other's whereabouts, with each becoming increasingly concerned for the other's safety. Eventually, I decided to abandon the route in favour of following the road all the way back to Robin Hood's Bay. I was sure Gill, during her searching back and forth, would stumble across me. Becoming even colder, I called at a roadside farm and asked for a bin bag. I made some holes in it and used it as a jacket. I was only a few miles from Robin Hood's Bay, so instead of running on the road, I reasoned I may as well wait where I was. As I sat huddled in my bin bag at the end of the farm drive, Gill drove straight past, mistaking me for a bag of refuse! Having decided to report me missing, she was on her way to the police station. I jogged down the steep lane to the seafront in Robin Hood's Bay and was surprised to find she wasn't there. It was 6 p.m. and dark, but at least I knew she was OK, wherever she was. Not knowing what else to do, I called at the police station. The duty policeman looked up and said, 'Are you Mike Hartley?' Gill and I were soon reunited and in our digs, feeling relieved if a bit stressed. If only mobile phones had been invented.

Soon, Mike, Clive and I were standing at a track junction on the approach to the A169, but I just could not remember which way to go. Lying on my back, feet in the air, enjoying the pain-free rest, I waited while Clive and Mike checked the map. Part of me wanted them to decide quickly so I could get going, but a small part of me wanted them to take as long as possible. I wanted to delay the return to painful blisters and stinging feet. Soon enough, they had made their decision; it was time to put my weight back on my feet.

Dennis joined the three of us at Hawsker, two hours up on schedule with only four miles to go. It felt good to have my three friends with me.

Then, suddenly, while running alongside Mike, I stumbled and started to fall into a gorse-filled ditch. I need not have worried. I felt Mike's strong left arm grab me under the armpit and, without breaking stride, he scooped me up like a rag doll and plonked me back on the path.

The last few miles, following the switchback path along the clifftop, began to feel frustrating. It was difficult to tell which bay was Robin Hood's, until we were almost there. Before long, however, we were jogging down the final steep lane to the beach. The tide was out, the sea barely visible, so we had to make do with the high-water mark as the official finish. I was glad I had not carried a stone all the way from St Bees to throw in the sea. It would have meant either an awfully long walk or throwing it onto the sand, neither of which would have felt quite right.

The post-run meal and beer looked and tasted fantastic – especially the beer! What a shame it made me violently sick.

The following day, my feet felt battered, which was no less than I expected. I felt weak and thin but, strangely, muscle stiffness was completely absent. My finishing time of 39h 36min was quicker than I'd anticipated; I was incredibly pleased with it, and I still am. I knew I had trained extremely hard and prepared well, and that gave me the confidence to fully exploit my preparation. I found the final sixty miles very tough, solely because I was determined to keep running as fast as possible. At the finish, I knew I really had completed the run as fast and efficiently as I could. All that remained now was to write that postcard.

CHAPTER 8:

The Western States Endurance Run

Having completed the Coast to Coast, I had achieved the last of my planned objectives; in fact, I had achieved all the major off-road ambitions to which I had been aspiring. During these undoubtedly successful years, I had also been in pursuit of personal physical excellence, an elusive state which I had only experienced for fleeting moments. During the Coast to Coast run I had realised that achieving a state of permanent or even prolonged physical perfection would probably not be possible, but those rare moments were always in my consciousness, like treasured jewels which I would always hold dear, beacons that reminded me of what was possible. I still had an insatiable desire for hard physical exercise, to push myself to the limit. I believed that if finding the key to a permanent transformation was still possible, it was more likely to happen during an extreme undertaking. I needed another challenge.

Two years had elapsed since the Solihull 100km where I had achieved the qualifying time for joining the GB Ultra Squad, but I hadn't yet competed. The Solihull race, for me, was primarily a unique and valuable training run in my Pennine Way preparation, but it did whet my appetite for ultra-road running.

Before shifting my focus to the tarmac and the daunting prospect of competing as an international athlete, there were several other off-road challenges I wanted to consider. The most appealing of these was a traverse of all 214 'tops' listed in the seven volumes of Wainwright's *A Pictorial Guide to the Lakeland Fells*. At approximately 320 miles and involving 120,000 feet of ascent, it would be considerably harder than anything I had yet done.

The first person to achieve a continuous Wainwright completion was Alan Heaton, on 29th June 1985. Alan set out from the Moot Hall, Keswick, and completed his circuit in 9d 16h 42min, despite having to visit hospital after five days, where he was prescribed antibiotics due to 'foot trouble'. The following year, in heatwave conditions, Joss Naylor completed the round in 7d 1h 25min. Joss began to suffer sore feet and ankles on day two, and by day five his ankles were skinned and swollen, as was the inside of his mouth. Difficulty eating, rendering him only able to sip water, added to his problems. Both Alan and Joss, not surprisingly, had problems with sore and blistered feet. I knew from experience how debilitating this could be, but I was inspired to make an attempt. Joss had produced a schedule showing the order in which he visited the tops. On the assumption that he had taken the optimum route, I decided that his choice of route would be good enough for me.

I had already covered most of the loftier Wainwrights during other challenges and training runs but had little experience of the smaller tops. During my first run, prospecting a few of these less frequented hills, I was surprised how rough the terrain was. To follow the optimum route, it would often be necessary to cross much difficult ground, rather than follow established paths. This caused me to have second thoughts; the probability of developing severe foot problems during a seven-day run did not appeal to me. On previous record attempts, I had always been enthusiastic to undertake reconnaissance, compose a time schedule and plan logistics, but this felt different. Perhaps I didn't really 'want' to do it; perhaps I was also frightened of failing on this extra-long quest.

The Lakes Meres and Waters was another Lakeland challenge of which I was aware. Again, Joss Naylor had set the record time of 19h 14min. The route visits twenty-six major lakes, meres and waters, covering 105 miles and accumulating over 20,000 feet of ascent. Joss completed the route in June 1988, also visiting Kentmere Reservoir for good measure. I was sufficiently motivated to check the entire route and compose a carefully planned schedule. The terrain consisted of approximately forty per cent road, thirty-five per cent track and twenty-five per cent rough hill running. I was sure the significant amount of road and runnable track would suit me well and stand me in good stead for my still unrealised ultra-road ambitions.

Making an attempt on the Tan–Cat record was also very enticing. Mike Cudahy's record time of 26h 36min for the 120 miles was impressive, especially considering it was over eight hours faster than the time I had recorded six years ago. But I had improved a lot since that memorable occasion with Guy and Howard. I felt that if everything went well, I should have a good chance of success.

Finally, I considered the Colne–Rowsley, which held many memories for me. Although I had only completed it once, I had often incorporated parts of it in training runs, and I enjoyed running over the rough and boggy moorlands. I loved hearing the cackling of red grouse, the mile after mile of peat and heather, and in winter, if I was lucky, the sighting of an arctic hare. Again, I prepared a schedule with a view to bettering Mike Cudahy's record time of 11h 44min for the seventy-three-mile route. Both Colne–Rowsley and Tan–Cat appealed to me more than the Wainwrights, partly because they were much shorter, but mainly because of their more runnable terrain. Thoughts of painful, blistered feet and sleep deprivation on a run lasting seven days had eroded my enthusiasm for the Wainwrights round.

As I mulled over these possibilities, I realised the spark that had always been there was now absent, and I was trying to reignite it. I'd never had to do that before. On all previous occasions, I had wanted to get started on the next objective on my list of ambitions, impatient and eager. Now I was searching, trying to find a challenge to commit to and then persuade myself that I really wanted to do it.

I was very fit, and I still had the desire to achieve more goals, but I didn't really know what they were. I wondered if it was time to retire from the long off-road runs and switch to the road, or hang up my running shoes and return to rock climbing. For me, the complex combination of hard physical effort and mental control required to succeed on a rock climb – indeed, to preserve life and limb – had no equal. But I could return to climbing in due course. At least, I hoped I could; increasing discomfort in my knees and decreasing flexibility did throw some doubt on this.

For some years I had been subscribing to a magazine called *Ultrarunning*. With accounts of exotic trail races from Alaska to Florida, it gave an inspirational insight into the American ultra scene. Of the many 100-mile trail races, the Western States Endurance Run received more coverage than most and was described as 'the most arduous running event in the US'. The magazine then went on to say that 'the Western States 100 is truly the ultimate challenge for the long-distance runner. Participation in this event should not be taken lightly.' The conditions for entry to the run were twofold. Prospective entrants had to provide evidence that they had achieved minimum times for stipulated distances; for example, 50 miles in under nine hours or 100 miles in under twenty-four hours. If the distances were on trails (not roads), then one hour could be added. All results had to be certified by a newspaper article, official race result or listing in *Ultrarunning*. The requisite times were not especially fast, but they ensured runners had at least some experience and possessed a reasonable level of fitness. Due to the expected high demand for places, qualifying entrants were then placed in a lottery. I was unsure whether I really wanted to travel all the way to California, but posted my entry anyway in the autumn of 1991. I reasoned that if I was accepted but subsequently changed my mind, I could then cancel. The spark had been reignited.

From the start at Squaw Valley, the race follows mostly dusty trails to the finish at Auburn, in California's historic 'gold country'. Within the first four miles the route climbs from 6,200 feet above sea level to 8,700 feet at the Emigrant Pass, which after a hard winter might be blocked by snow. From here, following many of the trails used by the gold miners of the past, the route continues west; another 15,500 feet of ascent and, interestingly, 23,000 feet of descent have to be negotiated, plus the wading of the American River at 78 miles.

Much of the trail is through remote country, and the race information states: 'getting rescue vehicles to some parts of the trail may be difficult or impossible. Injured or exhausted runners must stay on the trail; you will be found by another runner or search and rescue mounted patrols. Rattlesnakes, bears and mountain lions have been encountered on these trails.'

The terrain over the final twenty miles is easier, but with a 5 a.m. start and an estimated average speed of 5mph, I was expecting to finish in the dark. Being unable to reconnoitre the course, I was hoping it would be well marked and easy to follow.

*

On completion of the Coast to Coast, I had the shortest-ever recovery period and soon resumed racing and training. Although I was still unsure of my next objective, by mid-October I had increased my training to eighty miles per week and restarted my weekly interval session.

The year came to a close with a seventh-place finish in the St Albans marathon in December. My time of 2h 35min 42sec, a PB by 2min 7sec, was another step closer to the sought-after 2h 30min.

I had entered the Barry forty-mile track race which was due to be staged at the Jenner Park stadium, Glamorgan. Tailoring my training specifically, I undertook longer and longer track sessions, building up to ten miles of interval work. I made the forty consecutive 400m laps more interesting and beneficial by incorporating changes of speed. The first lap would be slow and served as a warmup, then laps two and three were run at what I called 'ultra race pace': ninety seconds per lap, or six minutes per mile. This equates to 10mph – a bit ambitious for an ultra, but there was no point in making it too easy. Lap four, the final lap of the first mile, was run – without any time to recover – as fast as possible. Over repeated weekly sessions, I gradually reduced the 'fast lap' from an average of seventy-four to a best time of sixty-six seconds. The remaining nine miles followed the same format, and each lap was carefully recorded on my sports watch. I repeated this session week after week, always transposing the times from watch to logbook and attempting to improve at the next session. I found speed sessions on the track psychologically difficult; the monotonous setting conflicted with my instinctive love of the hills' freedom and unpredictability. But I persevered, and eventually further improved my speed. This allowed me, if I made a superhuman effort, to squeeze out best times not only on the track but also on short road runs, where I was able to exceed previous best times.

The Barry 40 was obviously going to be perfectly flat; running 161 laps on a uniform surface with little change in stride length would provide a unique experience. Of course, my ambition was to complete the race in under four hours – a test not only of patience, but also of precise pace judgement.

By early February, I was including forty-mile runs in my training programme of 100 miles per week. Setting out from home on a training run of forty miles on the road was not appealing, whereas switching to the canal towpath felt less daunting. I found that the soft but generally even surface, the flora and fauna, the fishermen and boat traffic allowed the miles to pass with interest. Unexpectedly, I discovered an aspect of canal running which, although psychologically beneficial, after many miles became difficult to deal with. Because canals were necessarily constructed with long curves, it always seemed to take an age to get round a corner – a test of patience in itself.

My target time of five hours for these runs was slower than my ultra-road ambitions over a similar distance, but the canal runs provided an opportunity, notwithstanding the occasional aggressive swan, to test myself in a pleasant environment.

On 1st March 1992 I stood on the start line of the Barry 40 and looked down at the synthetic, rubberised surface of the track. My thoughts drifted back exactly three months to the St Albans marathon. If I could run another fifteen miles at the same pace, I would achieve a finishing time of under four hours. I had found the St Albans run tough; trying to maintain an even pace slightly faster than 10mph had been at the upper end of my capabilities. But the Barry 40 was perfectly flat, and the combination of my recent speed work and long flat runs on the canal might just allow me to break the four-hour barrier. To finish the forty miles in under four hours would mean averaging ninety seconds per lap, or 10mph. Despite my intention to run this race at an even pace, I didn't want to dispense completely with my normal 'steady start' strategy, which had always served me well. Gill was my timekeeper and recorded my first lap at 105 seconds; lap two took 94 seconds and lap three, 92 seconds. At five miles I was in third position, twenty-three seconds behind the two joint leaders, Dic

Evans and Malcolm Griffiths. Recording 30min 38sec for the first five miles, I was, on average, about two seconds per lap slower than would be needed to finish in four hours. I settled into a pace which only slowed by two or three seconds on laps when I occasionally collected a plastic cup of water from the official feeding station. This deficit was easily regained on the following two or three laps.

Another eighty laps at an imperceptibly faster pace brought me to twenty-five miles in 2h 29min 55sec, still in third place, but now averaging the necessary ninety seconds per lap. Not only had my steady start been beneficial, it had also, because of the precise nature of the track and timekeeping, been easy to judge. Dic and Malcolm were still joint leaders, but I could see that I had gained a few metres. The fast pace and the constant effort required to maintain exactly the same stride length were beginning to take their toll, but 2h 37min 8sec for the marathon distance was only 1min 26sec slower than the PB I'd achieved on the St Albans marathon. Malcolm had pulled away from Dic, but they were both slowing slightly, and I was closing the gap. Total concentration on stride length and breathing resulted in my taking the lead and recording 2h 59min 59sec at the thirty-mile point, the furthest I had ever run at 10mph.

Suddenly, Dic walked off the track. He'd given his all: thirty miles in 3h 56sec, a great run. The five miles from thirty to thirty-five were my slowest since the first five, averaging 92sec per lap. Although the next and final five miles were slower, averaging 99sec per lap, I had, yet again, proved to myself the value of a steady, conservative start. Finishing first in 4h 4min 1sec ranked me fourteenth on the world all-time list for forty miles on the track. Malcolm finished third in 4h 18min 28sec. Gwyn Williams, who had placed consistently fourth from the start to thirty miles, passed the thirty-five-mile point in third place and came through to finish second in 4h 15min 13sec.

Three easy weeks following the Barry 40 preceded a three-week gradual increase in weekly mileage up to 120 miles; two more weeks, and I was standing on the start line of the Telford marathon. It was the 26th April 1992. Eleven years had elapsed since my first one. Sixteen times I had raced over the classic 26.2-mile distance, and I had completed five of those races in 2h 45min or faster. It was high time I finally broke through the 2h 30min barrier.

My average time per mile on the recent St Albans marathon, when I felt I wasn't running at my best, was 5min 56sec; all I had to do was run each mile thirteen seconds faster and I would record 2h 30min. Thirteen seconds doesn't sound a lot; indeed, it isn't a lot. My self-belief was reinforced further when I realised that my time for the first twenty-six miles of the Barry 40 had only been slightly slower than 2h 30min pace, and I had also been strong enough to run another fourteen miles at almost the same speed. I was convinced that, with a start that wasn't too fast, a bit more effort and a willingness to suffer (even more) in the final stages, I could run the marathon in under 2h 30min. Ignoring the fact that making just 'a bit more effort' when I was already expending maximum effort could be the straw that broke the camel's back, I resolved to give this race everything I'd got.

Suddenly, we were away. Six minutes for the first mile felt slow; a slight increase in pace resulted in five miles completed in twenty-eight minutes, then ten miles in fifty-six minutes. Perfect: one minute up. I began to wonder if one easy mile really did count as a slow start, but it was too late now. Today was the day I would be successful!

As I ran past the twenty-mile marker, I glanced at my watch: two hours exactly. Despite my best efforts, I'd slowed down, and a sub-2h 30min finish now looked doubtful. I was surprised and disappointed; I had been faster at this point on previous marathons. My dream time looked destined to remain just that – a dream. But all was not yet lost. I was in sight of the leaders and gaining on them. Twenty-three miles done, three to go; I was now positioned fourth in the leading group of five. The time clock on the lead car, just in front, showed 2h 15min. To complete the course in under 2h 30min, I would need to run each of the remaining three-and-a-bit miles at less than five minutes per mile; impossible. I wasn't going to do it.

However, in my efforts to catch the leading group, I had gained a small amount of time. I could still achieve a PB, but only just, and only then by a few seconds. I had always considered a 'good run' more important than the actual time, but I'd never before been so close to the front of a marathon, and I could feel the adrenalin surging. I might never have a chance like this again. If I could win, the time would be immaterial. I had to risk everything and push it to the red line. Checking my stopwatch, I could see that the previous mile had been quicker. The pace of our group had increased. I wanted to win. We all wanted to win. My legs were starting to feel numb; I was losing that essential metronome-like efficiency, but I refused to give in. I would take the ultimate test. I would push even harder. I went to the front of the group and opened the throttle. Nothing happened. The tank was empty. The only thing between me and the finish was one mile of road and the lead car. The numbness in my legs became inexorable and flooded my muscles. Two runners overtook me, and then another, sweating and straining, all three determined to win. I had given everything on my seventeenth marathon in pursuit of a PB – and I got one. Finishing in fourth place, my time of 2h 34min 42sec was my fastest ever by exactly one minute.

Despite my disappointment at failing to run under 2h 30min, I knew I'd never been fitter. I continued to train twice per day with no adverse effects, recording eighty-two miles in training during the week following the marathon. I completed the Penkridge ten-mile road race in 54min 6sec one week after the Telford marathon – another PB. I had already reached the stage where I was able to run twice, sometimes three times per day for week after week without any repercussions. Now, I could also push myself to the limit of my speed until I had nothing left and still suffer no adverse effects. I was reaching a plateau; I had to find a way to maintain that high speed for longer. I started to dream about next year's Barry 40 and the international 100km races in which I still intended to compete.

*

With seven weeks to go to the Western States 100, I had already booked flights and accommodation for myself and Gill. Unusually, I had no intermediate events or races planned, so I was in a quandary as to what do. In the lead up to the Western States, I certainly didn't feel the need to rest, or even to attempt to achieve a higher level of fitness. I obviously couldn't undertake any reconnaissance, which meant I couldn't plan a schedule.

As in the past, a period without any immediate or even intermediate goals led to a feeling that I was losing my impetus. Averaging seventy to eighty miles per week through this period, I felt as though I was treading water.

As my trip to California drew near, my excitement increased – but so did my anxiety. Participating in a race of which I knew nothing was somewhat daunting, but it was easy to reassure myself of my ability. I was at the top of my game, of that I was sure. What I wasn't sure about was the practical details of the race. I knew it would be hot and dusty, but how hot and dusty? Would the altitude affect me, and how difficult would it be to follow the trail? There was another question I had to ask of myself: could I possibly win? Tom Johnson's winning time from last year of 15h 45min was very impressive; he was undoubtedly an extremely fit runner. I wondered how the Western States compared to some of the 100s that I had already done. It did involve more descent than ascent, so perhaps that would make it easier. I just didn't know enough about the race to make any assumptions. I would find out soon enough.

The days preceding the race followed – by UK standards – an unusual format. Pre-race 'clinics' were planned for the three days prior to the race, as shown in the following extract from the race information.

Wednesday 24th, 3 p.m. Fulfilling a Dream; Finishing the Western States Run. Informal discussion for first-time runners.

Thursday 25th, 10.30 a.m. Trek to Flag Raising at Emigrant Pass.

Run, walk or ride the tram to the summit for inspirational remarks, a great view and group camaraderie.

2.30 p.m. Crewing the Western States Run.

Advice for support teams.

4 p.m. Western States Trail Clinic.

Detailed course description and advice from trail veterans.

7 p.m. Medical Clinic.

Discussion of some of the possible physiological stresses of the run, by Medical Director and staff.

Friday 26th, 9 a.m. Race Registration and Medical Examination.

Including individual weigh-in. Runners' weight will be monitored during the run and advice given to rehydrate if necessary.

1 p.m. Supply bag deposit.

Runners can leave supplies here to be transported to support points along the trail.

1:30 p.m. Trail briefing.

Attendance by all runners mandatory.

Saturday 27th

3:30 a.m. Complimentary breakfast.

4:15 a.m. Pre-race check-in.

5 a.m. 27th June 1992. The start!

Not surprisingly, I could feel the effects of altitude before I had even started running. Despite my experience and steadfast belief in the importance of pace judgement, I failed to keep my enthusiasm in check. Paying scant regard to the likely effects of altitude, I set off at a brisk pace, driven as much by nervousness as by adrenalin. Emigrant Pass was free of snow, which was a relief, but at 8,700 feet the effects of altitude were even more noticeable. The news from a spectator that I was in tenth place fuelled my ego but increased my apprehension. Tenth place at this stage on any run I had done in the UK would have felt just right; I would have been biding my time, playing a waiting game, ready to move up the field when the time was right. This felt different. Not knowing the route, not even knowing any of the other competitors, was unusual. Simply not recognising any place names or flora and fauna was unsettling. I was an outsider, and I wasn't used to that. I felt at a disadvantage.

In the cold early morning, it was with mixed feelings that I left the highest point on the route to run through the beautiful but rugged Granite Chief Wilderness area. On average, this section lies 7,000 feet above sea level; my wish that it would soon warm up would shortly be granted.

Passing through the Red Star Ridge checkpoint at sixteen miles, I was in eighth place, unaware that I was four minutes in front of the eventual race winner.

Maintaining my eighth place through the Robinson Flat checkpoint at thirty miles, I followed the dusty trail as it dropped 2,000 feet in five miles, the first of three switchback descents. After climbing to Last Chance, a mining ghost town, the trail enters a section called the 'canyons'. Another 2,000 feet and five miles of descending switchbacks to Deadwood Canyon were followed by an extremely steep reascent of 1,500 feet. The second canyon descent of 2,600 feet preceded another very steep climb to the Michigan Bluff checkpoint at fifty-six miles. Running on hot dusty trails, with steep descents and reascents allowing no time for recovery, was punishing.

At only just over halfway, and now in twelfth place, I had to accept that I was struggling. Before the race, I had asked myself some questions. Now I knew the answers. The dust was ankle deep, the temperature approaching 40°C – and no, I couldn't win. Just completing the course would be a success.

The first road section since the start brought me to the Forest Hill checkpoint at sixty-two miles. The dust had penetrated my shoes and socks, so I had stopped en route to apply a liberal coating of Vaseline, my usual remedy for sore feet. Thus, I had succeeded in making matters worse by increasing the amount of grit and sand stuck to my feet, and so I availed myself of the checkpoint's first-aid facilities.

Leaving Forest Hill in fifteenth place, I was looking forward to the next section. The race information informed me that, after a brief excursion through relative civilisation, the sixteen miles along 'California Street' were downhill all the way to the river crossing at seventy-eight miles. Wonderful views opened up of the American River far below, and the three-hour downhill run was one of the most memorable and scenic parts of the course. But the constant pounding and braking on the steeper parts caused increasing stiffness in my quadriceps.

The river level at the crossing point had been lowered by temporarily restricting the flow at an upstream dam. Guide ropes had been fixed, and a team of burly helpers was on hand to assist weary runners in wading the strong current. Feeling jaded after the long descent, I was glad of their help and optimism as I splashed through the refreshing cold water. The support point was on the far side of the river, where I gratefully accessed my supply bag.

Much rejuvenated and wearing fresh shoes and socks, I set off into the gathering darkness, which brought an unexpected change in atmosphere. Although the final twenty-two miles covered much easier terrain both physically and navigationally, the trail had been marked especially well. Luminous green light sticks provided an infallible aid to route-finding, while loud rock music blaring through the dark forest gave an audible indication of a nearby checkpoint. The jovial and friendly checkpoint crews provided a welcome haven from the solitude of the forest. Runners are allowed to have pacers accompany them in the later stages; these 'buddies' cannot give the competitor any physical help or carry equipment, but the psychological boost of having a companion is considerable. As I was a visitor, I didn't have the luxury of a buddy, but at Highway 49, the site of the last checkpoint, one of the volunteer staff offered to accompany me. Arty, a young student from Sacramento, ran with me for the final seven miles. It was only a short distance and made little practical difference, but listening to Arty's running ambitions – and in particular his dream of one day being strong enough to complete the whole Western States 100, regardless of his final time – provided a delightful and humbling way to finish.

After a tough 21h 43min, I was the first Brit to finish. In retrospect, I was pleased with my twentieth position; of the 420 starters, only 230 finished and of those, only 75 completed the race in under twenty-four hours. It had been a tough, spectacular and memorable 100 miles.

CHAPTER 9:

Ultra Track and Road

The Western States 100 was the toughest and most memorable 100-mile trail race I had ever done. It was also my slowest. In contrast, I had completed the White Peak 100, four years previously, nearly four hours quicker – the fastest 100 I had ever done. Despite having had a tough time on the trails of the Sierra Nevada and feeling I hadn't performed at my best, I did recover very quickly. After only one week's rest, and still obsessed with my personal fitness, I resumed training at 100 miles per week. The slight disappointment on the Western States did make me wonder, not for the first time, whether I had reached my full potential and hit the limit of my achievements on the hills and trails.

I expected to have opportunities to compete on the road as an international athlete, so this was not the time for retrospective analysis and doubt, but a time to underline my ability; I had to refocus. To perform well as a member of the British Ultra squad, I would have to take my speed-endurance training a stage further. Even if it wasn't possible for me to become faster, it might be possible to maintain a high speed for longer, thereby completing a long or ultra-distance run more quickly. Mile markers and the even surfaces on road and track races should, in theory, make pace judgement easier, so I had to re-evaluate my view on 'steady' starts: I had to aim for as even a pace as possible. A 'textbook' run would be a perfect balance of effort and speed, enabling the entire distance to be completed at an even pace with no surplus energy left at the end. A 'negative split' – that is, completing the second half slightly faster than the first – would require a greater level of patience in the earlier stages and a very high level of fitness and effort in the later ones. Eliminating the tendency to slow down should result in a faster time – the 'Holy Grail' of pace judgement.

Although speed-endurance runs had always been an integral and productive element of my training regime, I was sure I would benefit by exploring this particular aspect further.

After a few reconnaissance trips in the car or by bike, I had soon worked out a suitable course of thirty-five miles – a significant increase on my previous road runs of between fifteen and twenty-five miles. My route had many junctions and therefore multiple route choices. On arrival at a junction, I could choose whether to take a long or short option. Knowing the mileage at strategic points would allow me to keep track of time and pace. My aim was to run the thirty-five miles at an even pace and, crucially, as close to my maximum speed as I dare. I wanted to test my resolve, to see how long I could keep on the red line of fast-paced effort. The price to be paid for misjudgement would be a slow and exhausted struggle home.

Following mostly minor lanes, my route was pleasantly rural, with the option of returning after about ten miles, along a canal towpath. If energy or determination were waning, this shorter option would serve as an easy, albeit disappointing, training run. The most critical route choice came near the end: here I had the option of shortening the course from thirty-five to thirty miles. Still a significant distance, but it would represent a failure, an inability to finish what I'd started.

The duration of the run would make carrying food and drink necessary. I could pre-place these essential items, but that would mean stopping or at least breaking stride to collect them. After some experimentation, I found carrying two small bottles of water and a supply of the humble Jelly Babies worked very well.

My first training run started well, with me covering the initial ten miles at an average speed of just over six minutes per mile. Approaching the canal bridge where I could turn off onto the towpath, I felt a temptation: I could take the first shortcut, slow down a bit and complete a good training run of at least twenty miles. Taking the 'shortest' shortcut on my first attempt would be disappointing. It would hardly test my resolve. Feeling slightly ashamed of myself for even thinking of it, I took a deep breath, ignored the bridge and carried on; there were more opportunities to shorten the route. Twenty-one miles without slowing down, and the pace was taking its toll. Doubts were creeping in. The fourteen remaining miles on the full course might be too much for me, especially at such a fast pace.

Balancing my remaining options against the effort I was expending, I was sure I would have to take the next shortcut. Recording 2h 35min at the twenty-five-mile point was good running, but it was hurting. Working very hard to maintain pace, I could see the penultimate junction, half a mile up the road. Maintaining this speed for another ten miles was going to be impossible. I would turn off and finish at a slower pace. I'd given it my best shot.

When the turn-off was almost upon me, at the last second, looking away from the junction – ignoring it, snubbing it – I continued past. Before cutting the run short, I would force myself to wait until the very last opportunity. Although I still hadn't slowed down, my energy reserves were severely depleted. Even if I succumbed to the temptation of taking the shortcut at the last junction, this was going to be a desperately hard thirty miles. At last, there it was: the left turn, the final choice, and the true test of my resolve. Speed-endurance training means exactly that, but it was easy to convince myself that a hard thirty miles would definitely qualify and would not be a failure. As I angled across the road towards the junction, my conscience suddenly screamed at me. 'What are you doing? The object of this run is to learn how to overcome precisely the thing you're giving in to!'

I felt a strange relief at committing to the final five miles. No more tempting shortcuts. I knew what I had to do. Breathe deeply, focus on an even pace, don't wish away the miles. Above all, accept the effort, absorb it; just let myself run. Turning in to my driveway, I was exhausted and euphoric. A victory for my resolve and tenacity; an improvement to my mental strength.

*

One month after the Western States 100, I lined up at the start of the Lincoln to Grantham 100km. The prospect of 100km on the roads of Lincolnshire felt like an anticlimax after the excitement and razzmatazz of my experience in California, but I was focussed; it was an important race for me. Although three years had elapsed since I had achieved the qualifying time required to join the Great Britain Ultra squad, I hadn't yet competed as a member. I was sure that the likelihood of receiving future invitations depended on my performance in this race. I wanted that invitation. I had to get this right.

Notwithstanding my vision of one day achieving a perfectly even-paced ultra, it was likely that my pace over the duration of this run would reduce. Meticulously planning a time schedule, I employed my tried and trusted technique of calculating a reducing speed. Breaking the 100km down into quarters, with each quarter planned at a slightly slower pace than the previous one, was the same format I had used on many trail races. On the road, it should be easier to judge.

Valuable seconds could be lost stopping for food and drink, so it was important to have an efficient system. I'd become well practised on the long off-road races, but now efficiency was even more important; a few seconds gained or lost could be very significant for the overall results. I had to be ruthless with time management.

The Barry 40 had been my first experience of collecting food and drink during a fast-paced ultra race. I could take the process a stage further. Small plastic bottles were much easier to pick up than paper cups; a few Jelly Babies in a small plastic bag were a convenient and easily swallowed source of energy; pinned inside the race number on my chest, Milk of Magnesia tablets to aid digestion and Crampex to ward off cramp were easily accessible.

Taking the lead early in the race, I felt comfortable. With Gill recording my times and passing drinks bottles, I ran steadily, passing 20km one minute inside my 7h 30min schedule. Three minutes in hand at 40km increased to six minutes at 70km and five at 90km. Slowing a bit over the final 10km, I finished in first place, recording a time of 7h 26min 55sec, three minutes inside my 7h 30min schedule and nearly twenty minutes faster than in the Solihull 100km. Max Kaeser finished second in 7h 40min 35sec, and John Foster third in 8h 0min 31sec.

I'd fulfilled my pre-race aim of running a solid 100km without any problems or heroics and certainly no attempts to cross the red line.

One week after the Lincoln to Grantham 100k, I received two letters from the chief executive of British Athletics. The first invited me to compete in the International Association of Ultrarunners (IAU) European 100km championships, to be held on 12th September at Winschoten in The Netherlands. The invitation from British Athletics included a detailed list of permitted and prohibited substances. The list was mostly self-explanatory, but to be sure I didn't take a common medication which did in fact contain a banned substance, I contacted my GP for verification. Further information regarding drug abuse informed me that as a competing international athlete, I could be asked to take a drug test at any time. If I intended to be away from home for more than five days, I must inform British Athletics of my temporary address. Failure to comply with this request could result in a four-year ban. This was on another level; I was now in the 'big league'.

The second letter was an invitation to join the other members of the British squad for a weekend in Wales. The venue for this social event was Tywyn, home to the annual fourteen-mile Race the Train event, which was due to be held on 15th August, one month before the 100km. Race the Train closely follows the course of the preserved Talyllyn railway, utilising nearby tracks and fields. The object is for runners to complete the course faster than the steam train on its journey from Tywyn to Nant Gwernol and back to Tywyn. The event is organised by the local Rotary Club, with proceeds going to charity.

The race felt like an interesting addition to the more important function of the weekend: meeting the other members of the squad and the organisers. The friendliness and obvious common purpose of the other runners soon made me feel like an integral part of the team. The gathering had been funded by British Athletics, as would be any future international trips. In contrast to the more experienced squad members, the 100km in Holland – only two weeks away now – would be my international debut. The organisers assured me I had been chosen because of my previous results, and I would not be pressured into trying to achieve a certain time or position. They knew I would want to attain the best result I could, and unnecessary pressure would not help. Nevertheless, it was difficult to ignore the fact that my expenses were being paid and, naturally, the team management wanted the squad to do well.

*

The two intervening weeks passed with some apprehension, but I continued to train regularly. I received contact details for the host family who would kindly provide accommodation for me and Gill. Travel details arrived, and so did my red, white and blue running strip. Midlands Electricity, my employer, generously offered to pay for two pairs of running shoes and grant me a day's leave, a gesture they would extend to future selections.

After being made welcome by our hosts, Marika and her family, Gill and I attended the team briefing. Since I had already met the other team members, the meeting felt relaxed. The team manager reiterated his desire that we should enjoy the experience and not feel under any pressure.

The course was to be run at night, over ten laps of 10km. Local groups, clubs and businesses could enter relay teams, while the full 100km was available to individual runners wishing to complete the full distance, and also to national teams. Refreshments, feeding stations, supporters and timings were all situated at the end of each lap.

My times from the Lincoln 100km were useful when calculating a schedule, especially the rate at which I might slow down. An estimated finishing time of 7h 10min was sixteen minutes faster than the Lincoln race, a difference of less than two minutes per lap. If I averaged forty-three minutes per lap, I would achieve that target; forty-two minutes, and my finishing time would be seven hours exactly.

There were over 200 runners at the start, many of them wearing their national team colours – Russia, Belgium, Latvia, Hungary and many more. The throng were high-spirited, chattering, shouting and wishing each other well in languages I didn't understand. The atmosphere was filled with excitement and adrenalin. Conflicting thoughts filled my head. I was sure I had the ability to run a 'fast' 100km, but the last thing I wanted was to make a mistake on my first international race. I couldn't help thinking that finishing in 'six hours something' would be a lot better than 'seven hours something'.

The sheer sense of occasion was a tangible force, but it was easy to resist; I didn't harbour any over-ambitious thoughts. The obviously high level of competition made it easier to keep my enthusiasm in check. In this new environment, I was a novice.

A first lap of forty minutes, followed by two laps of thirty-nine, was a faster start than I had planned and caused me a few doubts. Easing off for the next two laps, I recorded 3h 20min at the halfway point. It was too early to even think about the possibility of finishing in 6h 40min – and anyway, I didn't need to. I would be very satisfied with seven hours.

Two more slower laps of forty-two minutes brought me to 70km in 4h 40min and a predicted finishing time of 6h 46min. After a few jitters at halfway, I was now feeling confident of a sub-seven-hour finish. Crossing the finishing line in 6h 54min 59sec placed me eighth overall and made me the second Briton, behind Don Ritchie – a gratifying but not completely unexpected result. I still believed I had the potential to run faster. Don, myself and Steve Moore won the award for third-placed team, behind Russia and Belgium.

Still feeling on a high, I forced myself to take an easy week before resuming training. I'd had a mostly successful year so far, with my best results being on the track and road. This was a good sign; my slight changes in racing and training were paying dividends.

*

A mere four weeks elapsed before I started out on the fifty-four-mile London to Brighton foot race, a historic route which has been raced over since at least the early nineteenth century. In modern times the race was organised by the Road Runners Club from 1951 to 2005. The race was then discontinued due to increased traffic and difficulties in finding volunteer marshals.

While the leading runner had usually come from one of the UK's home nations, South Africa had also produced the winner on at least fifteen occasions.

George Taylor, my friend and long-time coach from Cannock and Stafford AC, offered to provide support, along with Gill. Clive Beauvais and Sue Ashley, whom we had met at the Race the Train weekend, had kindly offered to accommodate the three of us at their house in Banstead.

After a 7 a.m. start on Westminster Bridge, we headed towards the hilly terrain of the North and South Downs on our way to Brighton. By twenty miles, I was in a leading group of five. These five, with some swapping of places, would take the first five positions at the finish.

During one particularly testing climb on the North Downs, Steve Moore turned to me and, with a sly wink, said, 'Did you know that the eventual winner has never come from the first five at this point in the race?' – making sure, of course, that the others in the group could hear him. We glanced at each other and over our shoulders! Steve's attempt at gaining a psychological advantage caused some amusement within the group. Did he know that, or was it a ruse? We couldn't be sure. Anyway, it proved to be an unnecessary ploy, as Steve arrived in Brighton first in 6h 1min 9sec, representing his club, Hertford and Ware. Second place was taken by Russell Crawford of South Africa in 6h 3min 59sec. My third place in 6h 8min 15sec was achieved after a long battle with fourth finisher Freddie Kashiri, of the Zimbabwe Air Force, who finished in 6h 17min 41sec.

I have no memory whatsoever of competing in my next race of the year. Nevertheless, my training log provides concise and irrefutable details, testament to my obsession with recording every single race and training run. 1st November 1992: Harrow marathon: 2h 37min 55sec. Fourth place: first in over-forty age group: eighteenth marathon.

December 20th provided me with a memorable if somewhat glutinous experience, the Rowbotham's Round Rotherham 48. The event is organised by Rotherham Harriers and Athletics Club and was inaugurated in 1983, an impressive ninety-six years after the club was founded. Entrants are provided with a detailed and very accurate description of the route. The low-lying course follows the Rotherham boundary on mostly good paths and tracks. However, in 1992 the sections that are not on good tracks but on arable fields made up for their brevity with an exceptional degree of stickiness. The amount of mud, in both volume and weight, clinging to my running shoes was barely believable and appeared to be defying gravity. Reading the route description line by line while at the same time carrying a payload of mud that almost equalled my body weight made for slow going.

As I had taken the lead and was apparently not being caught, I assumed everyone else was having the same issues with mud. Nearing the end of the race, I received a tip-off from a spectator: my lead was being threatened. Carolyn Hunter-Rowe was in second place and rapidly narrowing the gap between us. I guessed Carolyn was also being spurred on by tip-offs. I just managed to retain the lead, finishing in 6h 31min 46sec, a mere two minutes in front of a fast-finishing Carolyn. It was pleasing to receive the winner's trophy from Brian Harney, club stalwart, president and previous holder of the Pennine Way record.

The after-effect of the Rotherham run was a painful strain in my left shin, but after five weeks of intermittent training and cycling, the injury subsided and I felt ready for another test. Completing a 10km road race at the end of January without a recurrence of the pain was a relief. Running 100 miles per week for the first three weeks of February felt good; interval training, long track sessions and speed-endurance runs all went well.

Two easy weeks and I was, once again, at the Jenner Park stadium for the 1993 Barry 40 track race. I was excited to be there. I'd had a great run the previous year, but I was sure I'd made some improvements to my high-speed stamina. My ambition was, of course, to complete the 161 laps in under four hours. If I could just maintain ninety seconds per lap right to the end, I would do it.

However, looking around the track at the other athletes warming up, I could see that time might not be fast enough to win, because I would be running against some very good competition. Malcolm Griffiths and Bernard Lloyd had both competed in last year's race, finishing third and fourth. I then spotted Steve Moore and Mick McGeoch; Mick had recorded the impressive time of 3h 58min 38sec in 1988. My strong suspicion that this would be a very competitive race was underlined when I noticed Carolyn Hunter-Rowe jogging effortlessly round the track. Breaking four hours would be difficult, but winning now seemed highly unlikely. Steve had soundly beaten me on the London to Brighton, Mick had run significantly under four hours, and Carolyn would definitely have beaten me at the Round Rotherham 48 if the course had been only slightly longer.

The pace was a little slow over the first five miles, but just a few seconds per lap outside a four-hour schedule. Steve and Mick went to the front and increased the pace, with Mick pushing on hard to thirty miles, opening up a lead of forty seconds over me, with Steve thirty-nine seconds behind me. By thirty-five miles I had taken the lead, but with less than one lap between us, it was anybody's race. The result would be determined by who could maintain the relentless pace right to the end. Recording 3h 29min 19sec at thirty-five miles gave me hope that I would finish in under four hours. Mick was only thirty-one seconds behind me, with Steve sixty-three seconds behind him.

Despite a superhuman effort of will, my lap times were getting slower. A few ninety-one-second laps; then ninety-two and ninety-three. The sought-after time of four hours was slipping away. Managing to hang on through the closing stages, I finished first in 4h 0min 20sec.

Steve overtook Mick to finish in 4h 3min 3sec, with Mick crossing the line a mere seventy seconds later and less than a lap behind. We didn't have to wait very long for Carolyn, who recorded a very impressive 4h 26min 43sec, finishing as the first woman and sixth overall. I had failed to achieve my hoped-for four hours, but the race had been enjoyable and competitive — a very successful start to the year.

Having now honed my long-distance speed, I felt I could improve my 100km time, so I entered the Woolwich 100km track race on 4th April. Running at a brisk pace from the start, my time splits were certainly faster than at Winschoten: two minutes up at 20km, four minutes at 40km and six minutes in hand at 60km. But I was working hard — too hard. At 70km, now less than three minutes up, I'd slowed slightly and my enthusiasm was fading. A little way after the 80km point, the marshals had placed a fifty-mile marker; I wasn't expecting that. Neither was I expecting Gill to pass me a note that said 'You have broken the British and Commonwealth record for fifty miles on the track in the 40–44 age group'. Feeling increasingly apathetic about the remaining 20km, but very pleased with my time of 5h 24min 17sec for the fifty miles, I walked off the track feeling satisfied.

A further three weeks without a break in training took me to the Stratford marathon, second place in 2h 35min 2sec being one of my best marathon times; another result where the quality of my log keeping made up for my poor memory. A PB of 72min 8sec for the Tewkesbury half-marathon was then followed by a string of 10km races.

Opening the car boot on 11th July 1993 at the start of the John Tarrant Memorial 50 Mile Road Race, I discovered that I'd forgotten to pack all my race food and drink. The carefully prepared bottles and packages of Jelly Babies were safely at home on the kitchen table. Gill and I looked at each other in disbelief. There was not enough time to reorganise; neither was there any point in being angry. I shrugged and said, 'Just get what you can from corner shops. I'll see how it goes.'

Starting the race, now with low expectations, I was surprised to find myself in third place after the first ten-mile lap of five. Receiving a varied selection of drinks and bars from Gill certainly provided interest and, in retrospect, I realise that the temporary lowering of tension caused me to relax. Focussing on my potentially disastrous logistical error distracted me from the tensions of the race; I felt I wouldn't do well because I'd messed up. Getting to the halfway point in 2h 41min 6sec felt good. Moving into first place felt even better. Leaving my food and drink at home obviously wasn't making any difference; I was running well. I experienced a relief, and a surge in confidence enveloped me. Crossing the finish line first in 5h 21min 41sec meant that I had run the second half faster than the first – I'd achieved the 'Holy Grail' of pace judgement. What a way to do it!

*

My high level of optimism and increasing confidence were given a further boost when I received two more invitations from British Athletics. I had been selected to run in the IAU World 100km Championships on 7th August in Tourhout, Belgium and the IAU European 100km Championships on 18th September in Winschoten.

Having two 100km races to plan for was exciting and motivating, rather than daunting. I was sure I had enough time to recover before the first race; in fact, I already had other short races planned for this period. I knew without doubt that the six intervening weeks would be plenty of time to recover before the second race in Winschoten. Using the first race to consolidate and maybe improve my time slightly, then making an attempt to achieve a significant improvement in Winschoten six weeks later, seemed an attainable plan.

Agonising over a schedule, I couldn't decide whether to be ambitious and plan for an even pace or to incorporate a reducing pace, as usual. Notwithstanding my ideal performance regarding pace judgement on the recent fifty-miler, I didn't quite have the confidence to believe I could run the entire 100km without slowing down, so I decided on the 'reducing pace' option. I composed three schedules – 6h 40min, 6h 50min and 7h – each one reducing in pace. This information I wrote on a slip of paper and pinned it to my race number.

The course of the first race in Tourhout was run over ten laps of 10km, made up of sixty per cent paved and forty per cent 'well-groomed dirt roads'. Disappointingly, I was never really in touch with the 6h 40min time splits, even in the early stages. I didn't feel as slick or as efficient on the dirt sections as I did on the hard surfaces. I wasn't running well. It could have been the unpaved sections; I couldn't be sure. I was searching for an excuse. I'd composed three schedules to deal with this very scenario, but five laps and 50km completed in 3h 16min was only just inside my seven-hour schedule. Time continued to slip away. At 65km I was three minutes down on the seven-hour finish, and two or three minutes were then lost at each remaining 5km split until the end. Finishing in thirty-ninth place in 7h 22min was the last thing I expected, a disappointing and inexplicably poor performance. The first stage of my two-part 100km plan had not worked.

Third place in the thirty-six-mile Two Bridges Road Race three weeks later marked a welcome return to good form. I was always in the first ten through the first half, then moved up from sixth at thirty miles to third at the finish, finally recording 3h 53min 22sec. This strong and confident performance helped to purge some of my negative thoughts.

Dwelling on my poor result at Torhout would not be conducive to a successful run at the European Championships in Winschoten, only three weeks hence. I'd had a good year up to this point: a PB half-marathon to a truly superlative fifty-miler, with many good results in races of intermediate distances. I had to avoid over-analysing my few failures and focus on my more numerous successes. Convinced I now had all the skills I needed to run my best 100km, I felt ready to tread the red line, blissfully unaware that events would take an unexpected turn.

A huge field of nearly 400 runners assembled in Winschoten at the start of the IAU European 100km Championship. The course was the same as 1992, and again it would be run at night over ten laps of 10km. On my first international race, I had felt overwhelmed by the sheer size of the field and was conscious that I was among competitors of the highest calibre. On this occasion, my third outing for Great Britain, I felt less daunted. My estimated time schedule was conservative; 6h 54min was the same time as last year, although I was sure I was capable of performing much better. The lap times I had estimated also reduced in pace; again, I was convinced that on the 'right day' I could run all ten laps with perhaps less than two minutes between fastest and slowest.

Completing the first lap in forty minutes would have felt pleasing if it hadn't been accompanied by the necessity for a pit stop. Two more stops during the next two laps and I thought my race would soon be over. I took a couple of Milk of Magnesia tablets, hoping they would help my digestion. My thoughts were in as much turmoil as my stomach. I couldn't come to terms with abandoning the race, yet if my stomach didn't settle, it would be inevitable. The thought of writing off the race due to bad luck when I was so fit was depressing. I decided to run another lap before deciding.

To my surprise, the three laps I'd completed were right on schedule, despite the stops. I was running evenly, and I'd regained my initial seventh place. It was a relief to complete laps four and five at a slightly faster pace without any more stops. Fifty kilometres in a little over 3h 19min, and I was still on schedule – but more importantly, I was feeling a lot better. Lap six was faster again and subsequently proved to be my fastest lap of the race. I was elated. My recovery had been miraculous. Having moved up into sixth place, I could sense I was ready to push my pace to the limit; I was ready for the red line. Laps seven and eight were also fast, seven being even faster than the race leader and eventual winner. Now in fifth place, I could see the runner in front. I was gaining ground quickly and soon passed Denis Gack, completing this lap nearly four minutes faster than he did. Shortly after the 90km mark, on a long straight, I caught sight of the third-placed runner. Gaining rapidly, breathing easily, hardly noticing my feet touching the ground, I was at last attaining my dream: running the race of my life, I was experiencing that effortless and serene application of energy. The only thing that prevented me from catching Mikhail Kokorov was running out of road. Ecstatic, I flew across the line to finish fourth in 6h 37min 45sec. If only the race had been a bit longer!

Post-race analysis provided gratifying facts about my performance and also food for thought. Konstantin Santalov (Russia) finished in first place, recording 6h 25min 52sec. Peter Hermans (Belgium) placed second in 6h 33min 57sec, followed by Mikhail Kokorov (Russia) in 6h 36min 38sec. Over the final 20km I had gained almost eight minutes on third place and seven minutes on second place; completing the second half 1min 25sec faster than the first, and only eight seconds slower than the race winner, was the icing on the cake. It's impossible not to imagine what might have happened if I hadn't needed to stop. In theory, I would have been slightly quicker – or would I? Having a problem to focus on, just like forgetting my drinks at the John Tarrant 50, could have worked in my favour. For a short while – and at the start, fortunately, on both occasions – winning or even running well were temporarily relegated, and just finishing would have been acceptable. Lower expectations again meant less stress and therefore less expenditure of nervous energy.

After this momentous result, I was unsure whether I was on the brink of further improvement or if, after a relatively short time, I had reached my full potential on the road. I gave my optimism the benefit of the doubt. The following two-week break was unprecedented. I was surprised I had to motivate myself to restart training. At the time, I attributed these somewhat negative events to the after-effects of one of the most successful and rewarding achievements of my career. However, the writing was on the wall. I just didn't want to read it.

*

The following five years were a rollercoaster of training and racing. I had some good periods of training and a few satisfactory races – but only satisfactory. I was no longer improving; my results were, in my view, mediocre. Refusing to believe that I was past my best, I imagined I would suddenly enter a more successful and rewarding phase. I continued to train and enter races.

Second place in the Barry 40 the following March was hard-earned, with Steve Moore finishing nearly ten minutes in front of me in 4h 1min 28sec.

Moving house in April 1994 was stressful and distracting. Receiving an invitation to represent Great Britain at the IAU 100km World Championship at Lake Saroma in Japan, in June – shortly after moving to our new home – failed to provide the fillip I obviously needed. Rather than being a stimulus, the invitation only added to the stress. With some regret – and, dare I say it, a guilty feeling of relief – I decided to forgo the opportunity.

In September I failed to complete the IAU European 100km Championship in Winschoten – another disappointing and surprising outcome. I had felt very relaxed on my third trip to this venue. Gill and I knew our way around quite well and we were again staying with Marika. Maybe I was too relaxed; I didn't have that slight nervousness which comes from the anticipation of something new or unknown. I didn't need to check my training log to know that, with one or two exceptions, this hadn't been a very good year. Abandoning the race after four hours with 60km completed equated to a pace comparable to that of my previous 100km races, but just reaching that distance had been considerably more difficult.

Although my overall training mileage was practically the same as last year and I had continued to undertake regular track sessions, I had neglected some vital components. Long canal and speed-endurance runs had both served me well in the past; both required an exceptional and unfaltering level of commitment, which recently I had found difficult to summon.

Through most of January 1995 I staggered – almost literally – between injuries: first a strained right thigh and then, even before I had recovered, a sprained left ankle. The sprain soon recovered, but the thigh strain persisted until the end of March. At last, after three months of intermittent training, it felt wonderful to start pain-free running again. A few days later, I was admitted to hospital with a detached retina.

One week after the operation, mindful of the doctor's advice not to jar my head, I completed a short cross-country run, and three weeks later I was up to twenty miles. With two weeks to go to the Potteries Marathon, I recorded ninety miles in my log, which pleasingly included a PB and no recurrence of the injuries.

The Potteries Marathon had a tough reputation, so I knew it wouldn't be easy. In perfect conditions, with no wind and constant rain, I started steadily. Running at an even pace, I worked my way through the field to finish in twentieth place with a time of 2h 47min 29sec. The fact that it was my slowest marathon for ten years didn't matter; I'd really enjoyed it.

On July 16th I lined up at the start of the John Tarrant Memorial 50 Mile Road Race for the second time. Thinking about my 5h 21min 41sec run of two years ago, I wondered whether I could improve on such an excellent time. My sister Vicky was on Jelly Baby duty, and this time I hadn't forgotten my water bottles. Five hours forty-five minutes later, I crossed the finish line in second place, twelve minutes behind fellow Great Britain squad member Greg Dell. My slight disappointment was tempered with a sense of acceptance and inevitability. Two years had elapsed since that memorable 100km, the pinnacle of my road and track endeavours. I had been unable to attain that level of success again. I could no longer summon the motivation to undertake the rigorous and specific training required to achieve at the highest level. But I had done it; I'd been there. I had stepped into that special zone for the last time.

The 33m Grantham Canal Run in August, the IAU 100km World Challenge in September and the Round Rotherham 48 in December were all satisfactory, but I was on borrowed time. Failure to complete the IAU World Challenge in Moscow in May 1996 was, of course, a disappointment. The twenty riverside laps of 5km were flat and paved, and it was not an unpleasant course; not so the tepid, smelly water dispensed at the feeding station, which I'm sure contributed to my demise.

As expected, the 1996 LDWA Yorkshire Dales 100 gave me a tough time. Reconnaissance of some navigationally complex sections helped me along, but I struggled over the last few miles. Passing by Malham Tarn at first light, with blurred vision, I forced myself repeatedly to run eight steps before walking two. The only reason for this punishing regime was the same as it always had been: to complete the run as quickly as possible. Eventually, after 20h 35min, I reached the finish at Settle – in first place.

When I failed to complete the Fellsman Hike in May of the following year, I knew I had given the event everything I could. Nine completions – including three outright first places and one joint win – and now, seventeen years after my first completion, a failure to finish. But the journey had been unforgettable.

Still refusing to quite believe that it was time to hang up my shoes, I entered the 1998 Snowdonia Marathon. Another tough one, with a big climb near the end and a long stony descent through the forest to the finish in 2h 58min 59sec. Fifteen years ago, at Wolverhampton, I had run my first sub-three-hour marathon. This was my slowest since then. It was time to move on – time to find another challenge.

CHAPTER 10:

Going with The Flow

It was mid-December 2002 and I was reading meters in Wolverhampton, with two weeks remaining of my working life, when a customer showed me into his garage. My jaw dropped; it was a veritable Aladdin's Cave. The speedboat looked brand new, as did the two bikes hanging on the wall. My eyes then settled on one of the most beautiful things I had ever seen: a very slender eighteen-foot-long sea kayak, pristine white, the livery on the side identifying it as a 'Romany Explorer, made in Wales'. I guessed he'd never used any of these things. He seemed an impulsive sort of chap who just couldn't resist a shiny new toy.

'Want to buy it?' he said. 'It's never been on the water.'

'Yeah, sure,' I said – then, as an afterthought, 'How much is it?'

As I finished my day's work, I had some misgivings. I'd never been in a kayak before and couldn't even swim. I hadn't thought to ask whether paddles or buoyancy aids were included, and he hadn't mentioned them. I guessed he probably viewed those essential items as secondary to the pleasure of owning such a beautiful kayak.

It was possible that my purchase would receive a less than enthusiastic response from Gill but, as I expected, we were on the same wavelength. 'You've never been in a kayak before, and you can't even swim. Does it come with paddles or buoyancy aids? Anyway, how are you going to transport it'? This last point was a good one which I had to resolve quickly; 'Mr Wolverhampton' was going on holiday in a few days' time.

Spotting and retrieving some damaged roof bars and pieces of steel tube from a skip at work was a timely stroke of luck. Modifying my trolley jack into a makeshift pipe-bending machine, then spending a couple of hours hacksawing, grinding and welding, produced a pair of substantial roof bars, suitable for my high-top camper van.

Driving home from Wolverhampton with the kayak on the roof, I felt as though I now owned something very specialised – something that, if I could summon the nerve, would allow me to visit environments which hitherto I had been unable to reach. I hoped I could muster the confidence to exploit its full potential.

Meanwhile, spring 2003 brought a long-anticipated return to rock climbing. My old friend and climbing partner Jon Haswell agreed to accompany me on my first trip. It was a warm spring day in the Manifold Valley, with the smell of wild garlic in the air. Beeston Tor towered above, smooth and white; jackdaws clattered around its caves and overhangs. I belayed Jon as he confidently led the first pitch. The climb was graded E1 5b, and Jon made light work of it. A bit apprehensive about my ability after a break of too many years, I tied on to the rope and touched the rock. It was smooth but peppered with small pocket holds, sometimes only big enough for two fingers. My lingering doubts receded with every upward move. The pocket edges felt sharp; the toes of my climbing shoes barely penetrated the small holes, but it was enough. I was glad of the rope above, glad I was here. I'd missed climbing much more than I'd realised.

*

A gleaming yellow kayak on a white beach, turquoise water pushing a thin line of surf along the sand, a small green tent pitched on the edge of the dunes. I was reading an article about sea kayaking. As I put the magazine aside, my thoughts dwelled on that glossy photograph. What an adventure that must be – a heady mixture of danger, remoteness and beauty. Well, I did have a boat and a small green tent!

Jon was still working, so we climbed at weekends on a regular basis; Dovedale, Chee Dale and Beeston Tor were our favourite haunts. Jon did most of the leading, but I was surprised at how quickly I gained confidence.

I kept thinking about the green tent in the photograph. Wandering into the garage, I would gaze at the Romany and imagine packing camping gear, food, water and safety equipment. I didn't know where I was going to go, but it would be somewhere, and soon; that was for sure. Given that the sea was very large, deep and wet, it would be sensible to have a partner to go with. Not knowing any paddlers was just another gap in my preparedness, which I hoped I would resolve – but if I couldn't, I knew what I would do. Temptation and impatience would get the better of me. I would go solo.

While looking at the Romany one day, I had an idea which prompted me to take a quick look at the map of Anglesey. A few days later, I was driving towards Aberffraw with the Romany on the roof. Checking the tide tables while nervously looking out over the estuary, I formulated a plan. I didn't know if there would be strong currents or tide races; I did know I had to avoid the combined effects of the river and ebbing tide dragging me out to sea.

The Romany looked massive in my garage; paddling out towards the open sea, it felt tiny, like a matchstick. As the tide turned and started to flood the estuary, I turned around, expecting it to push me back towards Aberffraw – but it didn't. I had a slight panic, but then realised that the incoming tide wasn't yet strong enough to overcome the strength of the river. Thankfully, as the estuary filled, the river flow became weaker and the shore closer.

Back at the van, relieved that my plan had worked, I suddenly had a thought: I had missed something. The wind had been very light when I set out, but it was now very strong and blowing offshore. If I'd misjudged the tides, I might not be sitting in my van drinking tea, but halfway to Ireland instead. While my first trip was short and undertaken in good conditions of tide and weather, it was unlike anything I'd done before. I was captivated.

Camping trips from the kayak on the inland Scottish lochs of Quoich, Lyon and Mullardoch added an atmospheric and surprisingly complementary element to my ongoing project of bagging all the Munros. Sitting outside my tent, fishing or just watching the changing colours on the loch after a day on the hills, was a sublime experience; looking out in the still, early morning at the rising trout I had failed to catch the previous evening, less so!

In an effort to improve my skills and provide some insurance against drowning, I booked onto a kayaking course. The instructors at Plas Menai, the National Outdoor Centre for Wales, demonstrated skill and competence of the highest order, and I learnt a lot. A door to a new passion had opened.

The Aran Islands, situated off the west coast of Ireland, were the intended venue for my next trip with Plas Menai. Unfortunately, our week-long expedition was dogged by strong winds and rough seas. So, instead of a multi-day camping and kayaking trip to this group of three small islands, we were forced to base ourselves on the mainland. Nevertheless, the challenging conditions provided some impressive seascapes and many opportunities to improve our skills, notwithstanding the occasional capsize. I was keen to rebook for the following year (and hoping for better weather) when Bob Hamilton took me aside and said, 'Mike, shall we plan our own expedition, next year?'

I still had some doubts about my competence. It could be a very serious issue, with just two of us on a multi-day trip. I wanted to say that I'd feel confident with more experience, maybe after another instructional course, but instead replied, 'Where do you fancy going'?

'How about paddling over to Mull?' said Bob. 'We'll pack the boats with gear for a week and see what happens.'

Paddle over to Mull . . . see what happens . . . He's mad, I thought. 'Yes, Bob,' I said. 'Sounds good to me. Let's do it.'

*

The following May, Bob and I paddled out of Loch Sunart on the west coast of Scotland, our loaded boats sitting low in the water, heavy but stable. Starting out on my first multi-day sea kayaking expedition, I felt an apprehensive eagerness; I wanted to do this, but I'd no idea what was in store. Since the failed Aran Islands expedition, a few solo trips on inland lochs had increased my confidence, but I wasn't prepared for the remote ruggedness of the coastline.

When we stopped to camp on the north shore of Loch Sunart near Auliston Point, unpacking the boats and putting up tents felt like the start of a real adventure.

As we broke camp the following morning, we gazed across the Sound of Mull to our proposed landfall at Ardmore Point. It was a long way, the five-mile open crossing being about four and a half miles longer any I'd ever done before.

Part way across, we noticed a huge vessel ploughing its way northwards. It presented no immediate danger, but if we continued with our current course and speed, we would come dangerously close. Arguably, we'd been there first, but the issue of who had right of way seemed an academic consideration under the circumstances. We let him go.

The following day, we paddled around the north-east coast of Mull via Caliach Point to land at the beautiful Calgary Bay. We had navigated twelve miles of rough coastline, mostly along inaccessible cliffs. We had endured some rough waters, strong wind, rain and swell – conditions which I had found very testing. The white sandy beaches and turquoise water of the bay were a relief from the constant noise of the surf and the continuous balancing act of bracing the boat and paddles against waves.

Leaving Calgary Bay the following morning, my heart sank as we approached Treshnish Point. A big swell was sweeping past the point; breaking waves, foam and white water were crashing against the cliffs. Massive rocks were being swamped and then exposed as the sea ebbed and flowed. I'd never seen conditions like this before, and they were well beyond my capabilities. When wind and tide are squeezed around headlands, the speed of both increases. We were attempting to round Treshnish Point at about halfway through the flood, when the tide was at its fastest. Future experience would teach me that the easiest time to pass such critical sections is at slack water. After consulting the map, we opted to bypass Treshnish Point completely by loading the boats onto our collapsible trollies and portaging them round by the road.

Eventually, after hauling the boats for six miles along a road that rose to 600 feet above sea level, we relaunched, exhausted, in a small bay near Kilninian. Backing off from Treshnish Point and waiting for the tide to slow down would have produced calmer conditions and been a less strenuous option. We had learnt a valuable lesson. This wasn't the last time I would find that the speed and direction of the tide can make a significant difference to conditions; sometimes, all that's needed is patience and an understanding that timing is everything.

As often happens when sea kayaking, the conditions and atmosphere changed in an instant. A glorious two-mile crossing on a gentle swell in improving weather took us to Ulva. The OS map showed a narrow sandy channel between Ulva and Gometra which, fortunately, the now high water allowed us to paddle through and avoid another portage. We emerged at an idyllic camping spot on the south-west coast of Ulva. The sea was bright blue and sparkling. Treshnish Point seemed like it had happened days ago, already fading into memory.

Our third morning dawned clear and blue. Staffa sat on the horizon four miles out to the south-west, straight offshore; there was no coastline to hug. The pressure was rising. It was a good day for it.

On the western margin of the OS map, in blue capital letters, are the words ATLANTIC OCEAN. I was nervous; Bob was confident. Bob was always confident. In less than an hour we were paddling alongside Staffa, feeling insignificant, dwarfed by the huge basalt columns flanking Fingal's Cave. The Atlantic swell was crashing into the far reaches of the cave, booming and echoing. Atmospheric and awe-inspiring.

On our return trip to the Mull mainland, we stopped to camp on Inch Kenneth before landing at Gruline, from where a short easy portage took us to Salen. All that remained was a return crossing of the Sound of Mull – at four miles, shorter than our outward route, but with mist shrouding the Sound and obscuring the mainland, it felt no less daunting. Our intended landfall was Fiunary, to the north-east. I programmed the grid reference carefully into my GPS, and Bob set the bearing in his deck-mounted compass.

All was going well, considering we couldn't see where we were going, until we heard the hum of a motorboat. Fortunately, the mist cleared as the boat came into view. The grey military-type launch was some way off but heading straight for us. He must have seen us (unless he was asleep) but didn't show any sign of altering course. We turned at right angles to get out of his way as soon as possible. He promptly changed direction and continued to aim straight at us. We changed course again and paddled as fast as we could. Just before he came close enough to be dangerous, he suddenly veered off and disappeared. We didn't know what he was up to, but agreed that he must have a strange sense of humour. Back on the mainland, pouring rain greeted us as we loaded the boats onto the trollies for the walk to the campsite.

Bob and I had shared a fantastic adventure. I had experienced fear and exhilaration, and expended no small amount of physical effort. Above all, I had experienced a dramatic, exquisite and challenging environment.

*

The end of our expedition marked the start of a paddling partnership that would last for more than ten years. Bob and I enjoyed many adventures on the west coast of Scotland and Skye, visiting remote sea lochs and islands, many of which were uninhabited. Twice we were 'stormed in', stranded and forced to camp an extra night or two, unable or unwilling to continue due to impossibly difficult sea conditions.

Our two trips to the Summer Isles were particularly memorable. On one of those, as we paddled from Tanera Mòr to Ardmair on the mainland, we were overtaken by a westerly storm. In a matter of minutes, the blue sky turned black and menacing, the wind transformed the calm sea into lines of steel grey, deep marching troughs. Through the lashing rain and increasing wind, we were pushed up and over the crests of the swell before surfing down into the next trough. Eventually, with conditions deteriorating, we were forced to make a detour to the nearest shore for a rest. A fortuitous reduction in wind strength then gave us chance to reach our campsite at Ardmair.

Bob and I also enjoyed a two-week visit to the Northern Isles, spending the first week on Orkney and the second on Shetland. Paddling along below the stupendous cliffs of St John's Head on the Isle of Hoy, as the Old Man of Hoy came into view, Bob said, 'Mike, do you fancy climbing that?'

In fact, I had made an attempt many years ago, but it didn't get very far. At the age of fifteen, I had been one of millions who had watched a BBC outside broadcast, enthralled, as Chris Bonington, Rusty Baillie and Tom Patey made the first ascent of the 450-foot sea stack. Four years later, unable to contain my desire to emulate those climbing heroes any longer, I started my attempt. Travelling by public transport, I arrived in Fort William, my rucksack packed with every item of climbing gear I owned, plus some I didn't. My friend George Skelton greeted me with the disappointing news that his van was refusing to play its part in the next part of our plan. As consolation, George had arranged a lift for us to the Cairngorms, but we would have to wait a few days. Three nights camping in Glen Nevis, eating fish and chips, drinking too much beer and thinking of what might have been, only increased our frustration. It wasn't until several years later I realised that George's van probably did us a favour by saving us from an ill-equipped fiasco.

The highlight of the second part of our Northern Isles trip was a paddle to Muckle Flugga lighthouse. Lying just north of Unst, itself the most northern of the Shetland Islands, it is almost the most northerly land in the British Isles (a unique designation that is actually held by a rocky outcrop situated a little further north known as Out Stack).

Bob and I were fortunate to share our trip to these remote and windswept outposts with a group of local and expert paddlers. Setting out from Lunda Wick on the west coast of Unst, our group of twelve was soon engrossed in paddling along the most committing and dramatic coastline I had ever seen.

White surf and breaking waves surged up the cliffs. Huge sea stacks were covered in guano and countless sea birds, and the sky was full of wheeling, diving gannets. My temptation to look up at the cliffs and trace imaginary lines of ascent was easily resisted; concentrating on remaining the right way up was a higher priority. After ten miles of paddling through this breathtaking environment, we reached Muckle Flugga. En route, we had enjoyed a break at the only place where it was possible to land with any degree of safety, a small bay sheltered from the southwesterly swell. Looking out from the lighthouse, we could see Out Stack; tide races resembling powerful rivers in the sea were racing along each side. To include Out Stack in our itinerary was optional, but it was preferable – even essential – to stay together. Those who wanted to reach it, including myself, didn't hesitate in voicing their assent. Those who were less keen said nothing, took a deep breath, and girded their loins. On reaching Out Stack, the area of relatively slack water between the two tide races and immediately downstream from the stack afforded us a short respite, but the first and smallest 'river' had already claimed a capsize. I watched in admiration as one of the local experts sped after the stricken paddler. I was happy to hang back and abide by the pre-trip advice: 'Do your best to stay upright – the fewer swimmers we have, the better.'

The very strong tide tested the differences in skill and strength between individuals and caused our group to become fragmented. With two others, I decided – having safely crossed the second tide race – to mark time and wait for another pair we could see behind us. Focussing on transit points on the headland, I was concerned to find we were having to paddle just to remain stationary. Finding I was physically struggling to paddle against the tide conjured thoughts of being swept away, helpless against the power of the sea. Our trio increased the effort and very slowly started to make some headway. As the speed of the tide increased, we were forced to expend ever more energy.

At times it felt as though I was fighting a losing battle. If I became incapable of making progress, the outcome would be hazardous indeed. Eventually, we managed to enter the outer reaches of Burra Firth, clear of the tide. Landing in a small bay, we joined other members of the group who had been just in front of us, and the remaining members joined us in twos and threes. Exhausted and relieved, we slowly paddled the final two miles to our finishing point, our quest for adventure fully sated – for the time being.

In complete contrast to our adventurous trip around the north coast of Unst, Bob and I enjoyed a quiet and relaxing day paddling in Ronas Voe, said to be Shetland's only true fjord. After an easy launch from an inauspicious shallow sandy beach, Ronas Voe soon revealed its true character: red sandy beaches, soaring pinnacles, arches and mysterious sea-level passages. For a full exploration, head torches are required. Ronas Voe was one of the most memorable places I'd ever been. A return trip with Gill in our double kayak allowed me to show her what I had been enthusing about over the intervening three years. Bob, having been equally impressed, came with his son, Michael.

Solo multi day sea kayaking was an obvious progression, which inevitably required a higher level of confidence and self-sufficiency. A three-day trip round the Isle of Arran and a two-day paddle round the Isle of Bute were mini-expeditions which allowed me to exercise my now increased level of competence. Nevertheless, solo trips involve a higher level of risk. My willingness to accept this was repaid with a higher level of fulfilment.

An incident that occurred on the trip to Bute has stayed in my mind with such detail that it seems to have happened only yesterday. In order to access my intended campsite, I had no choice but to negotiate a difficult landing through surf and seaweed-covered rocks. Relaxing outside my tent, I looked across the Sound of Bute towards the Isle of Arran and noticed a disturbance on the flat calm sea. It was a bird – a cormorant, I think – about 200 yards from the shore. It was flapping frantically, probably feeding on something, but there was a sinister and increasing weakness to its movements. It wasn't feeding; it was dying. Tangled in a discarded fishing net, its desperate attempts to break free were becoming increasingly futile. I stood up, wondering whether I had time to paddle out and help it. I stared at the cormorant, hoping it would suddenly be free – but then it stopped flapping. Its final ferocious struggle to attain freedom surprised me, such that I thought it had succeeded. But no. I looked at my boat and then at the bird. It was motionless.

I slept fitfully, thinking about the cormorant. Eventually, mesmerised by the sound of the surf, I dreamt of climbing the Old Man of Hoy.

Approaching Redshaw on the Fellsman Hike. Photo Gill Hartley.

Muker on the Pennine Way, the hottest day of 1989. Photo Gill Hartley.

Stoodley Pike on the Pennine Way. Frank Yakes (L) and Tom Robertshaw. Photo Dennis Berersford

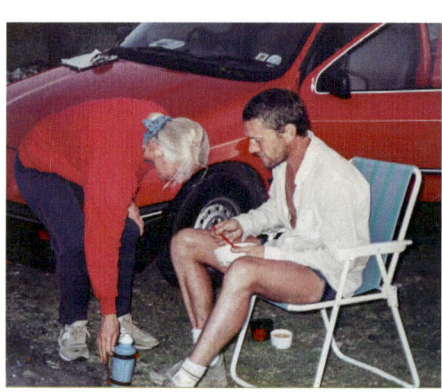

With Gill at the White House support point on the Pennine Way. Photo Frank Yates.

Kinder Downfall on the Pennine Way, only 4 miles to go. Photo Martin Stone.

 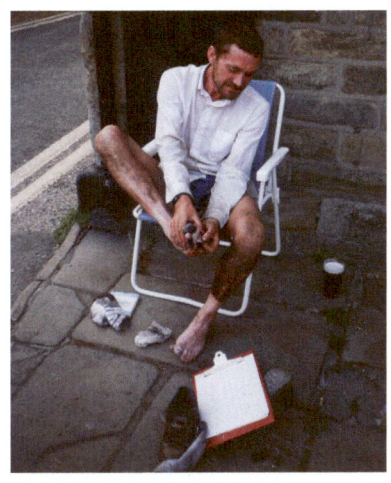

Crossing Kinder Scout on the Pennine Way with Clive Russell. Photo Martin Stone.

At last I could take my shoes off, The Nags head Edale, Pennine Way. Photo Gill Hartley.

'Cheers', The Nags Head Edale. L to R. Martin Stone. Frank Yates, Andy Brear, Anne Stentiford (now Johnson), John Amies, Geoff Petengell, John Axson. Photo Gill Hartley.

The summit of Helvellyn with Howard Sawyer, during the Bob Graham leg of the Three Rounds. Photo Andy Brear.

Climbing Yewbarrow during the Bob Graham leg of the Three Rounds. Photo Martin Stone.

Running the Grey Corries during the Ramsey leg of the Three Rounds with Ian Leighton. Photo Pete Simpson.

With Anne on Pen-Llithrig-y-Wrach, the last hill of the three Rounds. Photo Pete Simpson.

1992 IAU European 100km Championships Winschoten Netherlands. Photo Mike Hartley collection.

Robin Hoods Bay, the finish of the Coast to Coast. Clive Russell and Dennis Berersford (L) and Mike Cudahy (R).
Photo Gill Hartley.

Foot repairs from Clive at the Lion Inn on the Coast to Coast.
Photo Gill Hartley.

With Mike Cudahy(L) and Dennis Berersford (R) on the Coast to Coast.
Photo Clive Russell.

Kayaking trip with Bob Hamilton, west coast of Skye.
Photo Mike Hartley collection.

Idyllic campsite on Loch Nevis.
Bob Hamilton looking towards Knoydart.
Photo Mike Hartley collection.

Kayaking in the Sound of Sleat.
Photo Bob Hamilton.

Approaching the Old Man of Hoy from Rora Head, Orkney.
Photo Bob Hamilton.

The Drongs, Hillswick Ness, Shetland.
Photo Bob Hamilton.

Negotiating rough seas on route to Muckle Flugga, Shetland.
Photo Bob Hamilton.

Atmospheric kayaking in Ronas Voe with Gill. Photo Bob Hamilton.

With Gill in Ronas Voe, Shetland. Photo Bob Hamilton.

Boat packing. The river Meoble, NW Scotland. Photo Mike Hartley collection.

Solo aid climbing on Beeston Tor, Manifold valley.
Photo Mike Hartley collection.

Big wall, big haul bag. Yosemite.
Photo Alex Diego.

'Cleaning' an aid pitch, Yosemite.
Photo Alex Diego.

Hanging out in Yosemite.
Photo Mike Hartley collection

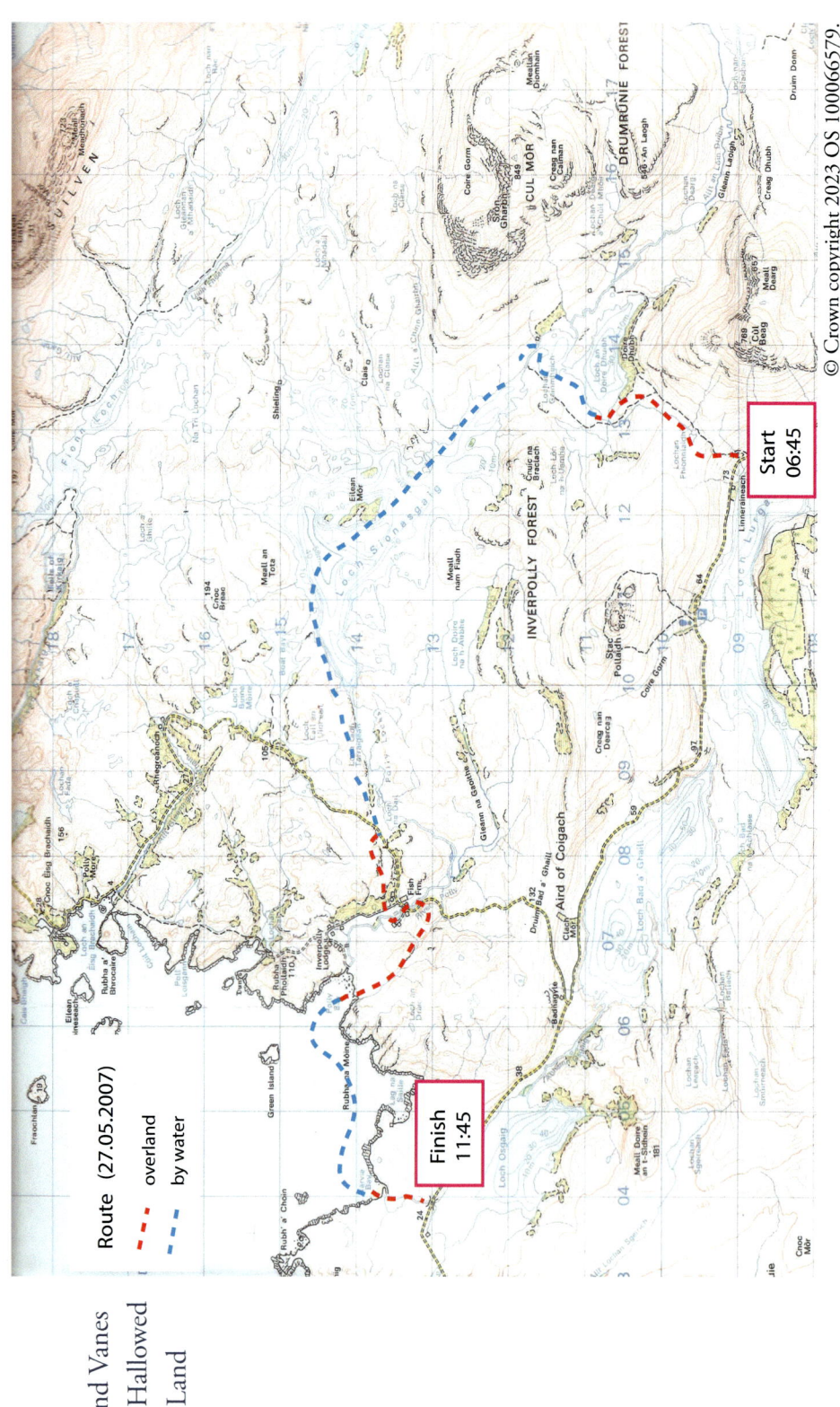

The Little Voice

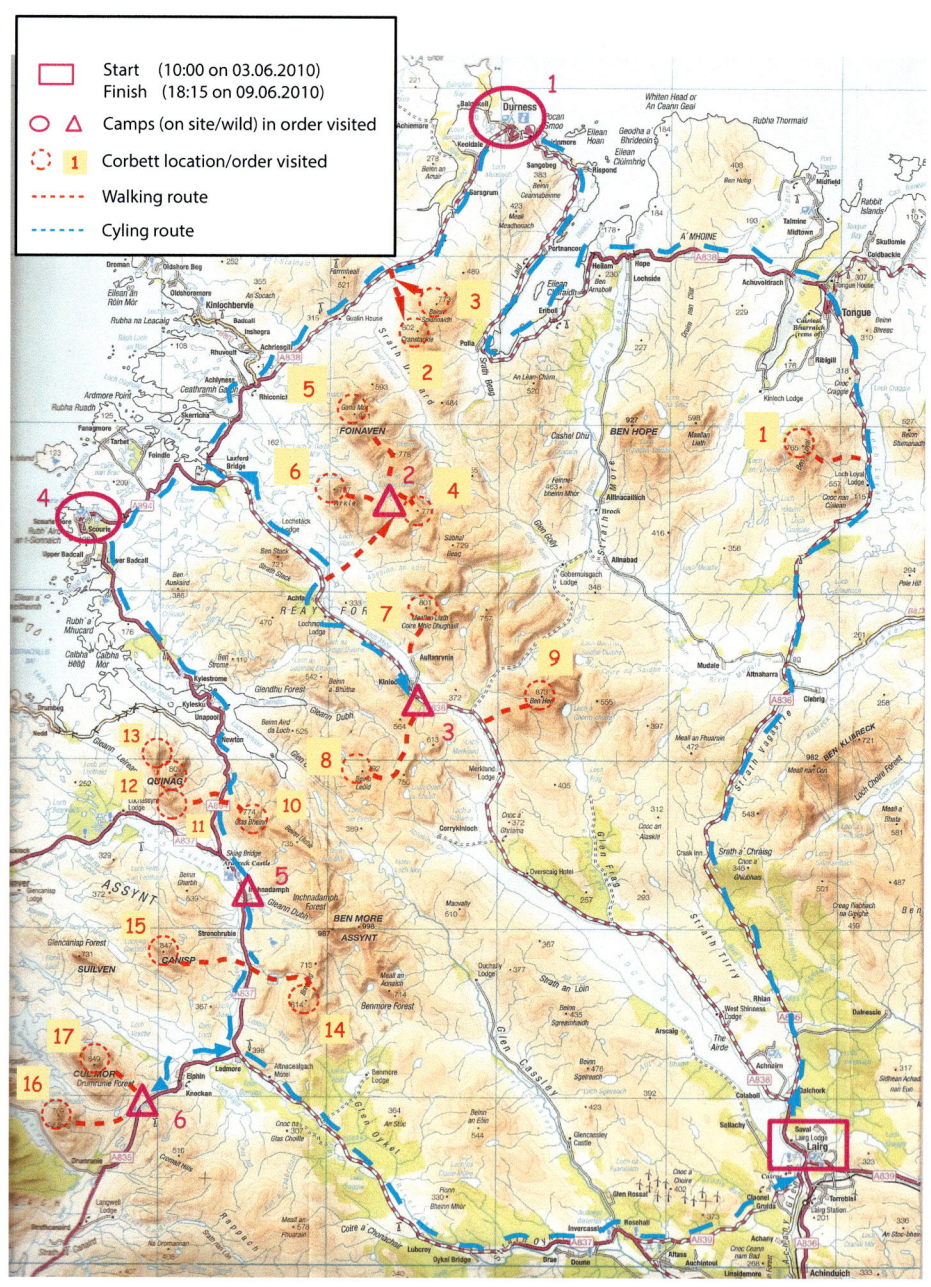

CHAPTER 11:

Wind Vanes and Hallowed Land

My discovery of Pakboat was a revelation: a boat light enough to carry! I could become amphibious. Combining walking and paddling, I could explore remote tracts of land and water.

On the day of my purchase, ignoring the advice of the salesman that lightweight boats were unsuitable for shallow stony rivers, I chose the River Derwent in Borrowdale for my maiden voyage. Derwentwater would have been infinitely more suitable – it's just that it looked a bit, well, boring. I wanted to shoot some rapids. On the first shallow section, I could feel the thin flexible vinyl hull sliding over smooth rocks; reading the contours of the riverbed with my posterior was an unusual and slightly unnerving experience. Inevitably, it wasn't long before I felt the not-so-gentle caress of a sharp rock. Stopping to check for damage to the underside of both myself and the boat seemed tedious and time-consuming so, assuming they would both probably be all right, I continued my journey.

Approaching Derwentwater, I noticed a rather ominous wet sensation around my nether regions. Poking my hand down inside the hull to investigate, I was relieved to find that it wasn't red. I did, however, discover a small but very powerful fountain of water. The boat had sprung a leak and was filling up, fast. Fortunately, I had a bailing bucket – but to plug the hole, bail and paddle with only two hands was impossible. On entering the lake, I was hoping to land close to a nearby car park, but an extensive reed bed forced me further out into the lake than was comfortable. I tried to plug the hole with one hand while alternately paddling and bailing with the other. Eventually, in frustration and more than a little wet, I employed the only technique that had any chance of working: plugging the hole with one hand while bailing out most of the water, then frantically paddling with both hands to the shore.

The following day, I called at the shop where I'd bought the boat, thinking the salesman might be interested in my experience and confirmation that the manufacturer's repair kit had worked very well. He was pleased I'd managed to fix the damage, but I could tell that behind his veneer of politeness he was incredulous, holding back a smirk and a wish to say 'I told you so'.

On another occasion, I caught the train from Glenfinnan to Morar, with the intention of paddling and walking back. Almost capsizing and getting soaked while launching into a very windy Loch Morar was an inauspicious start. After six bumpy miles, I was relieved to pull the boat out of the loch at the small bay of Camas Luinge. The first walking section of four miles was on a good track alongside the River Meoble, so instead of dismantling the boat, I strapped it horizontally across the packframe, thus saving a lot of time and effort. Launching into a thankfully more sheltered Loch Beoraid was simplicity itself, and the ensuing three-mile paddle took me to my egress point at Kinlochbeoraid. This time it was easier to dismantle the boat for the steep walk up through some woodland. It also made the final walk along the road safer – no chance of being clipped by a passing car and being forced to perform an involuntary pirouette.

Bob, intrigued by my new sport, which I always referred to as 'boat-packing', bought a boat of his own. Collapsible boats were then included in our kit whenever we undertook sea kayaking trips to the west coast of Scotland. Our first joint venture was 'The Great Circumnavigation of Slioch', as I called it. In retrospect, I think Bob probably agreed to accompany me on my wildly over-ambitious trip more through curiosity than any real expectation of success. The Munro of Slioch is almost surrounded by lochs and, as such, makes an ideal boat-packing objective. We started from Incheril by Kinlochewe, with our boats dismantled and loaded on packframes. Easy tracks took us about five miles to Lochan Fada and our first paddle. Lochan Fada occupies a dramatic setting among some of the wildest and most impressive mountain scenery in Scotland. Paddling along in the middle of the loch, we fancied we could sense Munro Giants watching us as they towered above. At the head of Lochan Fada, we left the boats still assembled and strapped them horizontally across the packframes; then came a slow uphill walk of three miles, first westward underneath the cliffs of Beinn Lair, then south to Bealach Mheinnidh.

My original plan had been to carry on west, then descend north to the causeway between Fionn and Dubh lochs, followed by paddling the entire length of the former, a distance of six miles. Beyond that, a walk of around five miles would have taken us to finish at my van in Poolewe. To complete this final remote and increasingly arduous eleven-mile section would certainly have entailed an overnight bivvy – without food, sleeping bags or torches – so we had decided it was prudent to take the most direct route back to our starting point. However, the thought of returning to make another attempt, allowing two days, was very appealing. I would put it on my list of unfinished business.

Approaching the bealach, the indistinct path disappeared into a boulder field. Clambering over large boulders with a twelve-foot boat on one's back is not conducive to nimble footwork; the bow or stern, sometimes both, regularly became lodged on boulders. As we neared the bealach, the path reappeared but the wind increased in strength, making progress erratic. A sudden gust would cause the boat to spin one of us round like a weathervane, and then the end of the boat would clout the hillside. We soon perfected a technique to deal with this rather unfamiliar scenario. The trick was not to fight against the wind but to allow the boat to turn until the wind eased, and then slowly turn back to face the correct direction. Descending from the bealach towards Letterewe on Loch Maree for our final paddle, we realised that even on this, our shortest possible route, we might not finish before nightfall. Launching into Loch Maree with only one hour of daylight left made me wish I had brought a head torch. The six-mile paddle along Loch Maree was exhausting, despite us being helped along by a light breeze from the west. The sun soon set, leaving us to cross the loch in the evening twilight. We landed in darkness at Rhu Noa on the south-east shore. Bob displayed an enviable level of fitness by jogging the three miles back to Incheril and returning with the car at midnight. While I waited for him, I packed up the boats – fiddly work in the dark without a head torch, amid swarms of midges. I wondered how many Munros it would be possible to circumnavigate.

I soon started planning another boat-packing trip. Many times I had stood on top of Stac Pollaidh and looked across the magnificent wilderness of the Inverpolly National Nature Reserve. To the east, the massive bulk of Cùl Mòr seems near enough to touch, while Suilven and the more distant Canisp stand to the north across one of the most remarkable landscapes in the Scottish Highlands. Blue lochans, rivers and mile upon mile of rough, mostly pathless terrain lie like a carpet at one's feet. A magical world; a magnet.

My original intention of crossing this wilderness from south to north on foot had been shelved for a single, very simple reason: water, in great quantities! But the lure of that great intertwining of moorland and lochs had remained. Boat-packing gave me a new approach. After much map-studying and mind-changing, I decided against a south-to-north traverse due to the complexity of arranging return transport. A shorter crossing following a more north-westerly direction presented itself as an obvious alternative.

What this shorter trip lacked in length, it more than made up for in aesthetics. There would be a bit of everything: rough walking, many lochs and a short coastal paddle on the sea. The map also indicated there might be two or three short river sections, although it was difficult to tell how deep or fast these might be. As a bonus, I would be paddling the full length of Loch Sionascaig, the centrepiece of this stunning landscape, with its enchanting green islet group of Eilean Mòr.

So it happened that, after a joint sea kayaking trip, Bob gave me a lift from my van, parked near Garvie Bay, to the start of my adventure at Linneraineach. Full of excitement, I shouldered the packframe to start the first uphill walk. At the high point lay a small lochan, from which I looked down to Loch an Doire Dhuibh, feeling impatient to reach its shore and assemble the boat. At last, my journey across this astonishing landscape would begin and I could experience the wilderness in minute detail, become part of it.

I paddled easily across Loch an Doire Dhuibh and through Lochan Gainmheich, then came to the first potential river section – only to find, with a mixture of disappointment and relief, that it was quite a narrow channel/canal. No risk of damaging the boat, or worse. As I made my way towards the middle of Loch Sionascaig, I wondered: if someone on top of Stac Pollaidh was looking down at me, what might they be thinking? I hoped my minuscule figure making its way across the picturesque loch like a tiny water insect would not seem incongruous to them, an intrusion, a blot on a beautiful landscape.

As I approached the twin islets of Eilean Mòr, my feeling that I was somehow trespassing increased – not because I was on private land, but because I felt I was on secret, mystical, almost hallowed land. It was obviously impossible to see whether anyone actually was watching me from Stac Pollaidh, but I continued to feel oddly self-conscious and a bit guilty. If anyone did spot me, I hoped they would be curious or inspired, not disappointed.

Sitting at water level can make navigation surprisingly tricky, because the shoreline's features all merge into a single background, so I used a laminated copy of the 1:50,000 OS map to eventually identify the entrance to the Polly Lochs on my left. These form a chain of three small lochans, connected yet again by narrow channels rather than flowing rivers. However, the map did indicate a larger river heading steeply down to the sea at Polly Bay from the final loch, Loch na Dàil. Paddling through Loch na Dàil, I spotted this outfall; I needed to land before the pull of the river made itself felt. Along the lochside, very steep grass banks alternated with overhanging heather. Unable to find a place to land properly, I pulled the spray deck off and slid out of the boat into waist-deep water. Attaching a painter in the form of a thin cord, I managed to haul the boat up the bank – beyond which, miraculously, a walk of only a few yards took me to a track leading to a minor road.

Walking along and feeling really pleased with my adventure, I heard a faint engine noise behind me. Carrying a boat strapped horizontally across my body down a single-track road could not be good for traffic flow. I turned sideways to let the motorist pass, just hoping there wouldn't be a sudden gust of wind, then returned his cheery wave. Thwarted by 'no access' signs at the start of the track leading to Polly Bay, I took a circuitous route over rough moorland. Launching from large rocks into a sizable swell provided a few tense moments, but they were soon forgotten on a glorious paddle over a glittering blue sea to land at Garvie Bay. All that remained was a short uphill walk alongside a pleasant lochan to my van.

During the afternoon, unable to resist looking down upon that fabulous landscape once more, I walked up Stac Pollaidh. The summit was deserted. I scanned the lochs and moors for signs of life; they, too, were deserted. It was as it should be.

CHAPTER 12:

A Solar-Heated Bivvy and a Floating Trailer

In 2005 I booked onto a Rucksack Club meet held at Oban bothy. The meet leader, Brian Cunningham, had arranged for a motorboat and skipper to transport meet attendees to this remote bothy – which is nowhere near Oban, but sits instead at the eastern end of Loch Morar. Scrutiny of the map showed that travelling to the bothy provided an excellent opportunity for further boat-packing experience. Instead of using the motorboat, I would make my own way to the bothy by paddling and walking.

My plan was to start on the north shore of Loch Quoich, paddle five miles to its western end and then walk five miles to the eastern extremity of Loch Nevis. From there I would paddle four miles to Tarbert Bay, walk a mile over to West Tarbert Bay on Loch Morar, and finally paddle four miles east to the bothy. This would be my first multi-day boat-packing venture and my most ambitious to date. To save weight, I had developed a technique of converting the boat into a bivvy shelter. One end of the upturned hull, supported by the packframe, acted as the roof; a custom-made lightweight tent was then hung underneath from the inside of the hull, its mesh roof serving to alleviate condensation and keep midges at bay.

Setting off on Loch Quoich into a headwind, I marvelled at the gigantic proportions of Gairich on the opposite shore. Its huge appearance belies the fact that it is actually one of the lower Munros. Paddling westward, I could see the pointed dome of a much higher one, Sgùrr na Cìche, standing sentinel at the head of the loch. On reaching the far end of Loch Quoich, I searched around for some soft grass across which I could drag the laden boat before dismantling it. With everything crammed into the packframe, I started on the first and longest walking section, towards Loch Nevis.

After a couple of miles, I stopped to adjust the packframe and check that everything was in place. It wasn't. To my dismay, I found that one half of my split paddle was missing. Having no choice, I left the packframe and retraced my steps. In my mind's eye, I can still see that paddle; what a curious sight it was, a white kayak paddle lying on the heather in the middle of Knoydart.

Although the OS map showed no path, I expected to find one leading from Loch Quoich to Loch Nevis, on what seemed an obvious direct route. My instinct was confirmed, but the path I found soon started taking me too high. After crossing the col between Sgùrr na Cìche and Garbh Cioch Mhòr, I had to make a steep, rocky descent into upper Loch Nevis, where, thankfully, I found another path. I was tiring and keenly aware that the trip was taking a lot longer than expected.

Just before reaching the flat ground leading to the sea, I came across an unexpected sight: a group of scantily clad American girls with trekking poles and rucksacks. 'Where are you going?' I asked one of them.

'Oh, we're just hiking around. Hey, have you got a boat in there?' The paddles sticking up from the packframe must have been a giveaway. 'Man, that really is cool,' she continued, or something like that. It could have been, 'That man really is a fool.'

I wondered how they had got there, so far from any roads or habitation. My growing suspicion that I might have seen a mirage was strengthened when I failed to spot a single footprint on the path.

At last, I could see the head of Loch Nevis, but it still took a long time to get there. After following deer tracks across a few hundred yards of bogland, I finally reached the loch. It was a relief to put the packframe down after a four-hour carry. While assembling the boat among seaweed and shells, I noticed a flattened tent not far from the shore. The tent was pegged down securely, with the yellow inner facing upwards, as though to attract attention from the air. Its history remained a mystery.

Loch Nevis is a sea loch and therefore tidal, so my arrival time at this point was crucial. Firstly, I wanted to avoid paddling against the tide, so launching at slack water or with the tide ebbing would be preferable. Secondly, I had to pass through a narrow section called Kyles Knoydart and I didn't know if this restriction in the loch would be subject to turbulence or strong currents. I had therefore hoped to launch at high water, or just after. If there was any flow, it would be in a favourable direction, but not too fast. Checking my watch and looking at the sea, I knew I had arrived here at precisely the time I had wanted to avoid; the tide was ebbing strongly.

Apprehensively, I started paddling into a powerful westerly towards the unknown Kyles Knoydart. By keeping close to the left-hand shore, I gained some shelter from rocky projections and small headlands. Approaching the narrow section, I strained my eyes to assess the water conditions. I struggled to see clearly as the sun was low and I'd forgotten my sunglasses. Soon an area of turbulence appeared across my intended line. In the difficult light, I couldn't tell whether I was looking at large waves a long way off or small waves close by. Glancing at the shoreline, I wondered if there was time to abandon or change course, when suddenly I was in rough water. After twenty-five yards of very choppy conditions, I was safely through the turbulence, but my relief didn't last long. Although the water wasn't as choppy, I was now more exposed to the open sea with a much bigger swell. Waves and foam were breaking on a rocky headland about a mile in front of me that marked the entrance to Tarbert Bay. Turning left into the bay, I gave the rocks a wide berth – the vinyl hull would never stand up to a collision with sharp rocks. Just after rounding the headland, I encountered the roughest water so far, and I was glad to reach the flat calm sanctuary of the bay itself. This was full of thousands of small jellyfish; paddling through them felt surreal.

The tide was well out by the time I landed, which meant stumbling around on seaweed-covered rocks to lug the boat up to the high-water mark. Since the walk to West Tarbert Bay on Loch Morar was pretty short, I decided to strap the complete boat horizontally across the pack-frame. On this carry, I perfected my technique of negotiating a gate with the assembled boat as follows: approach the gate facing forward, unlatch and swing it open, take four paces backward, turn through 90 degrees, walk up to and pass through the gate facing sideways, take four more paces away from the gate still facing sideways. turn through 90 degrees to face the gate, walk up to the gate, shut and latch it, take four paces backward, turn through 180 degrees, continue on your way. Any misjudgement of paces while executing a turn will result in walloping the boat against the gatepost. A momentary lack of concentration when approaching an open gateway less than twelve feet wide will have a similar outcome. Techniques to deal with spring-hinged or kissing gates are still in the planning stage.

The track ended conveniently at a jetty on Loch Morar. The wind had dropped, and the evening promised to be calm and golden – a fitting end to long, hard and memorable day. As I pushed off from the jetty, I could see the white-painted bothy in the distance. The conditions were now good, so I took a direct line straight across the centre of the loch. Stopping in the middle, I allowed the boat to drift around in a circle. I could see the entire skyline of the loch, the traverse of which was the object of the club meet. Drinking the cold water from my mess tin which doubled as a bailer, I wondered how deep the loch was. I could hardly believe the map, which showed contours dropping to 300 metres below sea level; nearly 1,000 feet of water directly below me! Paddling a lot more quickly, I soon arrived at the bothy to meet the other club members. We spent a pleasant evening making plans for the twenty-eight-mile round of Loch Morar the following day. Guesstimates for the rough, tough circuit ranged from an ambitious nine hours to a more conservative fourteen hours.

Settling into the boat bivvy for the night, I felt tired and uncomfortable. Tussock grass does not make for a very smooth mattress. I was surprised at how stiflingly hot my shelter was. As I lay looking up at the inside of the boat, I worked out the reason for the unexpected sauna effect. During daylight hours the black hull attracts heat, which warms up the two inflatable air chambers that form the boat's gunwales. This heat is then dissipated into the boat bivvy during the night. It seemed I had inadvertently invented a solar-heated bivvy!

The following day, after a hot and sleepless night, I joined the club on a successful round of Loch Morar's twenty-eight-mile skyline, which took fourteen hours. The evening's champagne celebrations in the bothy helped me achieve a much-needed rest.

Early the next morning, keen to return to my starting point, but by a different route, I launched into an extremely windy loch. Halfway across, having narrowly escaped being swamped by huge waves, I decided the risks were too high, and instead enjoyed a trip on the motorboat back to Morar village.

*

'From the sublime to the ridiculous' best describes my next project, for which I explored the rather unconventional idea of trying to include the use of a bike on a cross-country boat-packing journey. A crucial consideration was the terrain. It would have to be navigable by mountain bike, so I needed an area where lochs were linked by rideable tracks. Nothing really came to mind, but I was sure detailed scrutiny of the map would reveal a suitable route.

The size and weight of the packed-up boat were such that a trailer would be necessary for cycling, so how could I tow the bike and trailer while paddling? My initial idea of using a windsurfing board was discarded; it would be too long and heavy, more like a CalMac ferry than a trailer. Anyway, at twelve feet long, it was bound to get stuck on rough tracks. The trailer would need to be light, yet robust enough to withstand the rigours of off-road travel. A trailer made of balsa wood would be very light and buoyant, but I could foresee construction problems. Some sort of inflatable trailer would be light and would work well on the water, but it would probably be impossible to attach any wheels. And the danger of a puncture, with the bike and trailer sinking halfway across a loch, had to be considered. I concluded that as well as being strong, buoyant and light, the trailer would need to be just big enough to carry a dismantled bike. I looked at my windsurfer. It hadn't been used for a long time. Resisting the temptation to reach for a saw, since I was unsure just how long any trailer should be, I decided to first measure the dismantled bike. How to fit the wheels occupied more thinking time, as did how to attach the trailer to the bike/boat. Having worked out a design, I eventually commissioned my local engineering company to fabricate a simple lightweight chassis.

Measurements of the bike and chassis indicated that the front three feet of the windsurfer would suffice as a floating trailer. Sawing completed, I instantly wished I'd allowed an extra six inches, but it was too late. Fitting the chassis, twelve-inch wheels and towing connection to the 'surf float' all went according to plan. Careful measuring of the dismantled bike allowed me to attach fixing points; these had to be secure, as the bike was brand new. Cruising around the lanes with the dismantled boat on the floatable trailer was a great success. I was eager to get on the water.

My local sailing club was the venue for the final stage of preparation. I soon had the boat assembled and the bike dismantled on the trailer, and I was full of confidence that this last test was barely necessary. As I pushed off from the jetty, a slight doubt entered my mind; the bike on the floating trailer did look just a bit top-heavy compared with the length of the trailer. Six inches more on the trailer would have made a difference. At the design stage, I had dismissed the idea of fitting some sort of retractable centre board for stability as too complex and, most likely, unnecessary.

Halfway across the lake, I was sure my misgivings were unfounded. The boat was easy to paddle, and the trailer, even though I couldn't see it very well, seemed to be tracking smoothly.

Feeling very pleased with my invention and looking forward to planning a route in the mountains, I turned towards the shore. An unexpected gust of wind from my right coincided with an odd twitch from the trailer. Seconds later, a loud splash was followed by a definite increase in drag from the rear. I didn't need to look behind to know what had happened.

CHAPTER 13:

End to End Diary

A concise account of my cycle ride from Lands End to John O'Groats

To cycle from Land's End to John O'Groats had been a long-standing ambition. Being a member of the Rucksack Club, and therefore feeling obliged not to make it too easy, I decided to include the British Three Peaks. Walking up Snowdon, Scafell Pike and Ben Nevis was definitely unnecessary – in fact, the entire escapade wasn't necessary at all – but life would be boring if we only ever dreamt of doing things that were necessary. And if I didn't also include the most southerly and northerly points of the UK, I would feel as though I hadn't really quite done it – so Lizard Point in the south and Dunnet Head in the north were duly included in my itinerary.

What type of accommodation to utilise was a question that was easily answered. Overnight stops at B&B establishments would be too inflexible; car support would make it too easy and would in any case be unnecessary. Bivvying, although very lightweight, would be somewhat extreme for seven or eight nights, especially in wet weather. I decided to camp and carry minimal kit; I would be ruthless with the weight. There didn't seem any point in taking any food, as I would be able to buy it on the way. I didn't take any spare clothes, either. Buying clean ones when I got to John O'Groats was a part of my plan, which in practice didn't work quite as planned. In retrospect, the only items I took that I could have managed without were a gas stove and a small pan. On a future similar trip, in the interests of comfort, I might take a Therm-a-rest, a type of inflatable insulated mat, instead of a cut-down Karrimat, a simple foam mat. A Therm-a-rest would be a lot more comfortable. On the other hand, it would also be also ten ounces heavier, so maybe I wouldn't.

Conveniently, some friends offered me a lift from Birmingham to Plymouth, and from there it was a straightforward train journey to Penzance, leaving only a ten-mile cycle ride to Land's End.

Day one: Land's End to Lostwithiel

On 16th July 2003, I weaved my way through the tourists and candyfloss stalls to the 'start line' painted on the road. The detour to Lizard Point felt like a long way and a bit unnecessary, but then so would the detour to Dunnet Head.

After visiting Lizard Point, it was pleasing to turn north and feel a favourable tailwind giving me a helping hand. One advantage of including the UK's most southerly point was that my route through Cornwall avoided the busy A30. Eventually, after some very hilly cycling, I reached Lostwithiel, only to spend a frustrating twenty minutes in the dark and pouring rain locating the campsite.

Start 1.15 p.m. Finish 9.45 p.m. 88 miles.

Day two: Lostwithiel to Severn Beach

The thirty-inch bottom gear on my bike was only just low enough to negotiate the very hilly roads en route to Tavistock, but a beautiful day and a strong following wind made the difficult cycling more pleasant. Locating the cycleway over the M5 proved to be somewhat problematic. I eventually found it after making several false turns, one of which took me to what seemed to be a drug addicts' campsite. On I went through the dockland area of Avonmouth, making for the only campsite marked on the map. It turned out to be a residential caravan site, which was closed anyway. I wandered around in the dark for a while; there were no pubs, no hotels and no B&Bs. A man parking his car informed me that 'there's nothing round here, mate' and advised me not to go into Avonmouth 'without an armed guard'. My suggestion that maybe I could camp on his lawn drew the polite but firm response that I should 'find somewhere else'. Being short of any other options, I dossed down on some rough ground by the river and waited for dawn.

Start 6.05 a.m. Finish 9.45 p.m. 150 miles; 238 miles total.

Day three: Severn Beach to Maentwrog

Crossing the Severn Bridge in the half-light of dawn, being buffeted by a strong side wind and dwarfed by huge passing artics, felt surreal. Cool, quiet roads approaching Abergavenny soon became very hot quiet roads. The effects of a tough day yesterday and a sleepless night began to take their toll. Fighting off the desire to stop and sleep, I wandered into Abergavenny market and devoured a gigantic cooked breakfast. The road to Dolgellau was hilly and tiring; I was reduced to walking on the last hill. The ball of my right foot was getting sore, the last thing I expected on a cycling trip. On the spur of the moment, just before reaching the campsite at Maentwrog, I stopped at a pub for a hard-earned pint. In the bar, the Tour de France was on the TV, prompting some good-natured jibes from the locals about having lost my way. A long and tough day.

Start 4.05 a.m. Finish 8.30 p.m. 161 miles; 399 miles total.

Day four: Maentwrog to Little Stanney

The initial twenty miles to Pen-y-Pass were mostly uphill, so I was thankful yet again for the tailwind. Locking up my bike at Pen-y-Pass, I felt slightly nervous about its security. Two hours and fifteen minutes after setting off for Snowdon, I was back at Pen-y Pass, having taken it easy on the descent due to a recurrence of the sore foot. I suspected that vibrations through the SPD clip on my cycling shoe may have been causing the soreness. Switching to fell-running shoes and fitting plastic toe clips I'd bought in Betws-y-Coed failed to make any difference; the insoles I cut out of my Karrimat didn't help, either. Swapping back to SPDs but unclipping on the descents and easy gradients provided the solution. The soreness disappeared almost straight away.

The road was hellish busy near Chester and Queensferry, and I was glad to stop early at a campsite near Little Stanney. It initially seemed my relief was to be short-lived when the owner informed me that he was full, but he did relent after some pleading. Campsite fees of £11 seemed astronomical but did include the luxury of a washer and dryer. My already small Karrimat was now even smaller, as it now had two insole-shaped holes in it. The nearby disco started up just as I was falling asleep.

Start 5.00 a.m. Finish 5.30 p.m. 80 miles; 479 miles total.

Day five: Little Stanney to Langdale

The term 'all-night disco' certainly applied last night, the loud music finally stopping as I packed up my tent. But it was a beautiful Sunday morning on quiet roads through Runcorn and Widnes – roads that could obviously be very busy at any other time.

An ominous 'ping' from my rear wheel signalled a broken spoke. I cycled on for a while to think through the possibilities of what I could do at nine o'clock on a Sunday morning. I phoned Gill, who contacted fellow Rucksack Club member Don Talbot. Don selflessly abandoned his plans for the day and straight away drove twenty miles to offer his assistance. While I was waiting for Don, I noticed increasing numbers of cyclists going past. By the time he arrived, there were hundreds – thousands, it seemed like. Don explained that it was the Manchester to Blackpool Bike

Race, and suggested that I should 'Join in with 'em, they're going your way'. Don had already worked out a plan: he had brought me his bike to use while he got mine fixed. Having now cycled 500 miles on my fully loaded tourer, I felt I could fly on Don's lightweight racer. Meanwhile, Don took my bike to the race mechanic for repair. Ten miles up the road, I was back on my bike.

But it wasn't enough for Don to give up his Sunday morning and make a forty-mile round trip to help me; he insisted that as his house was on my route, I should have a meal there. As we said our farewells and I prepared to go on my way, Don cast his eye over my bike. He noticed my waterproof leggings, which I had draped over the crossbar to dry. 'Those leggings are a bit long, aren't they?' he said. 'If you cut them off below the knee, they won't get stuck in the chain and they'll be a bit lighter.' Then, spotting my running shoes sticking out of my pannier, he said, 'You're not carrying running shoes and cycling shoes, are you?' I thought I was travelling light, but it was obvious Don wasn't impressed.

I was just about to set off when he said, 'And what's that?'

'That's my tent,' I explained.

He shook his head. 'You could save a lot of weight if you just kipped under a hedge.'

I arrived at the Langdale campsite at 5.20 p.m., put the tent up and set off for Scafell Pike. It's a long way from here to England's highest peak; I knew I'd be late back to the campsite but didn't want to leave it until tomorrow. I'd cycled 117 miles from Little Stanney and, not surprisingly, my legs felt very tired as I ran up Mickleden. Scafell Pike was deserted. Approaching the top through mist and pouring rain, I was glad I'd made the effort, as it would save three hours tomorrow. I wasn't trying to break any records, but it would be satisfying to know that I'd completed my journey as quickly as I could. Low cloud brought nightfall early; it was nearly dark when I returned to the tent at half past nine. What a day; I was shattered.

Start 5.20 a.m. Finish 9.30 p.m. 117 miles; 596 miles total.

Day six: Langdale to Lanark

Today I was aiming to reach Airdrie, where there were no campsites marked on the map. I hoped that by making an early start and finishing late, I should be able to get through this busy conurbation before stopping for the night. I woke at 3 a.m. to pouring rain and was on my way by four o'clock, soon stopping to unpack my sodden tent to retrieve my bike's rear flasher, which I'd inadvertently left inside. The long, soul-destroying climb from Grasmere to Dunmail Raise seemed never-ending, but eventually easier cycling on a surprisingly quiet A6 followed. The morning rush hour through Carlisle felt quite frantic, but I'd become more confident in busy cities.

More heavy rain as I approached Johnstone Bridge at eighty-three miles coincided with my bike computer breaking. A detour to Moffat to buy a new one was a fruitless exercise as there was no bike shop in the town. The lack of a computer soon proved to be a blessing; it was quite a relief not to be staring at the thing for mile after mile. The rain eased slightly, and a following wind sprang up as I started along the A74 cycleway – easy going, if a bit tedious. As I approached Lanark, the roads were awash and drain covers lifting in the torrential rain. I stopped early at an inviting-looking campsite just as the rain ceased. I didn't want to press on into Airdrie and risk not finding anywhere to stay. All my gear was soaked, so it felt good to have a rest and put everything in the tumble dryer – including the tent. The evening's entertainment was provided by two guys demolishing a caravan with only a lump hammer each.

Start 4.00 a.m. Finish 5.30 p.m. 134 miles; 730 miles total.

Day seven: Lanark to Ballachulish

Another early start and more heavy rain until eight o'clock. Very busy roads made me glad of the rear flasher. I made slow progress navigating through Airdrie, then there was slow, hilly cycling over the picturesque Campsie

Fells. A peculiar noise from my front wheel signalled a requirement for new brake blocks. A bite to eat and a visit to the bike shop in Callander preceded a strong tailwind along the A84 through Lochearnhead and Glen Dochart. From here the road to Crianlarich runs slightly south of due west; this, combined with a westerly shift in the wind, produced an unexpected headwind. Twelve very tough miles later, I staggered into a pub in Crianlarich. After ordering food and drink, I sat down, exhausted. When the barman brought my order, he could barely conceal his annoyance as he informed me that it wasn't actually waiter service.

And so onto the fantastic Rannoch Moor, thankfully with the return of a tailwind. The vast moor feels huge while driving across in the car; on a bike, it's colossal. At last, I started the descent towards Glen Coe, into an inexplicable headwind. As I stretched against the railings outside Ballachulish Co-op, trying to coax my body into walking mode, an amused shopper asked me how long I'd been 'sitting on that thing'.

After six nights sleeping on a Karrimat about the same size as a tabloid newspaper (with two insole shapes cut out of it), my stay at Craigallan, the Rucksack Club's Scottish hut, was pure luxury. A warm, dry bed; my tent steaming in the drying room; sheer bliss.

Start 4.10 a.m. Finish 7.45 p.m. 134 miles; 864 miles total.

Day eight: Ballachulish to Altnaharra

Feeling much refreshed, I cycled to Fort William and locked up my bike at the Glen Nevis Youth Hostel at 6 a.m. On reaching the top of Ben Nevis, the mist was cold, but at least it was dry. I took a spectacular tumble while descending the rocky path – without injury, but it could have been serious. Three hours for the round trip was fast enough; after all, I wasn't racing anybody. A light following wind made for a satisfying ride up the Great Glen through Invergarry and Invermoriston to Inverness.

My arrival at Inverness coincided with the evening rush hour, so I was glad to turn off the A9 onto quieter roads at Evanton. After enjoying a meal at a very pleasant pub, I purchased a torch and adhesive tape to construct a makeshift head-lamp. My intention was to cycle through this final night. The single-track roads should be deserted and, being so far north, the night would be short. The roads were beautifully quiet; only the occasional clatter of deer hooves disturbed the total silence. However, it was a moonless night, so without streetlights or conurbation glow, there was an almost complete absence of light. Cycling on the narrow roads without white lines or kerbs required much concentration. It was difficult to see the edges of the road, even with the small torch taped to my helmet. Increasing tiredness caused me to almost cycle off the road on more than one occasion. Leaning forward, tensed, with my hands on the brake levers, became very uncomfortable. Scooting on one pedal and even sitting on the crossbar failed to produce any relief from the stiffness and discomfort. I was grinding to a standstill. Eventually, at 1.45 a.m., I ground to an exhausted halt. The simple task of putting up the tent seemed unexpectedly complicated. I hadn't erected it last night because I'd stayed at Craigallan, but surely I couldn't have forgotten? Tiredness overtook me. After making a token gesture of shoving a couple of random pegs into the rocky ground, I gratefully crawled inside.

Start 4.10 a.m. Finish 1.45 a.m. 151 miles; 1,015 miles total.

Day nine: Altnahara to John O'Groats

At 5.15 a.m., after two hours of fitful and uncomfortable sleep, I repacked the tent. At least there weren't many pegs to take out. I marvelled at a fantastic pre-dawn sky; Ben Klibreck was looking down on me against a backdrop of black and yellow streaks, a multicoloured plume of thin cloud streaming from its summit. A small group of deer stood motionless in the road, silent and watchful. Fortunately, my two hurriedly placed tent pegs had, surprisingly, proved to be sufficient. The odd thought struck me that on future trips I could save some weight by only taking two with me. Soon, I was enjoying the downhill ride along Strath Naver before turning east along the north coast past Dounreay power station. A short detour took me to Dunnet Head, the most northerly point of the UK, and a view of the Orkney Isles. All that now remained was an eleven-mile ride to John O'Groats.

I have many memories of my thousand-mile trip which I will not forget, but my arrival at John O'Groats isn't one of them. If it was memorable for anything at all, it was for its profound sense of anticlimax. A quote by Arthur Ashe summed up my mixed feelings: 'Success is a journey, not a destination. The doing is often more important than the outcome.'

Start 5.15 a.m. Finish 12.30 p.m. 86 miles; 1,101 miles total.
Total time: 7d 23h 45min

Epilogue

My much-anticipated purchase of clean clothes in John O'Groats was thwarted by the absence of a clothes shop. With nowhere to buy clean clothing, or in fact anywhere to buy much at all, I spent the afternoon sleeping, and reeking.

The following morning, there was a strong wind blowing from the south. As I was girding myself for the fourteen-mile ride to Wick, I met two young ladies who had finished their 'End to End' the previous day. They informed me they had prebooked the only two bike spaces on the train south, from Wick to Inverness. Even though they had cycled a thousand miles with no mechanical problems, and the chances of a breakdown on the last fourteen miles were slim, they didn't want to miss the train, so were leaving early. I hadn't prebooked as I didn't want to plan that far ahead, so I did have a potential problem. I would work something out when I got to Wick.

About halfway to Wick, I caught up with another cyclist and enquired how he planned to travel south. His slightly indignant reply was, 'On my bike. I'm going to Land's End.'

As I thought about the help I'd received from the wind on my own northerly journey, I groaned inwardly, and was glad I only had fourteen miles to do. I'd had some tough times, but I was sure the following wind had been a major factor in my success.

At last, I tried on clean clothes in a sports shop in Wick. It was a memorable moment. I walked out of the changing room looking like a mannequin from the shop window, my unwashed clothes now sealed safely in a plastic bag.

The ticket office at Wick assured me the only two bike reservations to Inverness were indeed already booked, but told me that ScotRail did run a van service just for bikes. As I boarded the train, I hoped my bike and I would, in fact, be reunited at Inverness.

The two ladies greeted me at Inverness with the words, 'You won't believe what happened.' Halfway through their ride from John O'Groats to Wick, one of their bikes had sustained a buckled wheel, but they were relieved to find they were close to a bus stop. Unfortunately, the bus driver refused to allow them entry, as their bikes would hinder passengers in an emergency, and it was 'More than my job's worth' to let them on. This intransigence had the effect of enraging the sympathetic passengers, who berated him until he relented.

With my own bike safely collected, I enjoyed a pleasant night in a guest house before driving home in a one-way hire car.

CHAPTER 14:

From Dovedale to Dihedrals

On 1st October 2011 I booked into Camp 4, Yosemite Valley. It's the centre of the climbing universe, but with camping fees of only $5 per night, it's understandably basic. There isn't any grass – just lots of dust, pine needles and bearproof food boxes. There are also lots of climbers, from all over the world. But what Camp 4 lacks in refinement, it makes up for in atmosphere.

I was sharing pitch 19 with two Japanese lads and two Finnish climbers. The Japanese, while being very friendly and sociable, either didn't understand or refused to obey any of the campsite rules. Leaving food boxes open will encourage bears and the lightning-fast raccoons. Collecting firewood or pine cones for fuel was also an offence. These violations resulted in many 'yellow cards' from the rangers, who repeatedly pointed out the dire consequences of further rule-breaking. The Finns were climbing fanatics. After their one-day ascent of the overhanging Leaning Tower and a twenty-hour race up Lurking Fear on El Capitan, they earned the nickname 'The Super Finns'.

Unable to find a partner to accompany me on my first trip to this climbing Mecca, I was on my own. My first job was to visit the official noticeboard. The board is used for all manner of messages: friends trying to make contact, people looking for partners, gear wanted, gear for sale. One advert in particular caught my eye: 'For sale – poop tube'. A 'poop tube' is a portable mini-toilet – but even though the advert said 'one careful owner', I decided to give it a miss. I was keen to do the 'Prow', a C2 'aid climb' on Washington Column. Upward progress on an aid climb is accomplished by the climber placing expandable cams or alloy nuts in cracks in the rock, which are then used for direct aid instead of natural

'The Prow' on Washington Column

Equipment : nuts ; micro & offset nuts ; cams (0.33 – 4.5ins) ; sky hooks/bird beaks

Pitch information on diagram

- **X** -- xxft   pitch number – length
- (.....)   main items used
- ♦ ♦   belay bolt(s) at top of pitch
- ★ ★   bolted sections
- TTT ⊥⊥⊥   ledges / overhangs

TOP △ **FINISH**
scramble

PORTALEDGE BIVVI

- **6** --130ft   (fixed heads)
- **5** --110ft   (reachy bolts)   ← micro nut
- **4** --110ft   (small cams)
- **3** --100ft   (small cams)
- **2** --90ft   (small nuts)   ← rusty peg
- **1** --150ft   (nuts & cams)   ← hook
- **START**
- scramble

- **11** --130ft   (small cams)
- **10** -- 170ft   (small cams)
- **9** --100ft   (big cams)
- **8** -- 80ft   (micro nuts)
- **7** --70ft   The Strange Dihedral

PORTALEDGE BIVVI

(25 & 26.09.2011)

The Prow illustration by Inken Blunk

hand and footholds. The guidebook says 'Spectacularly steep and exposed'. At eleven pitches and 1,300 feet, it's not big by Yosemite standards, but it was plenty big enough to get started on. I pinned up my note asking for an interested partner.

After doing my food shopping, I went to visit the climbing equipment shop, an Aladdin's cave full of every imaginable piece of climbing gear. I bought a new pair of etriers, short flexible tape ladders which connect to the cams or nuts and are also connected to the climber's harness. I was soon back at the noticeboard, slightly disappointed not to find a response to my message. I took the shuttle bus up the valley to check out the approach to Washington Column. I'd been here all of four hours and didn't want to waste any more time! As an afterthought, I took the route description for the climb with me; it would be worth finding the start of the 'Prow'. Further thought prompted me to pack ten litres of water, my portaledge and a rope. A portaledge is exactly that, a collapsible ledge which can be hauled up the climb and used for sitting or sleeping on – a glorified camp bed. I could stash these at the start of the climb. It was useful to discover that the final 200 feet of steep scrambling to the start of the climb proper could be difficult and dangerous, or safe and easy, depending on one's route choice. Eventually I looked up at the 'Prow'. It looked fantastic – clean and steep. It occurred to me that in the event of not being able to find a partner, I could consider making a solo attempt. I then met two experienced-looking climbers who had just backed off the route, which brought me down to earth somewhat. But they very generously gave me ten litres of water, which I added to my stash.

Back at Camp 4 I met Boris, a young Russian. He had seen my note and was keen to do the Prow – great! He assured me that he knew what he was doing, but hadn't got much gear. This turned out to be true on both counts.

By mid-morning the following day, unable to find Boris, I walked back up to the climb and stashed another rope and all the hardware. Big wall climbing is very gear-intensive. It requires a lot of hardware: cams, nuts, carabiners, various skyhooks and bird beaks for hooking onto the tiniest of ledges, also jumar clamps for climbing ropes, and pulleys for raising the haul bag. Other essentials were sleeping bag, first aid kit, food, stove and a myriad of other items, plus the heaviest thing of all: water. The haul bag was going to be heavy. Back at Camp 4, I wondered if Boris really was serious. Anyway, I couldn't wait for ever, so I packed my haul bag with sleeping gear and food and set off for Washington Column. *This is it*, I thought. *Partner or no partner, I'm gonna climb.*

I'd spent a long time practising big wall rope systems; I'd bought all the gear and researched the climbs I wanted to do. Practising roped solo aid climbing in the Peak District allowed me to perfect my techniques. Routes which were usually climbed unaided provided ideal training and included 'Caesar' and 'Indecent Exposure'. The pre-bolted horizontal roof climbs in the Dove Holes and Thor's Cave added another important skill. Particularly exciting was my winter ascent of the 'Big Plum' in Chee Dale – overhanging, exposed and technical. 'Black Grub' on Beeston Tor also provided a memorable outing, the many sharp pockets giving ideal skyhook placements.

On one occasion while climbing in Dovedale, I was forced to put my roped solo system to the ultimate test. I was nearing the top of 'George', an E2 on Tissington Spires, when a small cam I was hanging on suddenly came out. Although the next piece of gear was only a couple of feet below me, the combination of slack in the system and rope stretch meant that I fell about fifteen feet. After a few silent mutterings to convince myself that everything had worked as it should, I was soon on the top.

As I looked up the first pitch of the 'Prow', I knew I was ready. The first pitch went well, medium-sized nuts and cams up a beautiful clean, soaring corner, followed by a slab; then a steeper section, finishing with a skyhook move onto the belay. I was very pleased with that. Roped soloing is very complex and labour-intensive. By the time I'd led the pitch, abseiled back down to remove all the gear, jumared back up and hauled my kit, three hours had gone by. Still, I thought, at this rate I could climb three pitches per day.

Half Dome, across the valley, looked gigantic from my vantage point. It was then that I noticed a change in the weather. Black clouds were rolling over the horizon and it seemed to have turned a bit warmer. Being mid-afternoon and only one pitch up, I was unsure whether to assume the worst and go down or hope for the best and go up. I decided to go up; I had a fly sheet for the portaledge.

After a couple of difficult free moves across a slab to start pitch two, I was at the base of another magnificent corner. Finding I couldn't place any solid gear and being unable to reverse the slab, I had to employ a bit of aid jiggery-pokery. The most important piece of kit on a big wall climb is a roll of gaffer tape; it can be used for many things, including repairing kit and sealing rubbish bags. Using a fifi hook and taping a daisy chain (a thin nylon tape formed into several separate small loops) to the end of a trekking pole, I just managed to hook a peg above me. The peg was rusty. If it failed while I was hanging on it, I would fall onto the slab, roll down it and go over the edge. Although my rope system would prevent a ground fall, as a solo climber any injury would be serious and, in this case, likely. I tried not to think about it. Another skyhook move and I was established in a long crack line leading to a spectacular hanging belay on two very secure-looking bolts. Alone on the vertical, featureless wall, I looked down to the previous belay, 100 feet below. I could see my haul bag and portaledge, collapsed and stowed in its carry bag, hanging from two bolts. The two ropes attached to me, the lead rope and the haul rope, snaked their way down to their respective rope bags, also suspended from the two bolts.

At the sound of distant thunder, I looked over my shoulder. Half Dome now seemed even bigger, illuminated by flashes of lightning. It was nearly dark, and spotting with rain. I wished I'd gone down.

Trying to keep calm and think clearly, I knew I hadn't got time to go through the rigmarole of cleaning, abseiling and hauling. I would have to descend one pitch, then either stay there on the portaledge or continue to the bottom. I opted to erect the portaledge, which was a mistake. I had practised this procedure thoroughly, but only on my shed wall. It's a piece of cake when you're standing on the floor and it's daylight! The ledge seemed quite stable when I stood on the inside edge of the frame – but when I stood on the outside, the whole thing would flip over, tip me off and leave me hanging from the belay. The problem was the angle of the rock; it just wasn't steep enough. It was more of a steep slab than a wall. After two more attempts, the novelty wore off and I abseiled to the bottom.

It was quite sheltered at the base and the storm soon passed, but terrible cramp in the night made me realise just how little water I'd drunk during the day. Worrying about bears meant I didn't sleep much, and the night passed slowly. But it was beautiful gazing at the millions of stars, the moon rising over Half Dome, and watching the lights of climbers on that huge black wall in the moon shadow. It felt great to be out there, having an adventure. The faint munching sound I'd heard during the night was explained when I discovered that half of one of my socks had been eaten, I assume by an unseen rodent. I'm sure I would have noticed if it had been a bear.

By the time I'd jumared back up to the portaledge, it was daylight, and it was now obvious that I'd hung it in the wrong place. You live and learn. After repacking the ledge and cleaning pitch two, I abseiled back to the base. Although I'd failed to do the climb, I felt quite pleased with myself; I now knew I possessed the confidence to attempt a big wall solo. With all my gear stashed near the base of the climb ready for another attempt, I set off for Camp 4. It wasn't over yet. I had unfinished business!

Two days later, I met Boris at the base of the 'Prow'. He seemed very pleased that I'd left all my gear and the water at the start. I could see he'd also brought all his gear: a rope and one jumar! It was just as well I'd got enough equipment to open a shop. As I had already soloed the first two pitches, I was happy for Boris to lead these, plus pitch three. He did this in good style, safely and confidently, free climbing a few short sections which I had aided. The rain started at the top of pitch two but it looked like it would soon pass, so we waited . . . and waited . . . then we went down. Within minutes, the sky was blue and everywhere was steaming. We should have waited a bit longer.

On the second attempt, Boris was rummaging in the haul bag when something green disappeared into the abyss. He'd dropped the food bag! We went down – again. The bag had exploded in the scree; we found some of the contents, but some were lost or damaged. I could see he felt guilty, so there didn't seem any point in telling him how hungry I felt. Nevertheless,

Boris offered to go down to Curry Village to replace the food and buy some beer – he must have been reading my mind. It was too late to make another attempt, so I bedded down and tried not to worry about bears. Apparently, they are frightened of humans unless they are very hungry, when all they want is your food. *Well, they'll be out of luck tonight*, I thought.

The following morning saw us jumaring back up in the dark. I was getting to know the first two pitches quite well. At the top of pitch three there is a ledge big enough to stand on, so at Boris's suggestion we erected the portaledge and hauled it attached to the rope above the haul bag. This proved to be a master stroke, as at the next three belay points there was nowhere to stand, just two bolts in the wall. Lying on the portaledge in the sun while belaying felt decadent compared with standing in etriers for ages.

The guidebook gave a general description of the climb – its length and difficulty – plus a suggested list of key items of equipment. A line drawing showing the technicalities encountered on each pitch accompanied the description. Before we started, the note 'fixed heads' had caught my attention. 'Head' is an abbreviation of 'copperhead', a small solid copper cylinder with a thin wire loop attached. The 'head' can be hammered into a small depression in the rock and should be secure enough to hold the weight of a climber, thereby allowing upward progress. The word 'fixed' informed me that the copperheads should be in place already. But there was also a cautionary note. 'It's unlikely any of the twenty or so fixed heads will blow, but come prepared just in case.' One or more copperheads could be missing or broken. 'Being prepared' meant either bringing a hammer and spare heads or employing an alternative method of climbing that section of rock. I decided to go for the latter and employ my hook-and-trekking-pole invention.

Pitch six was my lead. It looked very steep and exposed. I could see the occasional wire loop sticking out of the smooth rock, but trusting the copperheads felt risky; some of the wire loops were partially broken, leaving only three or four strands to support my weight. About halfway up the pitch, I looked up at a head with a completely broken wire. By balancing in the top step of the etrier and reaching full stretch with my extended fifi hook, I could just hook the loop of the next head. What a relief. I swarmed up the daisy chain – but even before I reached the top, I could see the condition of the loop was even worse than the previous one; there were only two strands of wire remaining. I froze for a moment, trying not to breathe. If this were to 'blow', I would fall. My increasing velocity would probably cause the previous head to fail, and maybe the one below that. The further I fell, the more load I would place on each head. I had a vision of 'unzipping' the entire pitch. 'Just keep cool, don't make any sudden movements. Clip the next head. Don't forget to breathe.' More solid nut and cam placements soon presented themselves before I reached the belay bolts at the top of the pitch.

Pitch seven is called the Strange Dihedral. It's an atmospheric, very exposed leaning corner, and this was also my lead. On completion, I abseiled back to the portaledge belay, cleaning all the gear from the pitch on the way down – a mistake which wouldn't become evident until the following day. This would be our bivvy site for the night. Making a meal, bedding down on the portaledge and trying not to drop anything was surreal, as was balancing on the edge of the frame, peeing over the edge into the void. I didn't sleep much, not because of where we were but because of Boris's incessant snoring!

We failed to hear the alarm and overslept, but Boris was soon jumaring the haul line I had fixed. At the top of the Strange Dihedral, he switched to the lead line and led pitch eight, taking the top of the haul line with him. Boris was now two pitches above me, out of sight and over to one side. As he prepared to haul the bag, I realised that if I just let it swing out and round the corner, out of sight, I was asking for trouble; it could easily get damaged or stuck on an unseen obstacle. Lowering the bag out on a separate line allowed me some degree of control over its trajectory, but I was surprised just how far over to one side it finally stopped.

As Boris was now two pitches above me, I would have to jumar two consecutive pitches. No problem with that, but halfway up the Strange Dihedral the awful realisation dawned on me that because I had already cleaned all the gear from the pitch, there was nothing to hold the rope into the leaning dihedral. Gravity would dictate that I would follow exactly the same trajectory as the haul bag, only a lot quicker. If I'd thought about this before starting the pitch, I could have rigged a separate line to lower myself out and avoid a spectacular and nerve-racking swing, but it was too late.

To start with, I made good progress, but I could feel gravity pulling me to my right. For every few feet I jumared upwards, I moved a few involuntary inches to the right, towards the edge of the dihedral. As I made steady progress, I tried to limit my inexorable rightward direction by bracing my feet on small ledges and blemishes in the rock. Then, inevitably, my feet would slip, I'd scrabble a bit, and then I'd regain my balance another few feet nearer the edge. Gravity was winning. *Next time you're gonna go*, I thought. It probably looked like something from a *Tom and Jerry* cartoon, but to me it wasn't so funny; another few feet, another slip and scrabble, and I'd gone. Swinging through the air, out of the corner of my eye I caught a glimpse of the bivvy site we had used at the base of the climb, 1,200 feet below. I had a vision of the rope scraping across a sharp edge. Twenty feet of free-hanging jumaring and I was back in contact with the rock, confronted by the haul bag jammed behind a flake; at least we were in the same place. After freeing the bag so that Boris could continue hauling. The rest of pitch eight, thankfully, went without incident.

Pitches nine and ten were mixed aid and free climbing. Boris made light work of these while I tried to calm my nerves. It felt really good to pull over the top. My first big wall; high fives and mutual congratulations.

My arthritic knees refused to entertain the usual descent down the North Dome Gully, so we decided to abseil down the South Face route. As Boris had done this before, he went first to locate the anchors, but he still missed one and had to jumar back up for twenty feet. I went second with the haul bag. It was quite unnerving to start with, like abseiling with another person hanging on the device; I was glad I'd done this in practice.

We descended the last of the ten pitches in the dark. Boris, being young and fit, raced down to spend the night at his tent in the valley; I, being old and exhausted, bivvied at the base. As I lay in my sleeping bag, staring up at the stars and the black outline of the 'Prow', I tried to visualise every foot of the climb and forget about the bears and that swing out of the Strange Dihedral.

CHAPTER 15:

The Little Voice

It was only 1 p.m., and I'd already climbed Foinaven from my high camp. Foinaven and Arkle looked like huge shimmering white beasts, standing guard over the final vast wilderness stretching towards Cape Wrath, their wispy cloud caps dissipating quickly with the increasing heat of a perfect June day. These mightiest of Corbetts were soon revealed in all their glory, quartzite flanks sparkling. What a fantastic place to be!

The Scottish accent on my voicemail started alarm bells ringing, and the message had barely started before I stopped dead in my tracks. 'This a message for Mr Hartley. Your wife has reported you missing. Please make contact with your wife and Inverness police as soon as possible.' I was stunned! I had no idea why she had done that. We had agreed that I would make regular contact during the trip, and I'd sent Gill a text message last night – hadn't I?

It was surreal. Here I was, absorbing one of the finest moments I had ever experienced in the mountains, smiling at the thought of phoning Gill to tell her just how fabulous this was; I knew she would be envious. But in an instant, the peace and solitude, the sheer delight of being there, all seemed as nothing. Gill was distraught, sobbing with relief at the sound of my voice.

We'd obviously had a misunderstanding about how and when I would make contact. I wasn't sure if it was my fault, but I felt guilty about causing her so much anguish. The thought of her lying sleepless all night as I was safe in my tiny tent made me feel even worse. Daylight would have come, and her long vigil would have continued, waiting for the phone to ring. Inevitably, the decision to contact the emergency services had to be made; she had reasoned that causing a false alarm was better than taking a gamble that everything was OK. She made the call at 12.45 p.m., so only fifteen minutes had elapsed before I phoned her. The policeman who had Assynt as his patch was on his way to the deserted cottage at Lone to check whether my bike was still there, so a full-scale search hadn't actually started. It was fortunate he didn't get as far as Lone; I'd hidden my bike well. I doubt he would have found it, and that would have added another complication.

My adventure had begun on 3rd June 2010, two days earlier, at Lairg. The ambition to climb all the northern Corbetts had been on my 'must-do' list for a number of years. I had cycled through Sutherland on my way to John O'Groats in 2003 and promised myself that one day I would return for a more extensive tour that included all the seventeen Corbetts north of Lairg. The thought of undertaking this trip, cycling between the mountains, kept popping up like a recurring daydream. I visualised myself cruising along those beautiful single-track roads, seeing not a house, a car or another person for mile after mile. I would be under the gaze of what must surely be the most majestic mountains in Scotland. I would also have idyllic and, of course, midge-free wild camps. OK, that was optimistic – but daydreams often are.

A Corbett is a Scottish mountain of 2,500 feet or more but less than 3,000 feet; there are 220 of them. Cameron McNeish's book *The Corbett Almanac* describes these hills, giving concise details of location and possible routes of ascent. In chapter 29 he covers the seventeen most northern Corbetts under the title 'Inverpolly, Assynt and The Far North'. What an evocative title; it's enough in itself to make you want to go there. The extent of my planning was to run a map wheel over the route in a road atlas. This determined that my trip would involve about 200 miles of cycling, but it seemed too much of a fiddle to work out how many miles of walking and feet of ascent were involved. A cursory look at the Ordnance Survey maps showed a 'fair bit' of both – maybe more. After this 'expert' research, I decided that three or four days would be ample time. It wasn't really planning – more a case of 'Yeah, that's a great idea. Where's my bike?'

Day one: Ben Loyal

I set off towards Ben Loyal into a very strong northeasterly and found the first two hours depressingly difficult. My progress could only be described as pathetic; in fact, I hardly seemed to be making any progress at all. At least I was grinding my way through a truly inspirational landscape, surely some of the strangest and most beautiful country in Britain. As if to add insult to my already low morale, after ten miles my rear tyre developed a slow puncture. I considered abandoning the trip. Then I heard a little voice say, 'Three or four days? You'll be lucky to finish this in a week!'

This was the first time I'd been on my bike for six months, and the lack of training wasn't helping. The bike felt heavy, but I expected that; in addition to my camping gear, I had packed an extra-thick sleeping mat and two pillows. I was waiting for surgery on a ruptured shoulder tendon, so I hoped these luxuries would make sleeping more comfortable. The extra kit I required to go walking on the hills was minimal, but it all added up. Due to near drought conditions, I had taken a water filter, and I was soon glad of it, as many of the usually full gushing streams were just dribbles of tepid water.

It was time to take stock; this was going to be tougher and take a lot longer than I first thought. Did I really want to do this, even if it took seven days, knowing I would run out of food? My shoulder would probably stop me sleeping properly, and I was also waiting for surgery on a torn knee cartilage . . . Yes, of course I did! But then I heard the little voice say, 'Not only is this going to take a long time, it's also going to be a lot harder than you're expecting.' I decided not to fix the puncture straight away but use it to my advantage. I would stop and blow the tyre up every few miles. This would give me an excuse to stretch regularly and gradually ease my way in. *Yes, that's the way,* I thought. *Don't try too hard. Just go with it.*

Feeling in much lighter mood, I pedalled my way northwards. As I passed North Dalchork forest and the Crask Inn, the sun was breaking through and I could see the distant Ben Hee to the north-west. Ben Hee would be Corbett number nine, about halfway through the trip. As I approached Ben Klibreck (a Munro which I didn't need to do), I looked out for the roadside spot where I'd camped on my Lands End to John O'Groats trip in 2003, but I just couldn't tell exactly where it was. I've tried to identify it on other occasions without success; not surprising, really, as in 2003 it was 2 a.m., pitch black and I'd almost fallen off my bike through exhaustion, having cycled 150 miles from Ballachulish and walked up Ben Nevis in a not undemanding twenty-two-hour push.

Rounding a corner, I came across several parked cars, a camper van and a posse of fit-looking runners. It didn't take long for it to register that this was a support crew – a support crew for something big. My polite enquiry brought the response, 'It's a long story, but that guy over there is on schedule to complete the Munros in record time.'

I was duly introduced to Stephen Pyke – or Spyke, as he's known. Stephen had just done Ben Klibreck and was preparing to cycle to Ben Hope, his last Munro. He would finish in under forty days, at an average of seven Munros per day. I quickly calculated that he must have started in mid-April following quite a harsh winter and he must have endured some gruelling conditions. He was probably relieved when I declined his offer to accompany him up Ben Hope; he may have been out for thirty-nine days longer than I had, but I had the distinct feeling he was a lot faster than I was. As I pedalled on my way, I was thinking that maybe I should have accepted his offer when I heard a humming and whirring sound approaching from behind. In an instant, Spyke and his two-wheeled support crew flashed past. With a cheery 'All the best, Mike', they disappeared into the distance. *Hmm. Maybe not.*

The encounter with Spyke improved my morale. I soon had the puncture repaired and was on my way. Loch Loyal looked wonderful. When a strong gust of wind swept across the water, it would flatten the white horses, changing the colour through every possible shade of blue to black and back to blue again. The strong wind was still against me, and I was glad to get to Lettermore and stash my bike. Ben Loyal doesn't look as impressive or as challenging from this side as it does from the north, but this is probably the shortest and easiest route. The ascent from Ribigill in the north would have involved a detour on the bike of about four miles, and this trip was going to be long enough without any detours. I'd cycled thirty miles to Lettermore and I don't think I've ever before expended as much energy to cover such a short distance. I was relieved to get off the bike and start the uphill walk. It was good to feel the dry grass on my legs, hear the crunch of granite and smell the sheep. It's not that I dislike cycling; it's just that I always feel as though I am missing something. I feel like I'm not fully experiencing the environment, always casting longing glances at the lochsides and distant bealachs, wondering if there's any climbing on that crag or where that footpath goes. The tarmac feels like a narrow ribbon of man-made predictability and security.

The ascent of Ben Loyal, my first Corbett, went quickly. I was soon scrambling up the granite tor that crowns the top. To the north, the road across the Kyle of Tongue looked lonely and tenuous as it wound its way towards Durness.

The extra time I now expected to spend on the trip would make my food supply an issue. There are not many places for resupply, so to be on the safe side I decided to buy in nearby Tongue. As it happened, both shops were closed.

The subsequent ride to Durness certainly did feel lonely and committing. It was also very windy and hilly, the climb from the Kyle of Tongue being particularly testing. Ben Loyal looked majestic now, its craggy top steep and inaccessible. Loch Eriboll came into view below, with my next two Corbetts standing above its western end. The fourteen-mile trip around Loch Eriboll and on to Durness typifies Sutherland: craggy white hills separated by desolate moorlands, remote farms and isolated crofts, some of which have been converted into tea rooms or craft workshops. I rarely stop to buy anything, but made a mental note to do so more often. The gorse was spectacular. It seems more prolific each year, forming bright yellow hedges smelling of coconut. Stopping occasionally to drink from nearly dry streams, I was glad of the water filter.

At last, I breasted the final climb to arrive at Durness. I phoned Gill, then went to the campsite. I couldn't actually book on as the office was closed; a notice on the door said that I could pay at 9 a.m. the following day. Nine o'clock – I was hoping to be miles away by then! I'd just begun to put my tent up when I realised my neighbour was a drunken Scottish woman, friendly but loud. Ten minutes later and I'd transferred to another pitch, as far away as possible, with the only noise being the croaking of a corncrake.

As I lay in my sleeping bag, I knew that I'd found this first day extremely tough – but it also felt good to be on the brink of a long, testing journey. Although I now felt committed to this trip and I really wanted to finish it, I wasn't sure whether I was actually capable. I'd only been going for one day, but already I felt very tired. I could sense how disappointed I would be if I failed. From past experience, I knew that this sense of impending disappointment increases with the amount of effort and time expended. As I fell asleep, I had the ominous feeling that the little voice was going to be right.

Cycle 67 miles; walk 6 miles; 2,200 feet ascent.

Day two: Cranstackie, Beinn Spionnaidh, Meall Horn.

At 7 a.m. I was ready to leave, but the office and shop were both closed. I didn't want to avoid paying, but I only had £2 in change, so I left that on the step and went on my way. I hoped I could find somewhere to buy food within the next couple of days.

As I cycled south alongside the Kyle of Durness, I thought how late my seven o'clock start was, considering it had been light for three hours. Maybe it was early enough, though – after all, a 7 a.m. start and a likely 9 p.m. finish still means a fourteen-hour day. *You're not as young as you were*, I thought. *The days when you could endure consecutive twenty-hour days are definitely over.*

Gill and I had climbed Cranstackie and Beinn Spionnaidh only last year; in fact, I'd already done ten of the seventeen Corbetts in the far north. But I wasn't here simply to tick them off; I was here to make my own journey through this weird and wonderful landscape. I was here because I found it inspiring. First, I tackled Cranstackie. As trackless grass and heather gave way to quartzite scree and boulders, the sky cleared to reveal another superb day.

I reached Beinn Spionnaidh via a short out-and-back before descending into Calbhach Coire, then passed Rhigolter back to my starting point, taking just over four hours for the round trip. Back on the bike, cycling was hard work again. Climbing up to the watershed at Gualin House, I felt like an ant creeping almost imperceptibly up a massive incline, but at last, I reached the top. Foinaven and Arkle looked fantastic. Even if I lived here, I couldn't imagine ever getting used to this scenery.

It was a nice fast descent to Rhiconich, but there was no sign of any shops. Finally, there was a tremendous swooping descent to Loch Laxford. I then cycled south-east past Loch Stack, and along the minor road and track to the deserted cottage at Lone. Here I met a wild camper. He was waiting for his friend; they would be doing Foinaven and Arkle the following day.

After hiding the bike in the pine forest, I started packing my camping gear for the night ahead. No matter how I tried, I could not get everything in the old KIMM-style rucksack I was using; too much stuff was the main reason, and just chucking it in wasn't helping. But there was another reason: in an attempt to take less gear on a KIMM, in a flash of inspiration I had decided to make my rucksack a bit smaller. Cutting the rucksack in half, shortening it by four inches, then sewing it back together was a simple if somewhat radical solution. However, this did present a problem: I had already reduced my kit to the absolute minimum, so the rucksack was now too small. But it was, of course, (insignificantly) lighter.

Eventually I set off up the track towards Bealach Horn, with the rucksack jammed full and a pannier over my shoulder. The pleasant stalkers' path soon became a very unpleasant stalkers' path; earth moving equipment and piles of shale marred the landscape.

There was no point in carrying my gear any further than necessary, so I stopped to camp just before the bealach, as I wanted to be in a good position to do the next three Corbetts. I really wanted to do Meall Horn that evening as it was by far the nearest, but some ominous-looking clouds were rolling in from the west. It seemed pretty obvious that it was going to rain, so I took the opportunity to make a meal and take a much-needed rest. Post-meal drowsiness and thoughts of putting off Meall Horn until tomorrow were overtaking me when, although it was still light, I was sure somebody was flashing a torch on the side of the tent. Before I could investigate, the total and heavy silence was broken by a tremendous clap of thunder. Further lightning and more thunder were followed by an eerie silence and steady rain.

With a start, I awoke from my doze to see another light shining through the tent. This time it was low, big and still: the sun. A quick text to Gill: 'storm's passed – going up Meall Horn'.

Hurriedly putting my shoes on, I noticed that not only were my heels sore and my big toe tender, but my running shoes were starting to fall apart. The same could be said for my cycling shoes. The answer seemed obvious: cut holes where the shoes were causing discomfort. If the discomfort increased, cut bigger holes. With a bit of luck, both pairs of shoes and my feet should last to the end!

Being out late on the hills without time constraints is a feeling I always enjoy. The remote and dramatic environment enhanced this feeling of contentment. Ambling down to my tent from Meall Horn, I thought how fortunate I was to be able to visit this place. Back at the tent, I filtered water from a tiny stream; it did have a healthier look to it than the tepid pool I had used earlier. As I made a brew, I watched the sun set in the perfect 'V' formed by the black outlines of Foinaven and Arkle, the silence broken only by the barking of a nearby stag. Snuggling down into my sleeping bag after a hard but memorable day, I felt tired and satisfied. Forgetting to message Gill that I'd returned to the tent, I was blissfully unaware of the drama and anguish that was unfolding at home.

Cycle 29 miles; walk 12 miles; 5,265 feet ascent.

Day three: Foinaven, Arkle, Meallan Liath

Before the alarm sounded, I was up and keen to get on my way. Unfortunately, my big toe had other ideas. The discomfort as I put on my shoe was a stark reminder that if I couldn't resolve this, it would spell the end of my trip. I looked at the battered and ripped Walsh fell-running shoe, then at the knife in my hand. To start with I just made a single cut, about two inches long, directly above the toe. I didn't want to go too far and render the shoe unusable. Next, I put Vaseline on my sore heels, glad I'd brought a plentiful supply. Both my pairs of socks were wet, filthy and impregnated with grit. I made a mental note to rinse them every night.

The mist was low, nearly down to the tent, as I set off for Foinaven at 7 a.m., but it had a light, dry feel to it. I guessed it would soon clear. I jogged and walked across numerous boulder fields, the many small crags and bluffs all looking the same in the mist. As the terrain transformed into a blunt ridge, I sensed I was at the start of the giant beast's rocky mane. With one eye on the compass and one eye on my footing, I made my way to the top. It was only four and a half miles from the tent, but it took me two and a quarter hours – slow going indeed. I made the return trip entirely on a compass bearing, trying to convince myself that I was retracing my outward route.

The walk to Arkle was magical, the mist clearing to reveal sparkling quartzite and blue lochans. Two figures appeared, coming towards me. I was thinking they must have made an early start when I realised it was the wild camper I'd met yesterday and his companion. We chatted for a while, enthusing about where we were and laughing about the thunderstorm. Sitting next to the summit cairn, I switched on my phone to text Gill – and I listened to the voice message in disbelief. Arkle no longer seemed so magical.

I've often been away on trips and not made any contact at all, but we'd made the arrangement, so I should have kept to it. It was small comfort to know that our system had actually worked. On the one occasion I had failed to make contact, Gill alerted the police, and they knew where to start looking. But the highlight of my trip was now tainted. I resolved to be more considerate in the future.

By the time I'd completed Arkle, broken camp, walked back to Lone and packed up the bike, it was 3.45 p.m. It felt a bit late to do the next Corbett and then find a campsite, but I decided to press on and see how the time went. With the bike stashed in the wood at Aultanrynie, I set off up the stalkers' track towards Meallan Laith at 6 p.m. I felt I was making good progress, but from the top of the first rise it still looked a long way and not straightforward. The mist was intermittent. I briefly thought about abandoning the attempt until the following day – but soon I was on the top, and glad I'd stuck with it. A better route down to rejoin the stalkers' path, and I was back at the bike just under three hours after setting out. Later, checking *The Corbett Almanac*, I noted that McNeish says '10 miles/2,700 ft; approximate time 5–8 hours'. Maybe I wasn't so unfit after all.

Cycling towards my next Corbett, I knew I needed to find a campsite. The approach path from the road to Beinn Leoid crossed a ditch to a small birch wood before climbing steeply up on to the hill. I set up camp in the wood at 9.45 p.m. and filtered water from the ditch. It felt too late to eat – and anyway, I had no appetite. As I lay down, I realised I had pitched on a slope, my shoulder and big toe were both hurting, and my heels were sore. Tomorrow would be my last chance to abandon the trip. I could head south and take the most direct route back to Lairg, or turn north and commit to the remaining eight Corbetts. I decided to make the decision tomorrow as I walked up Beinn Leoid. Somehow, although I could hear the doubtful murmuring of the little voice, I knew I wouldn't be giving up. I'd drifted into that 'I'm in too deep now to pack it in' mode. Many times I'd been in this position, balancing the disappointment of failure against the effort of continuing.

Cycle 8 miles; walk 18 miles; 6,650 feet ascent.

Day four: Beinn Leoid, Ben Hee

I left camp for Beinn Leoid at 5.15 a.m. After the initial climb, I had to make quite a significant descent and reascent, but eventually I reached the top. It felt very remote; I watched ravens cronking and tumbling. The circular windbreak wall on top was filled with small white flowers which I thought might be wood sorrel. It was only afterwards I wondered about them: *wood sorrel on top of a 2,500-foot rocky mountain? How strange.* I was hoping for clear weather so that I could look west along Loch Glencoul to the spot where Bob Hamilton and I had camped from our sea kayaks the previous year, but thick low cloud prevented that. By the time I had done the reascent on the return trip, I knew I was committed to continue my journey. With this commitment came a new wave of enthusiasm. In the interests of looking after my feet, I decided not to run any of the descent, and therefore reduce the pressure. The trick would be to keep my body and especially my feet going long enough to make it back to Lairg.

It was only a two-mile ride down the road to do Ben Hee, then a return to break camp before continuing north. Ben Hee went without incident, the route following a pleasant stream; higher up, it was misty, bouldery and deserted. My big toe was really painful now, so before breaking camp I undertook more drastic action in the hole-cutting department. With everything packed up and larger holes cut in my shoes, I set off towards Scourie.

The ride to Scourie was only twenty miles, but hilly and into the wind – two and a half hours' hard graft. The campsite shop was shut, putting paid to my hope of replenishing my food supply. The public phone was out of order due to the thunderstorm, so I rang Gill from the phone in the café. 'What's wrong?' she said. 'You're slurring – you sound exhausted.'

I was certainly tired but had no intention of stopping so early in the day; it was only 5.15 p.m. Even as I said the words, 'Well, the shop is closed – I may as well cycle for another four or five hours,' I was having second thoughts. I didn't need to push on until dark and I really did need a rest – so, feeling just a bit guilty, I enjoyed a sensible and beneficial break. A meal in the café, showers and flat grass to sleep on. Luxury.

Cycle 24 miles; walk 15 miles; 5,200 feet ascent.

Day five: Glas Bheinn, Spidean Coinich, Sail Gharbh and Sail Ghorm

The late opening of the shop forced me to make a late start and take a much-needed rest, do some washing and undertake a bit more hole cutting.

After a sixteen-mile ride to the foot of Glas Bheinn, I stashed my bike in the heather. It was a lovely breezy day, and I was on the top at midday – and, despite a poor route choice on the ascent, back on the road by 2 p.m.

Then it was only a one-mile ride to the foot of Spidean Coinich, the first of the three Corbetts that make up the huge Y-shaped massif of Quinag. I again stashed my bike in the heather. There were a lot of cars in the car park; mostly walkers, I suspected, but also sightseers. Who could blame them? This was an impressive trio. The lovely breeze continued as I traversed Quinag's dramatic ridges. On top of Sail Gharbh I met a young man who had travelled by public transport from Walsall, then jumped off the bus in Sutherland to 'grab an adventure'. The terrain wasn't particularly steep, but I revelled in the silent, empty space that was all around me. Five hours after setting out, I was back on the road. It was over all too soon. I wished it could have lasted for ever.

Back in the saddle, I headed for my next camp at Inchnadamph, arriving at 8 p.m. It would have been a treat to stay in the bunkhouse, but it was full. Anyway, it looked a bit odd – too posh for a bunkhouse, more like a hotel. I camped about a mile up the track towards Glen Assynt. I now had too many aches and pains to sleep properly, and I was getting seriously tired. The midges were so bad that I brought the stove into the tent, which then rapidly filled with condensation. Everything was damp and filthy. I was sick of eating midges.

Cycle 21 miles; walk 13 miles; 5,000 feet ascent.

Day six: Breabag, Canisp, Cul Beag

I awoke early, anxious to get on my way and escape the midges. Standing up, I knew instantly that my physical state had deteriorated. My left knee was swollen and painful, my big toe in a similar state. But more hole cutting and I was soon pedalling along the three-mile road section to the start of the next Corbett.

The early-morning ascent of Breabag was enjoyable – up past the Bone Caves then through endless boulder fields and crags. There were no paths or cairns high up, so putting waypoints in my GPS ensured I could find the same way back.

Canisp went well, too; it was just a nice angle for jogging and walking, with a weird landscape like a frozen sea – wave after wave of quartzite. Despite my tiredness, I found this to be the easiest Corbett so far. Another five miles along the road, I came to the Elphin tearoom. After spending ages snacking and drinking tea, I phoned Gill – then, instead of starting the long pedal up to Knockan Crag, I went back inside and ordered a proper meal!

The climb up to Knockan Crag only took thirty minutes but felt a lot longer. Two Corbetts left now, and I wanted to be back in Lairg the following day. With the tent pitched, I set off for Cul Beag at 6 p.m., forgetting to take my head torch. The mist, rain and fading daylight made careful navigation between the twin tops essential. It was a relief later to find the tent in the dark at 10.30 p.m. Settling down for my sixth and final camp, I knew I still had to do Cul Mòr and cycle thirty-seven miles back to Lairg. That didn't sound much, but I was in no doubt – and neither was the little voice – that it would be a very tough day. I even started to think that maybe I wouldn't be capable. Perhaps I just wouldn't have it in me; perhaps I should have taken the shortest route back from my camp in the birch wood at the end of day three. I thought about stashing the bike and hitching a lift or enquiring about the bus service. But I knew that all these doubts were irrelevant, because the effort, the discomfort and the injuries were nothing compared to the crushing disappointment of failure. I would recover from injuries, but the disappointment would stay with me for ever. I would complete my journey.

Cycle 12 miles; walk 21 miles; 6,600 feet ascent.

Day seven: Cul Mòr

I left camp at 7.30 a.m., apprehensive about the climb up Cul Mòr and even more so about the ride back to Lairg; it was obvious I would yet again be riding into a headwind. As I set off uphill, though, a feeling of satisfaction welled up inside me. When I completed this trip, it would be against all odds, and I was nearly there. What a fine line it is between success and failure.

At 8 a.m. I rested on a rock and looked down at my tiny tent. It seemed a long way below me, and I could just make out my bike in the heather. If this became too difficult and required just too much effort, all I had to do was walk downhill. I looked at my swollen knee and up at Cul Mòr, its top shrouded in mist. There didn't seem any point in listening to the little voice any more, or any point in weighing up effort, injuries, success or failure. There was only one thing I could do. I stood up and started limping towards Cul Mòr.

I must have been daydreaming, because suddenly I was on the top. As I set off downhill, the mist cleared, but I was too tired to attempt any running. Four hours after setting off, I was back at the tent. I ate my remaining scraps of food, packed up, and started the long ride back.

On the way to Lairg, I stopped by a river bridge and watched a man fly fishing. I tried to replace despairing exhaustion and continuing doubts about my ability to succeed with tranquillity and optimism. Eventually, after five hours riding into a headwind, I made it back to Woodend campsite, my starting point at Lairg. I collapsed into the van and slept for twelve hours. The little voice had been dead right.

Cycle 37 miles; walk 7 miles; 2,030 feet ascent.
Total miles cycled: 198.
Total miles walked: 92.
Total ascent: 32,945 feet.

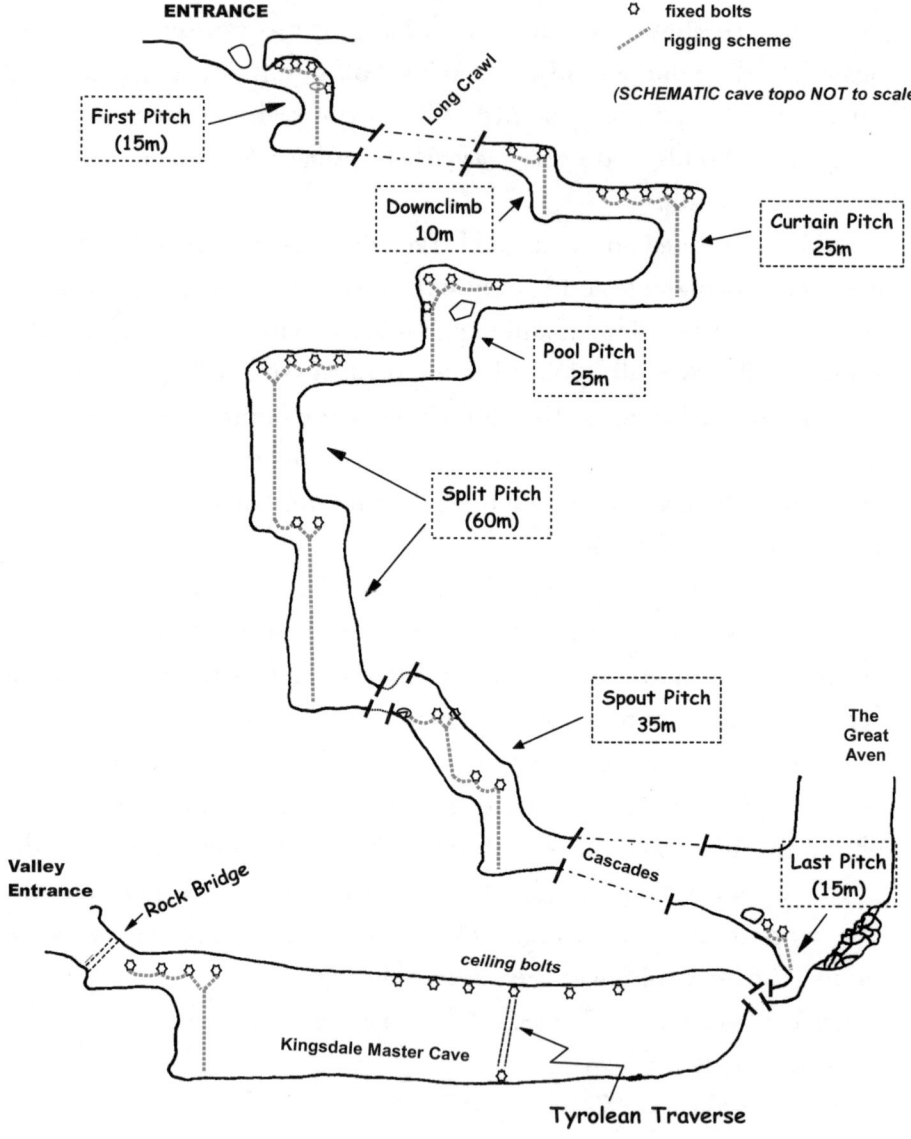

Swinsto Hole illustration by Inken Blunk

CHAPTER 16:

A Firmer Than Usual Handshake

Rain on the windscreen, waterlogged fields, and Kingsdale Beck in spate. It wasn't a good day to be underground.

The plan was to do a 'pull through' trip in a cave called Swinsto Hole. A 'pull through' is exactly that: start at the top and work your way through the system, pulling the abseil rope down off each pitch behind you. Pulling through is a pleasant way to cave, as it requires minimal equipment and it's downhill all the way. The downside to pulling the rope down is that it guarantees total commitment; after the first pull, there's no way back!

Swinsto Hole is a popular grade 4 trip, and all the abseil anchors are secure. The system takes a lot of rainwater, so the Master Cave (the lowest point in the trip) and the final exit passageway, called the Valley Entrance, can flood to the roof. Because of the flood risk, it is normal practice in wet weather to check the water levels in these two areas before starting, therefore checking your exit route before you begin.

The water in the Valley Entrance passage was about knee deep, and when we arrived at the rock bridge, we looked down into the Master Cave to see a similar depth. There was a rope in place, hanging down from the rock bridge, which would facilitate our final climb up.

Our recce complete, we retraced our steps – which only took about ten minutes – and, reassured that our exit would be clear, set off up the hillside to the cave entrance. The forecast of a dry morning and light rain in the afternoon didn't seem to bear any resemblance to what was actually happening; the weather had worsened by the time we got to the start.

We now kitted up with harnesses, jumars, helmets, lamps, knee pads and a device called a Petzl Stop, for descending the ropes. John chose to get ready inside the cave entrance, out of the rain. I stayed outside, where it was much wetter but didn't require any physical contortions in a confined space. Anyway, I had a feeling I was going to get very wet, very soon.

I don't have much experience of very wet caving, but there seemed to be an awful lot of water falling down the first pitch. I was right: I was soon very wet. We pulled the rope down, and things suddenly felt extremely serious. I knew we were fully committed.

The 'Swinsto Long Crawl' was, well, long and wet – wetter than I was expecting. We had brought three ropes, expecting to use only one on most pitches (doubled through the anchor, to enable pulling through) but giving ourselves the option to tie two together on a long pitch and still have a spare 'just in case'.

As we descended the pitch called the 'Split Pitch', the water was really thundering down. It was difficult to hold a conversation due to the noise. Then, just when we didn't need it, the rope jammed. Jumaring back up to free it might have been possible, but it would also have been time-consuming, and dangerous due to the volume of water. So, in the absence of any volunteers, we thanked our lucky stars we had brought a spare, and abandoned it.

I watched John go down the next pitch – at least, I did until he disappeared in the waterfall. I could see his lamp glowing dimly under the brown floodwater. When my turn came, I found it wasn't actually as bad as it looked; most of the way, I could bridge out and avoid the full force of the water. Eventually, though, it was necessary to step into the middle of the fall. Surprisingly, I slipped straight through to the other side into a slight alcove, thereby avoiding the full force for all but a few seconds. Soon we were at the Great Aven; just one more pitch and we would be on our way to the Master Cave.

I now started worrying about the time. I'd given Gill a call-out time of 5 p.m. but I now knew we might be late. If I failed to make contact by five, Gill would alert the cave rescue team. The already stressful situation was made worse by worrying about the time, made worse by worrying about Gill worrying about the time!

The next and final pitch was a raging brown torrent. I watched anxiously as John disappeared into the water and the glow of his lamp disappeared from view. After waiting for what seemed ages, I was sure he must be down, but the rope was still taut. I couldn't believe he was taking so long. I had an awful feeling we were going to have a disaster. Then I saw him stagger clear of the waterfall and shout; I couldn't tell what he said, but the rope was slack and he seemed OK. I looked over the edge at the roaring torrent, the foam and spray sparkling in the light from my lamp. I didn't want to do this, but I knew I had no choice, and we were nearly in the sanctuary of the Master Cave. OK – check the stop was on properly and the carabiner screwed up, take a deep breath, and get going.

I could hardly believe the power of the water: when I touched down, I could barely stand up. I couldn't see anything except the white blur of my lamp reflecting off the water, and all I could hear was an incessant screaming in my ears. I couldn't tell which way to go to escape the force of the water, and the rope in the stop was impeding my movements. After what seemed ages staggering about in a jumble of submerged boulders, being pummelled by a maelstrom of white water, I sensed the power had lessened. At last, I was on the edge of the fall – then a hand on my shoulder and John shouting, 'Are you OK, Mike?'

John had had an equally bad time. We were now both feeling anxious, as well as tired and battered, but we just needed to stay calm and keep moving.

At last we reached the Master Cave. On a previous occasion, it had been a pleasant stroll in just a few inches of water. Looking at the brown river now racing down the streamway, I knew it would be no easy stroll today, and it looked nothing like the expected sanctuary. I remembered the guy who'd led the earlier trip pointing up to the bolted escape route in the ceiling and saying, 'If it's flooding and the chips are down, you can climb along there.'

The river was far too fast and deep to wade, and too wide to jump across without extreme risk. So here we were: the cave was flooding, and the chips were down. We had no option but to traverse the high-level escape route.

The bolts are placed so that by clipping a carabiner to each one, a rope can be rigged from one to the next, thereby allowing the caver to safeguard himself. We were unable to rig in this fashion because we were doing a pull through, which didn't require many carabiners; we didn't have enough. It might have been possible to thread or tie the rope through each separate bolt, but that would have been very time-consuming, and time was another thing that was in short supply. We climbed by clipping 'cow's tails' (short lengths of rope attached to our harnesses) into the bolts. Two cow's tails each should have ensured that we would always be secured to at least one bolt. Unfortunately, some of the bolts were spaced so far apart that it was necessary to unclip from both bolts to enable the next one to be reached. Not a good time to slip! Fortunately, John is an experienced rock climber and I've done many bolted aid routes, including the roofs of Thor's cave, Peak Cavern and Kilnsey, so this didn't feel unduly difficult. But for a caver without some significant climbing experience and without the means to rig a rope to each bolt or extend cow's tails, this might prove to be a very difficult and daunting exercise. The high-level escape route along the Master Cave, unless fully rigged, is not an easy option, but a last resort.

After a short while the bolts along the right-hand wall seemed to end, and it seemed obvious we should cross the streamway to the easier-looking terrain on the other side. However, achieving this looked problematic. The river was too wide to jump, and the consequences of falling in would be dire; just around the corner, the river disappeared into an underground sump, so certain death would be the only outcome. We threaded a rope through a bolt, and John lowered himself into the water a short distance downstream. The current pushed him across to the far side, where he climbed out onto a shelf. When we were both safely across, we searched in vain for the continuation of the bolts. We were annoyed to spot that they actually continued on the side we'd just left, hidden around a corner!

The thought of reversing our last move was not appealing. Indeed, we quickly realised that it would in fact be impossible due to the direction of the flow. We had used the current to push us over; it certainly wouldn't push us back again. It seemed best to simply find the best jumping point, hold on to the rope (still attached to the other side), and make a very determined leap. Fortunately, the side we were on was slightly higher than the side we were jumping to. Unfortunately, the landing was sloping and slippery. So, with a kind of lurching, jumping scrabble, we regained the correct side and the continuation of the bolts.

After a short while, it really was necessary to cross to the other side: we could see the bolts continuing along the opposite wall, just under roof height. A wire cable, strung across from right to left, provided the means to get there.

Crossing the flooding Master Cave via the Tyrolean traverse was atmospheric but safe. With cow's tails clipped to the wire, and pulling hand over hand, it was technically quite easy. It would have been enjoyable if it wasn't for the nagging feeling that we might miss our call-out time.

The bolts continued along the left-hand wall, across some very steep terrain, vertical rock, poor footholds and spaced bolts. We were both now very tired, mentally and physically, so it was a relief to see the rock bridge at the start of the final passage to the Valley Entrance. We could see the rope hanging down, but because we were high up on the escape route, it was unnecessary to climb it; we were already at the right level.

It was now only ten minutes from here to safety, but the water in the passage was much deeper now, sometimes chest high. I was sure the water was getting deeper and the ceiling lower the further we went. At every corner I expected to find the two converged. Then would come the crushing disappointment and the awful realisation that we were stuck!

After a few more minutes of trying to hurry but not panic, we scrambled out of the Valley Entrance onto the dark, rain-lashed hillside, with ten minutes to call-out time. We had shared an adventure we would never forget – and a firmer than usual handshake.

CHAPTER 17:

The Strand

Craig Gogarth is one of the most impressive sea cliffs in the UK. Situated on the north-west coast of Anglesey, it is home to many famous and adventurous climbs.

'The Strand', graded at E2, was a climb I'd always considered to be at the upper limit of my capabilities. If ever I summoned up the courage to make an attempt, I knew my chance of success was, at best, evens. My friend Fritz once said, 'If there's one climb you must do before you hang your boots up, it's 'The Strand'. You'll love it.' But then, Fritz was a better climber than I was.

I couldn't stop thinking about it. I read and re-read the guidebook, trying to imagine what it would be like. I'd done quite a few climbs at Gogarth and always revelled in the atmosphere. The unusual rock features, crashing waves and screaming sea birds complement the beauty of the flowers and colourful lichen. Fritz was correct; I had to at least try it.

One summer morning in May 2008, Jon Haswell and I stood under the huge soaring crack line. It must have been foreshortened from such a close vantage point, but it still looked massive. It was still early – too early. The climb was in the shade, the rock cold. I didn't need to read the guidebook again. I already knew what it said: 140 feet with the crux right at the top.

The gear placements didn't seem too good for the first twenty feet. My fingers were cold, and I was fumbling. I should have waited for the sun. In an attempt to calm my nerves, I was trying to place too many runners. Jon shouted up, 'If you keep putting gear in at that rate, you'll run out by halfway.' Things weren't going too well, and my strength and confidence were draining away. Then I came across a jammed alloy nut – a relic from a previous ascent – and managed to thread a sling around it. What a difference that made. I felt safer and, now in the sun, I relaxed and started to climb much better. OK, now I'm in business – finger jams, then laying away to the right, another good runner, nice footwork. A pull up to the right led to more layaways and a good spike runner. So it went, on and on, absorbing technical climbing. Fantastic! I was 'in the zone'.

The expected stopper move – the one that perhaps I just couldn't quite do – never materialised, and I was soon at the final steepening. When I looked down at the ropes snaking below me, Jon seemed a long way away. The last fifteen feet looked difficult and strenuous, slightly overhanging, but I knew I could do it. I slotted a cam into the crack and said a silent, 'Fritz, this is for you'. A few powerful moves on good finger jams and I was safely on the belay.

It had been the perfect climb for me: overcoming some early doubts, never really pressed to my limit, and a bit left in the tank at the top.

Jon climbed it well. I knew he would; it was his type of climb – open, technical and thoughtful. But he did complain about having to lug about half a ton of gear up the last steep section. The abseil down brought home just how steep it was; we hardly touched the rock. In our euphoria, we forgot to retrieve the number two wire we'd left in, but it was a small price to pay for such a magnificent pitch.

As we walked back across the clifftop towards the car, I was so excited I was jabbering away like a beginner, reliving the climb, going through all the moves. You would never have thought I'd been climbing for over forty years.

Then I noticed two people: a man in a wheelchair and his lady companion. He was waving his arms and shouting, pushing away the lady, who was trying to feed him with a spoon. The spectacle hit me like a sledgehammer. Here was I, exultant in my achievement, revelling in the joy of total physical and mental control, and this poor man couldn't even feed himself. I was overcome with emotion and turned away so that Jon couldn't see the tears welling up in my eyes. Turning back, I could see the wild gesticulations and his caring, patient partner holding out the spoon again. The tears rolled down my cheeks.

By the time we'd walked back to the car, I'd resolved that the next time I was patting myself on the back after a good lead, next time I was celebrating the coordination, the balance and the strength, I would think of that man in the wheelchair.

AFTERWORD:

Three Score Years and Ten

Fifty-seven years since my first climb, and I can still remember that snowy day on Stanage as if it were yesterday.

The excitement of my first training run is also etched in my mind. I would need to consult my log for details of time and distance, but I remember feeling that, somehow, it was right. Like my first steps on the rock, I was sure this path would lead to fulfilment.

Realistically, despite a regular intake of glucosamine sulphate and three arthroscopies in an attempt to alleviate sore knees, it's highly unlikely I shall ever run again. The hip replacement I'm sure would be up to the job, but painful knees would tip the balance of discomfort and enjoyment too far the wrong way. An intermittent battle with atrial fibrillation, while not painful, makes running impossible and steep uphill walking hard.

But what about climbing, my first obsession and most powerful addiction? Is it inevitable, with the advance of years, that I should have to lower the grade at which I climb, reduce my expectations? Regular practice and conditioning might allow me, at best, to slow down the rate of decline. Or is it possible for a creaking septuagenarian to improve? I don't yet know the answer, but I intend to find out.

Although I'm very pleased to be climbing at a similar level to that of forty years ago, I am convinced that with the right type of training and preparation, I can improve. Workouts on the multi-gym or finger board should improve my strength. The techniques of balance and body position can be improved by regular visits to the indoor climbing wall. The dream of climbing just a bit harder than ever before is rapidly becoming an obsession.

Fifty-five years after watching that epic ascent of the Old Man of Hoy on television, it is still a recurring daydream, a dream which refuses to reduce in either frequency or clarity. I've visualised the climb so many times I can almost feel the damp, cold rock, smell the sea and hear the birds. The easy but sandy first pitch, the difficult and awkward second, then the final pitches finishing up on an exposed corner with the surf and waves crashing far below.

For fifty-five of my seventy years, I have been fortunate to have taken pathways which I found so absorbing that they consumed me. The ambitions I continually thought and dreamt about fuelled an energy which, so far, has been undiminished.

Undoubtedly, some of the challenges I have written about will be thought of as unachievable or even unimaginable to some. Others may see them as unnecessary, pointless undertakings. Compared with the upper levels of high adventure and attainment, they must be viewed as modest – but adventure is a feeling, and attainment depends on where you set the bar. Both are subjective.

Like me, the 'Old Man' is becoming increasingly fragile. I should climb it soon before one of us keels over.

GLOSSARY

Aid climbing

A style of climbing in which upward progress is made by pulling oneself up on devices fixed into the rock by attaching slings or etriers.

Bealach

Narrow mountain pass.

Bird beak

Sharp pointed hook for making upward progress. Used in aid climbing.

Bivvy

Temporary camping place. Bivvy bag, bivvy tent, portaledge.

Belay

System to protect a roped climber from falling by controlling the movement of the rope from a secure stance.

Bolt

Point of protection permanently installed in a hole drilled in the rock.

Bothy

A basic shelter, usually left unlocked.

C2

Second level of difficulty in aid climbing.

Cam

Spring-loaded device used for protection, also known as a 'friend'.

Carabiner

Spring-loaded snap link.

Clean

To remove equipment from a route.

Col

A saddle, the lowest point of a ridge between two peaks.

Copperhead

Small nut made of copper or aluminium hammered into a small depression in the rock.

Corbett

Scottish mountain over 2,500 feet but less than 3,000 feet.

Daisy chain

Sling with multiple sewn loops, used in aid climbing.

Dihedral

A cliff feature where two planes of rock come together to form a corner.

EB

Early climbing shoe made by Edmond Bourdonneau.

Etrier

Short webbing ladder used for aid climbing.

Fifi hook

Small alloy hook attached to a daisy chain or etrier.

Finger board

Training board with finger holds, used for improving strength.

Free climbing

A style of climbing where devices fixed in the rock are used for protection only, not for direct aid.

Grading system

System of classifying routes according to difficulty. For example, E2 is the second level of difficulty in the Extreme section of the free climbing system.

Gunwale

Upper edge of the side of a boat.

Hardware

Equipment required to ascend a climbing route.

Haul bag

Large bag used to transport equipment and supplies up a route.

Jumar

Mechanical clamp for climbing up ropes.

Karrimat

Closed-cell foam sleeping mat.

KIMM (Karrimor International Mountain Marathon). Now called the 'OMM, (Original Mountain Marathon). A 2 day mountain marathon for teams of two. Teams must be self sufficient for 2 days and navigate between checkpoints.

Lochan

Small loch.

Munro

Scottish mountain over 3,000 feet.

Nut

Alloy wedge for jamming into cracks; usually has a wire loop attached.

PA

The first rubber-soled climbing shoe. Designed by Pierre Alain.

PB

Personal best achievement.

Pakboat

Collapsible boat, constructed from vinyl with an alloy frame.

Peg

Steel spike for hammering into cracks in the rock.

Pitch

Portion of a climb between two belay points.

Poop tube

Container for carrying faeces during multi-day climbs.

Portaledge

Deployable hanging platform for belaying, resting or sleeping.

Roped solo

Climbing solo with a rope for protection.

Runner (running belay)

Rope running through a carabiner and sling secured to an item of equipment placed while climbing a pitch to protect the moving climber by reducing the length of a fall.

Skyhook

Small hook to grip ledges and protrusions.

Sling

Loop of nylon tape or rope.

'All men dream, but not equally. Those who dream by night in the dusty recesses of their minds wake in the day to find that it was vanity; but the dreamers of the day are dangerous men, for they may act on their dreams with open eyes, to make them possible.'

T. E. Lawrence, *Seven Pillars of Wisdom*